Forestry policies in Europe

FAO Forestry Department

FAO
FORESTRY
PAPER

86

FOOD
AND
AGRICULTURE
ORGANIZATION
OF THE
UNITED NATIONS
Rome, 1988

The designations employed and the presentation of
material in this publication do not imply the expression of
any opinion whatsoever on the part of the Food and
Agriculture Organization of the United Nations
concerning the legal status of any country, territory, city
or area or of its authorities, or concerning the delimitation
of its frontiers or boundaries.

M-36
ISBN 92-5-102724-2

FOREWORD

The FAO Forestry Department has been working for a long time under its Regular Programme on improving mechanisms of policy formation and formulation in the forestry sector, both in developed and developing countries.

Many studies on this subject have been carried out in the past and more recently special importance has been given to the updating and reorientation of national forestry policies so as to align them with the new social and economic concepts of forestry development. A new forestry policy will of necessity imply the adaptation of the other institutional mechanisms (legislation, institution building, education, training, research and extension) to allow its sound implementation.

The study of current national forestry policies has been a means of obtaining better knowledge of the trends and objectives being pursued by different countries in the sector to facilitate their revision and improvement. Through different FAO statutory bodies, the FAO Forestry Department was asked to carry out a continuing review of the subject.

More specifically, the Twenty-Second Session of the FAO European Forestry Commission (EFC) held in Budapest, Hungary, 28 October - 1 November 1985, requested FAO to conduct a survey of Forestry Policies in Europe during 1986 and 1987 to keep forestry policy formulation and related questions under review.

A similar proposal for a study on forestry policies within the member countries of the European Economic Community (EEC) was recommended by the EEC Forestry Commission which agreed to participate in the FAO survey.

The survey was carried out on the basis of an outline which was prepared in consultation with the Executive Committee of the EFC and office holders of the Economic Commission for Europe (ECE) Timber Committee, as well as with officials of the Forests and Forestry Division of the Commission of the European Communities (CEC).

FAO presented a progress report on the first results of this survey during the Joint 23rd Session of the EFC and 45th Session of the ECE Timber Committee held in Geneva, Switzerland, in October 1987. In the ensuing discussion, the meeting agreed that FAO should publish the summaries of all the national reports on forestry policies received.

This report came out at the same time as the Timber Committee of the Economic Commission for Europe and the FAO European Forestry Commission produced a study on European Timber Trends and Prospects to the Year 2000 and Beyond (known as ETTS IV). ETTS IV provides clear indications that forestry and forest industries in Europe are at a turning point, requiring a reassessment of national forestry policies needed for the twenty-first century.

All the summary reports appearing in this document have been cleared and approved for publication by the national forestry authorities concerned.

I trust this informative document is of interest not only to the countries of Europe, but also to those of the other regions which are making efforts to define sound forestry policies that can contribute to and support the achievement of social and economic national development goals.

This document will be followed by a comparative study on forestry policies in Europe. Work on this is now in progress. The study is based on the national reports received. A similar study for the EEC countries was prepared and published in March 1988 by the CEC Forests and Forestry Division, based on the information in the surveys received from the EEC member countries.

FAO would like to thank all the European countries that have participated and collaborated in the preparation of the survey, and also the Forests and Forestry Division of the CEC for its support regarding its member countries.

Acknowledgements are also due to Dr. F.C. Hummel for his services in preparing the summary reports.

J.P. Lanly
Assistant Director-General a.i.
Forestry Department

CONTENTS

ALBANIA

1. INTRODUCTION

The land area of the Popular Socialist Republic of Albania (RPSA) is 28,748 sq.km., of which 10,450 sq.km. are covered by forest and 4,000 sq.km. are pasture. All the forests are the property of the State; they thus belong to all the people.

The wood supplied by the forests for industrial uses and for firewood satisfies all national needs. The forests also supply secondary plant and animal products such as pine resin, essential oils, laurel leaves, herbage and fruits of various medicinal and aromatic species, skins of wild animals which are used nationally as well as for export. About 20% of the forests are important for the prevention of erosion, as reserves for flora and fauna and for recreational purposes.

The main objectives of the national forestry policy are:

- Bringing annual cut and increment into balance by reducing fellings and increasing the productivity of the forests;

- Minimizing waste by increasing the utilization coefficient of wood and by the adoption of new technologies for the more efficient utilization of wood residues;

- Giving priority to the exploitation of over-mature stands;

- Improving the mechanization of operations in the forest and in forest industry;

- Increasing the rate of reforestation, especially in stands of low production.

In order to achieve the above objectives, an indicative plan has been prepared for the forestry economy up to the year 2000. The plan specifies the measures for bringing cut and increment into balance; the measures include the substitution of industrial wood with other materials such as iron, concrete, plastic and of firewood with other fuels such as oil, electricity and natural gas.

At the same time, there will be an intensification of forest management in order to raise the productivity of the forests. The measures will include the increased use of fast growing species, especially conifers.

All the workers in towns and villages assist greatly in the enlargement, improvement and protection of the forests. The aim is to achieve a rational and ecologically sound system of management in which current needs and opportunities are reconciled with the interests of future generations.

2. ADMINISTRATION

After the liberation of the country on 29 November 1944, the forests were nationalized and there are no longer any private forests. The forests are administered in accordance with the forest law. The Directorate of Forests and Pastures is in the Ministry of Agriculture. The forestry enterprises operate in the 26 districts of the country. These enterprises deal with forest protection and management, hunting, hydrotechnical installations for the protection against erosion in water catchment areas, utilization of minor products of the forests and of hunting.

The Directorate of Wood and Paper is in the Ministry of Industry and Mines. In the districts, there are 3 Wood Combines, 6 paper factories, 3 fibreboard factories and the enterprises which are concerned with harvesting and sawmilling.

The scientific work relating to forests is directed by the Research Centre for Forests and Essential Oils, which comes under the Ministry of Agriculture. The research projects deal with afforestation, silviculture, watershed management, hunting, etc. The Research Centre for Wood and Wood-based Industries at Tirana, which comes under the Ministry for Industry and Mines, investigates harvesting methods and prepares projects for forest utilization, construction of new wood processing industries, forest roads, etc. These two research centres cooperate with each other as well as with other relevant national institutions and with the forestry and forest industrial enterprises.

The development of the forestry economy is integrated with all the other branches of the economy in the general plan for the economic and cultural development of the country. Central Government determines the targets to be achieved by means of quinquiennial and annual plans. The targets relate to reforestation and other measures to improve the productivity of forests, to the amount of wood to be harvested and also to savings in wood use and the replacement of wood with other materials. The development plan for forestry provides for the financial resources required for implementation. All concerned are encouraged to exceed all targets except the prescribed cut.

The protection of forests and the execution of the plans which have been approved are based on the constitution of the RPSA. There are thus no juridical obstacles to the implementation of forest policy.
Apart from the Ministries of Agriculture and of Heavy Industry and Mines, the following organizations exert an influence on forestry policy: The Commission of the State Plan, the executive and advisory district committees, the agricultural cooperatives and the social organizations. In addition, juridical organs such as the tribunals have a say in certain matters.

The fundamental principle of policy is the management of the forest as a renewable natural resource.

3. FOREST MANAGEMENT AND PROTECTION

The indicative plans provide both for an increase in the area under agriculture and for more reforestation. The reforestation is carried out on unproductive forest land and on deforested areas. The objects are wood production and the prevention of soil erosion. Where necessary, the reforestation is accompanied by hydrotechnial measures in mountainous water catchment areas, especially in those of importance for hydroelectric power or as reservoirs for irrigation. Special provisions are made for forests destined primarily for the conservation of water resources and as protection against avalanches. These, like all other forestry operations, are included in the State plans.

Forest management on a scientific basis is assured by forest working plans. These plans are in respect of the 400,000 ha. of most valuable forest; they are prepared by the Research Centre for Forestry and Essential Oil Plants and they cover a ten year period. In the forests not covered by working plans, operations are based on the results of the forest inventories which are repeated at ten-yearly intervals. On the basis of the most recent inventory, the forestry situation has been examined and the necessary measures for the rational exploitation up to the year 2000 have been defined. At the same time, forest maps have been prepared at scales of 1:25,000, 1:50,000 and 1:200,000. Wildlife maps and maps of medicinal and aromatic plants have been prepared at a scale of 1:200,000.

According to the recent inventory, 80% of the forests should serve both for production and protection while 20% should fulfil only a protective and social function. 46% of the area is high forest, 29% coppice and 25% scrub. The species distribution is as follows:

Fagus silvatica	17%
Pinus spp.	15%
Abies sp.	2%
Quercus sp.	32%
Other broadleaved species	34%
	100%

Seventy-five percent of future planting is to be of conifers, especially Pinus nigra var. austriaca Hoess. The broadleaved species will include Populus euroamericana hybrids, Robinia pseudoacacia, Castanea sativa, Juglans regia, Laurus nobilis and Salix spp.

The protection of forests against fire is a continuing task not only for the forest services but also for the whole population; a variety of measures are taken for fire prevention, fire fighting and increasing public awareness of the danger. These measures and the willingness of the public to assist have reduced the number of fires to only 41 in 1986 and the area damaged to 54 ha.

The main insect pest is the processionary moth (<u>Thaumatopoea</u> <u>pityocampa</u> schiff.) which has attacked about 35,000 ha. Damage to poplars is caused by <u>Saperda</u> <u>carcarias</u> L. and <u>Saperda</u> <u>populnea</u> and to sweet chestnut by <u>Endothia</u> <u>parasitica</u> Murr.

These and other biotic causes of damage are controlled by physical, mechanical and chemical methods. The damage from industrial pollution is very limited. The quinquiennial plans make provision for the material and financial resources required for protecting forests against fires and other destructive agencies.

200,000 ha. of forest have been declared as protection forests for the prevention of erosion, protection of catchment areas, railway lines and other social installations, etc.

In 1966, the Council of Ministers designated six national parks with a total area of 10,000 ha. Holiday cabins for workers and young people have been constructed in these parks. The establishment of additional national parks is planned. Near towns and health resorts, green zones with forest have been created for social purposes. Strips of forest have also been established near industrial installations. Forests and single trees of particular scientific, historic and touristic interest are protected by law.

The administration of the protection forests lies with the district forestry organs of the Ministry of Agriculture. The national forest parks are administered jointly by the Ministry of Agriculture and the Ministry of Rural Economy, while the public parks in towns and the green zones are administered by the Ministry of Rural Economy and the commercial enterprises in the districts.

According to Decree No. 5607 of 1977 on hunting, wild animals and birds of prey are the property of the State. While the Ministry of Agriculture directs the general forestry economy, hunting is administered directly by the forestry enterprises. Particular attention is paid to the conservation and propagation of game mammals and birds which may be hunted without special authorization in the designated hunting zones. The general planning is done by the Ministry of Agriculture on the basis of an inventory which is carried out twice a year by means of collective hunts organized by the district hunting and fishing associations at fixed dates within the hunting calendar. Every citizen who has reached the age of 18 years has the right to hunt. For the killing or capture of less common mammals such as bears, or birds such as eagles, special authorization from the Ministry of Agriculture is required. In order to create favourable conditions for hunting, 23 hunting reserves with an area of about 35,000 ha. have been established by the Ministry of Agriculture. The populations of wolves (<u>Canis</u> <u>lupus</u> Z.) and jackals (<u>Canis</u> <u>aureus</u> Z.) are kept at a low level because of the damage they do to both farm and wild animals.

The workers in agricultural cooperatives and also the general public, especially young people, contribute voluntarily to forestry protection and improvement. This applies in particular in the month of December, which is designated as "the month of the forests and the fight against erosion".

Thanks to the attitude to the rural economy which has been cultivated in the RPSA, there is no abandoned land and every Albanian village is inhabited. The social structure permits the development of hilly and mountainous regions in the same way as of other parts of the country. In many mountain areas, metal and coal mines have been developed, forestry and wood processing activities have increased and, above all, there has been an expansion of farming.

Albania is rich in pastures, mainly in the mountains. There are pasture enterprises in all districts. These enterprises are controlled by the Direction of Forests and Pastures in the Ministry of Agriculture. Scientific support is provided by the Central Station for Pastures. Three inventories of pastures have already been made, the last in 1981; they provide the basis for deciding the measures to increase production. Maps at scales of 1:25,000, 1:50,000 and 1:200,000 have been prepared.

The burning of forests and pastures is prohibited by law. The conversion of forest to agricultural use requires the permission of the relevant State organs.

4. UTILIZATION OF FORESTS

Forest Law No. 4407 of 25.06.1968 amplifies earlier legislation. It defines the structure of the forest estate and the duties and rights relating to its protection, management and rational exploitation. Major decisions concerning the implementation of this law have been taken by the Council of Ministers while the Ministry of Agriculture has issued the necessary detailed regulations.

The harvest of wood and other forest products is based on the forest working plan and is carried out in accordance with annual plans approved by the wood processing industries and by the agricultural cooperatives in respect of their requirements. There are strict rules concerning all aspects of harvesting and transport, including the timing and protective measures against insect attacks. Transport from roadside to user is undertaken by the national transport enterprises.

The wood processing industry which developed only after the liberation of Albania is geared to satisfying the needs of the popular economy. The industry produces sawnwood, plywood, wood for construction, all types of furniture, and paper. Some of this production is exported.

There is close cooperation between the forestry and the forest industry sectors of the economy in the application of the rules for forest conservation and utilization. Forest industrial development includes also the mechanization of fellings, transport within the forest, construction and modernization of wood processing plants in accordance with the State plan.

The use of firewood, which is produced mainly from scrub and from logging and processing residues, is in decline because the production of industrial wood is the main objective and firewood is being replaced by coal, electricity and natural gas not only in towns but also in rural areas.

5. DISTRIBUTION AND SUPPLY OF WOOD

Wood distribution and supply are governed by a plan which takes account of the needs of the diverse sectors of the national economy and of the population. Albania imports no wood or wood products but it exports chairs, plywood and some other products.

6. EMPLOYMENT

The forestry and forest industrial enterprises employ staff who have had professional or technical training and forest workers who learn their skills on the job. Camps have been built for staff and workers in forests and industries situated far from towns. Decisions on the numbers to be employed are taken by the appropriate organs of the State.

Workers and employees are members of the unions in each production unit and their relations with the administrations of the enterprises are governed by the labour code.

Wages of workers and specialists are based on the socialist principle of remuneration according to the quantity and quality of the work. The maximum salary in all categories of work is twice the minimum salary. Social insurances in the RPSA guarantee pensions, payments in case of incapacity and for other purposes provided for in law. Particular attention is also paid to health and safety at work.

There is no unemployment. The State assures work for all citizens according to their abilities.

7. EDUCATION AND TRAINING

Forestry engineers and forest industry engineers receive their training at the Faculty of Forestry at the Higher Agricultural Institute at Tirana. Technicians and skilled workers receive their training either at one of the two forest schools or at a wood "factory". Workers attend courses organized at the forestry enterprises. Specialists in particular subjects are trained at the Higher Agricultural Institute or at the Scientific Institutions. The State and society continually seek to increase the understanding of forestry among the working population. Television, the press and other means of publicity are used for this purpose. Information to promote a better understanding of forestry is supplied to all schools.

The Faculty of Forestry has already achieved a high level in the training of professional forestry officers and in up-to-date Albanian silviculture. About 40 to 45 students graduate each year.

8. RESEARCH

The main objective of the research is to increase the productivity of the forests. As a result of the studies that have been undertaken, natural regeneration is now obtained on 85% of the areas felled; progress has also been made with the afforestation of difficult sites, the preparation of volume and yield tables, advances in mechanization, better use of residues, etc. There is both applied research with short-term objectives and more fundamental research with longer term objectives.

Most of the research is carried out in Tirana where there are two research institutes, one dealing primarily with forestry and the culture of ethero-oleagenous plants, while the other deals with wood processing and harvesting. Some research is also done at the Faculty of Forestry. These research establishments cooperate with other research institutions of the Academy of Science and the research institutes dealing with agriculture and other aspects of land use.

The results of research are published in various scientific and agricultural bulletins and journals. The State assumes responsibility for the diffusion of the results to practice.

9. INTERNATIONAL COOPERATION

The Research Institute for Forestry and Ethero-oleagenous Plants and the Faculty of Forestry cooperate with FAO in projects of forestry protection against insects and fungal diseases, pasture, reforestation and forest management, forest ecology and silviculture. Cooperation also exists with Unesco. In addition there have been exchanges of delegations and groups of specialists, literature, films, etc., with a number of countries including France, Italy, Finland, Romania, Greece and Spain.

International cooperation in forestry will increase.

AUSTRIA

1. INTRODUCTION

Forests occupy 3.8 million ha. (46% of the total land area), 3.0 million ha. of which are classed as commercial and 0.8 million as protection forests with limited or no utilization.

The most important principles of Austrian forestry policy are the conservation of the forest and the permanent maintenance of its four functions (utilization, protection, amenity and recreation). In order permanently to fulfil these tasks, it is necessary to treat forests in such a way that the productive capacity of the forest floor is conserved.

Taking into consideration this important principle, which is contained in the Forest Law of 1975, and in view of the present state of Austrian forestry, further objectives of forest policy are:

-   Reduction of air pollutants on a national and international scale;

-   Investigation into the complex causes of "Waldsterben" (decline of forests) as well as a permanent inventory, analysis and control of damage to forests;

-   Improvement of protection forests and endangered catchment areas of torrents and avalanches in order to ensure regeneration of trees in good time;

-   Minimization of damage to growing stock;

-   Regulation of the stocks of game on a federal basis according to requirements of forestry;

-   Separation of forests from pastures;

-   Promotion of the conversion of productive agricultural areas into forest (e.g. for the production of firewood);

-   Promotion of all branches of the Austrian timber processing industry with the aim of increasingly processing Austrian high-quality large timber;

-   Improvement of framework conditions for forest enterprises in order to increase their competitivity.

These tasks of Austria's forestry policy are partly described in the Forest Law of 1975 and relevant regulations and partly in political declarations and statements (e.g. the Austrian Government's Ten-Point Programme for Fighting Waldsterben 1984, the resolution on conservation and protection of forests of the 14th FAO Regional Conference held in Reykjavik, the Report on the Results of the Survey on Ecology and Economy by the Federal Ministry of Agriculture and Forestry).

2. ADMINISTRATION

Of the Austrian forest area, almost two-thirds are privately owned, about one-fifth owned by the federal authorities, the provinces or political communities, approximately one-tenth by cooperatives and one twentieth by religious communities. The property situation is extremely stable, except that private forests exceeding 500 ha. and those of less than 10 ha. are gradually decreasing, while the number of forest enterprises ranging from 20 to 200 ha. is gradually increasing.

The organization of Austria's forest administration is marked by a complex structure and comprises the forest authorities as well as the other interests concerned.

The distribution of authority within the forest administration is regulated by the Austrian Federal Constitutional Law. The responsibility for forestry lies with the federal authorities, as far as legislation and execution of the law is concerned. The regulation of forestry takes place at federal level within the framework of the Forest Law 1975. However, with regard to some aspects of this law, the provincial legislative authorities are empowered to issue implementing laws for the provinces concerned (division of forests, fighting forest fires, limitation of forest utilization, etc.). The responsibility for the execution of the Forest Law lies with the administrative authorities of the districts and provinces and, in some exceptional cases, with the federal government.

The District Forest Authorities are attached to the district authorities and the Provincial Forest Technical Departments are attached to the provincial governments. The Federal Ministry of Agriculture and Forestry has a special forestry department and constitutes the highest level of forest administration.

According to the Law on Federal Ministries of 1986, the Federal Ministry of Agriculture and Forestry deals with the following matters related to forestry: affairs concerning forest policy and forest laws, research, tests and examinations concerning forests, torrent and avalanche control, regulation of the import and export of timber with regard to phytosanitary aspects, plant protection, maintenance of the federal agricultural schools and forestry schools, matters concerning professional representation of self-employed persons in agriculture and forestry. The District Agrarian Authorities deal with forest matters to the extent that they are responsible for forest-technical advisory activities for agricultural communities (jointly owned forests).

The Austrian Federal Forests constitute a federal enterprise that has no legal entity. Their financial management is regulated within the scope of the federal budget. Management of the enterprise is effected by a board of directors comprising three persons who follow the directives of the Federal Minister of Agriculture and Forestry. The Central Administration of the Austrian Federal Forests does not act as an official authority and is only responsible for managing the State-owned forest according to the relevant federal law.

Numerous influences help to shape forestry policy measures. The most important influence is exerted by the political parties. As far as the federal government is concerned, relevant views are influenced by the demands and wishes of various interests which are voiced by the institutionalized representations of interests, associations and unions.

Forestry legislation is based on a similar democratic process. The greatest legal and political limitations of forestry policy are inevitable whenever interests other than forestry interests prevail. For instance, an immediate solution to the problem of air pollution - the most serious problem at the present time - could not be found because of a conflict of interests with trade and industry, these powerful branches having carried out their waste gas disposal free of charge for a considerable time, thus polluting the environment. However, a change in public opinion is now forcing trade and industry to carry out their waste disposal in such a manner that pollution of forests is reduced or avoided, even if this involves the application of costly methods.

The budgetary resources destined for the promotion of forestry are low (AS 138 million in 1985). The value of primary forest production in 1985 amounted to 0.85% and the value of forest products (pulp, paper, etc.) to 6% of the gross national product.

3. MONETARY AND FISCAL POLICIES

In accordance with the different tasks allotted to the federal government on the one hand and the provinces on the other, the federal government promotes on its own initiative only measures for structural improvement and for the achievement of economic objectives. It may also contribute to subsidies for other purposes which are granted by the regional bodies concerned.

The "public forests" owned by regional bodies are managed according to the rules of private industry. They are excluded from almost all types of promotion by the State budget while also being exempt from the taxation of profits.

Direct financial subsidies are granted for forestry measures in forest enterprises not exceeding 400 ha. Larger forest enterprises may be granted cheap loans (especially from the ERP-Fund) for the haulage and handling of timber.

With regard to converting agricultural areas into forests or firewood plantations, enterprises of all sizes are entitled to a conversion subsidy. These subsidies have so far been comparatively low but are to be increased considerably.

All private forest enterprises that conclude a fire insurance policy receive a subsidy amounting to 25% of the insurance premiums.

Subsidies of up to 90% of the cost of afforestation at high altitudes and of the cost of improving protection forests are granted to all forest enterprises, including those owned by regional bodies; the federal government and the provinces share the cost at a ratio of 2:1. Generally,

80% of the funds for measures for promoting recreational facilities are provided from public funds; the cost of this subsidy is shared equally between the federal government and the province concerned. With regard to other promotion measures, the federal subsidies cover 45% of the cost of the projects in question.

Subsidies amount to less than 2% of the turnover of forestry.

Public subsidies for reduced rates of interest on loans as well as actual loans are also granted to communities for the purchase of facilities for hauling and marketing timber. Associations for the joint marketing of timber are provided with skilled personnel free of charge by the chambers of agriculture.

The associations and societies representing the interests concerned also receive federal subsidies for measures furthering extension training and advisory activities for forest owners. This is effected by the federal authorities paying the fees for advisory staff and by subsidizing the cost of organized events within the framework of special training.

The advisory activities are partly organized by the well-staffed organization of the forest authorities and partly by employees of the chambers of agriculture. In addition to the above-mentioned subsidies towards the cost of advisors, the chambers of agriculture finance their activities by members' contributions, membership being compulsory.

The Austrian tax system is extremely complex. During the course of the last decades, fiscal and organizational-political requirements have resulted in an increase in the number of tax criteria, of which there are currently seventy. For forestry, the most important factors are the taxes and contributions based on the unit-value, as well as the income tax.

The unit-value constitutes the basis for the land tax, property tax, inheritance tax, a part of the contributions for social insurance and family allowance as well as the contribution to the chamber of agriculture.

Although the State forests carry out their management as an independent economic body, they are incorporated in the annual federal budget. This leads to certain difficulties. Efforts are therefore being made to achieve budgetary independence for federal forests.

Timber sales may be indirectly promoted by tax reductions for enterprises purchasing heating plants exclusively heated by biomass.

Although there is harmony in many respects between forestry policy and fiscal policy, there are divergencies in certain respects.

4. FOREST MANAGEMENT AND PROTECTION

In order to integrate the forest into the framework of national area planning, the federal instrument of Forest Area Planning has been created and specially incorporated in the Forest Law of 1975. According to this Law, the tasks of Forest Area Planning include the presentation, planning and coordination of forest area development. The instruments of forest area planning comprise the Forest Development Plan, the Technical Forest Plan and the Danger Zone Plan. These plans are based on situation analyses showing various influences on forest conditions. The results of these analyses are shown in the form of texts and maps.

According to the Forest Law, the objective of forest area planning should be a coordination of all relevant public interests. In practice, this task is made difficult by conflicts between the interests concerned (e.g. hunting, air pollution).

The Forest Development Plan covering the entire federal territory will be completed in 1988. This plan deals with the four forest functions: production, protection, environment, recreation. The Forest Development Plan also clearly shows the effects of planned measures outside the scope of forestry (e.g. measures concerning winter sports or industrial plants emitting pollutants).

The system of torrent and avalanche control in Austria consists of a combination of constructional measures and forest-biological measures (e.g afforestation at high altitudes or prescription of certain forest management measures). The main objective of all these technical measures in a mountainous country like Austria is the conservation of protection forests which cause a considerable reduction in flood discharge, thus preventing erosion of large areas and the formation of mudflows and avalanches.

According to the legal principle of sustained yield, the paramount objectives of forest policy are the prevention of all dangers to the forest and the reduction of damage caused to forests, respectively. In Austria, the most important factors causing damage to forests are air pollution and deer, these two factors leading to losses totalling at least AS 6 billion per annum. In 1984, the federal government decided to issue a 10-point programme of appropriate measures for fighting air pollution which destroys forests. The programme includes the improvement of the legal instrument for imposing a reduction of emissions of harmful substances on those causing them, surveys of damage to forests and research activities to determine the causes.

Austria is the only country in Europe that can prescribe by way of regulations contained in a forest law (Subsection IV.C. of Forest Law of 1975 and 2nd Order on Air Pollution Damaging Forests) appropriate conditions, in the interest of forest protection, for the building of industrial plants, while also being in a position to make investigations on such pollution in the forests concerned. However, despite the success achieved, the fight against Waldsterben (decline of forests) has not yet been won. Austria therefore plans to introduce further amendments with a view to laying down clearer pollution limits. Parallel to this there are further investigations into the complex causes of damage to forests, as well as permanent surveys, analyses and control of such damage. In addition, there is a federal inventory of forests started in 1961 covering five-year periods and including a survey of the most important forest data as well as data on damage to forests from various causes.

Deer, which cause an annual loss of yield of some AS 3 billion, seriously hamper regeneration through browsing of young growth in forests already damaged by pollution. In almost all Austrian forests, there is an excessive number of cloven-hoofed game. Since 1950, there has been a fourfold increase in the number of game shot. One of the objectives of forest policy is to reduce the number of cloven-hoofed game to a tolerable level. The federal government is in a position to influence the shooting of deer by excluding forest areas devastated by game from federal forest subsidies.

Damage to forests is also caused by grazing cattle. Alpine grazing over several centuries has led to a lowering of the forest limit. These zones which have thus been deforested are now the main areas from which avalanches start. So far, one of the most important objectives of forest policy, i.e. the separation of forests from alpine pastures, has not met with much success owing to the agricultural laws which are unfavourable for forestry.

Fortunately forest fires do not play an important role in Austria.

Legislation and the execution of measures concerning the protection of nature, including the establishment and management of national parks, lies within the competence of the provinces.

With the Forest Law of 1975, an existing customary law was formally legalized, i.e. the right for everybody to enter forests. This means that forests constitute vast recreational areas accessible free of charge. If the creation, conservation and arrangement of recreational areas in tourist zones appears desirable, a Recreational Forest Declaration may be applied for by any province, community, tourist association, association of persons seeking recreation, or by the forest owners concerned. If a Recreational Forest Declaration based on a decree causes economic disadvantages for the forest owner, the latter may receive compensation from the beneficiary, who is generally the applicant for the Declaration.

All forest owners, including agricultural communities owning forests, are legally obliged to protect the forest. In addition to numerous limitations under the Forest Law, there are also special forest protection regulations. For example, the forest owner has to fight forest pests and to carry out preventative treatment.

For protection forests, i.e. forest areas on specially endangered sites, the forest authorities are entitled to prescribe certain kinds of forest management. In extreme cases, they may issue decrees transferring the management of such forest areas to the competent Torrent and Avalanche Protection Service.

The protection of water is regulated by the Water Law, according to which the population must be provided with good quality drinking water. "Spring protection forests" are entirely managed in such a way that the requirement of ensuring the supply of good quality drinking water is fulfilled.

Funds for promoting the afforestation of about 1,800 ha. p.a. (mainly on marginal agricultural soils) are made available. In future, the emphasis will be shifted from afforestation of poor quality agricultural areas to the government-subsidized conversion into forest of highly productive agricultural areas in order to reduce the agricultural surplus.

Such forest areas serve mainly for firewood production and are to be managed on short rotations, thus reducing Austria's dependence on the import of costly raw materials for energy supplies.

5. FOREST UTILIZATION

The maintenance of sustained forest yield, as practised in Austria, is largely based on an unwritten law. Although larger forest enterprises generally have management plans to regulate the annual cut, such plans are only legally prescribed with regard to the State forests and in forests owned by cooperatives which formerly belonged to political communities. Official permission is required for carrying out any clearing that exceeds an area of more than a hectare. Clearings of more than 2 ha. may only be carried out in exceptional cases.

Although the average forest enterprises utilize far less than the increment and although large quantities of raw timber are imported, federal forest policy does not include measures for encouraging increased fellings.

After a phase of intensive forest road building by the State, there are no longer any important problems with regard to logging.

The forestry and timber industry have a joint forum in the form of the "Bundesholzwirtschaftsrat" (Federal Timber Council). Rural cooperatives are generally concerned with marketing and mainly deal with mass assortments of small timber. The development of the timber industry is largely limited to private initiatives. Measures for better environmental control, especially for reducing water pollution caused by the effluents of the wood pulp industry, are promoted on the one hand by a stringent water law and on the other by public subsidies (especially low-interest loans).

Residues from wood processing are almost entirely used industrially, the sawdust partly by industry and partly for spreading litter in stables and sheds. During the last few years, residues have been increasingly used for energy production as well.

At present, the sale of roundwood of small dimensions and of logging residues rarely seems to be profitable and cannot compete against industrial wastewood.

6. TIMBER TRADE AND MARKETING

In the timber trade, the law of the free market prevails. This applies to the home market as well as to export and import. The grading of timber is subject to guidelines drawn up by forestry, timber trade and timber industry within their joint forum, the Federal Timber Council.

Forest enterprises as well as farms generally sell their timber themselves. At present the volume of joint timber sales (mainly pulpwood) ranges from one-fifth to one-tenth of the total timber sold. As the sawmill industry is increasingly concentrating on a few enterprises, an increasing volume of jointly sold timber is to be expected.

Timber sale policy is mainly keyed to encouraging the increased use of timber. Information on timber supplied by the Federal Timber Council not only includes publicity for consumers; architects are also provided with basic technical data and examples of construction models.

7. <u>EMPLOYMENT</u>

Persons employed in agriculture and forestry are subject to a number of different laws, i.e. the Agricultural Labour Law, the Estate Employment Law, the Employees Law and the Trade Regulation Law.

The number of skilled forest workers has fallen very considerably, whereas the number of foresters and forestry graduates has more or less stayed the same. The earnings of skilled forest workers are above the average of those of industrial workers in view of the hard work and professional training required.

There are a number of health and security regulations included in the Labour Protection Law (e.g. on working time, holidays, protection of children, etc.). There are numerous regulations concerning social insurance, unemployment insurance, family equalization payments and social assistance.

According to regulations contained in the Forest Law of 1975, forests exceeding 500 ha. are legally obliged to employ a forester, those exceeding 1,800 ha. having to employ a senior forester.

8. <u>FORESTRY EDUCATION AND TRAINING INCLUDING FOREST INDUSTRIES AND</u>
<u>NATIONAL PARKS MANAGEMENT</u>

The training of forest officers takes place at forestry schools under the Federal Ministry of Agriculture and Forestry and the Federal Ministry of Education, Art and Sport or at the University of Agriculture which comes under the Federal Ministry of Science and Research. The syllabus includes forestry, torrent and avalanche control and timber industry. The course covers 9 semesters at the end of which a final examination is obligatory.

The training of foresters covers a period of 5 years and is concluded by a final examination. After two years of professional practice, there is the possibility of taking a national examination for the forest service, entitling those who pass to manage forest enterprises of up to 1,800 ha.

In addition, there is a special forestry school run by the federal authorities. The object of the one-year course provided by this school for forest wardens is the fulfilment of certain tasks within the framework of the forest protection service.

Training of forest workers lies within the competence of the provinces. This training comprises a three-year professional forestry course at the end of which there is an examination for skilled forest workers.

In Austria there is much willingness and enthusiasm amongst young people for forestry.

Besides the classical and traditional forestry training schools, there are numerous training courses and extension courses adapted to the extremely varied structure of Austrian forests and the various types of skills required. Forestry courses for the management of small farm forests are held free of charge in federal forest training schools.

The number of forestry graduates, foresters and forest wardens has gradually decreased since 1975 from about 4,300 to 4,000. On the other hand, there is a constant increase in the number of forestry students and persons attending forestry schools.

9. FORESTRY RESEARCH, EXTENSION AND INFORMATION

For forestry research, the Federal Ministry of Agriculture and Forestry has the Federal Research Institute, whereas the Federal Ministry of Science and Research has at its disposal the University of Agriculture.

According to the Forest Law of 1975, the Federal Research Institute has the task of carrying out forest investigations and tests on a scientific basis and to convey the results of the research to those responsible for practical forestry. The results of the most important research activities are presented to the public within the framework of press conferences once a year.

The University of Agriculture not only provides forest education for students but also carries out scientific forest research projects with objectives similar to those of the Federal Research Institute. To coordinate procedures in connection with the fight against Waldsterben, an advisory committee for research on damage to forests was constituted at the Federal Ministry of Science and Research. Furthermore, following an initiative of Austrian forest scientists, the Austrian Initiative to Fight Waldsterben was started. The task of this group of scientists is to provide a detailed report and clarification of the way in which air pollutants and other harmful influences affect the ecosystem forest.

The funds for forest research are provided by the two above-mentioned ministries. In addition, federal funds are provided as part of a promotion programme entitled the "Green Plan".

Forestry extension training includes various courses, seminars, lectures, excursions and symposia (e.g. the Forestry Symposium within the framework of the International Timber Fair, Klagenfurt). Moreover, there is an extension training programme for teachers and advisory staff of the federal government, the provinces and the chambers of agriculture.

Within the framework of interviews and press handouts, the Federal Ministry of Agriculture and Forestry endeavours to provide the public with direct information on forestry. Once a year this ministry organises the "Week of the Forest", including the publication of information leaflets. At the end of each year, a report on the annual agricultural and forestry activities is provided by the Federal Minister of Agriculture and Forestry for the members of the Austrian parliament. On the radio there are also broadcasts of relevant advisory programmes. Finally, information is given to the public within the scope of direct informative talks. For example, at the Federal Ministry of Agriculture and Forestry there is a "green telephone" for dealing with enquiries and requests in an unbureaucratic way.

10. INTERNATIONAL COOPERATION

International cooperation in Austria is characterized in general by the willingness to work together with all countries, organizations, bodies, etc., which show an interest, and to give them all an insight into Austria's forestry activities.

Austria being a small country, one big problem is the financing of all activities connected with forestry and the foreigners. Austria is a member of most of the international organizations dealing with forestry, e.g. FAO, ECE, and tries to participate as much and as actively as possible in the meetings, seminars, etc., organized by them.

Close contacts exist with Central European countries (FRG and Switzerland) and many agreements have been reached with countries from all over the world concerning the exchange of publications and research. There are also close ties with countries in the Eastern block, especially the GDR, Hungary, Poland and the USSR; these ties result not only in an exchange of publications but also in exchanges of experts and annual meetings of leading officials to discuss the latest developments in forestry which are of mutual interest.

BELGIUM

1. INTRODUCTION

1.1 Areas and Ownership

Forests cover 20.2% of the national territory but are very unevenly distributed. They cover 30% of the Walloon Region and only 8% of the Flemish Region. Even within these regions, there are considerable variations in forest cover.

The 487,000 ha. of the Walloon Region are more or less evenly divided between broadleaved species (mainly beech and oak high forest and coppice with standards) and conifers (mainly Norway spruce). 51.5% of the forests are privately owned and 48.5% are in public ownership; of the publicly owned forests, 77% belong to Communes, about 20% belong to the State and the remaining 3% to the Provinces and other public bodies.

In the Flemish Region, 28% of the 114,000 ha. of forest are publicly owned and 72% private.

The 2,000 ha. of forest in the Brussels Region are mainly State-owned.

1.2 General Principles and Objectives of National Forest Policy

Since 1980, when the responsibility for forestry was transferred to the regions, only international relations have remained under national control. As no formal coordination is planned, the forest policies of the regions may diverge.

In the Flemish Region, the primary consideration is to meet changing human needs - without prejudice to forest conservation and the balance of nature. Interest in forestry has been growing.

The difficult aim of forest management is to achieve multiple-use forestry by a system of silviculture based on the bio-ecological principles of the natural forest. The pressure on forests necessitates control measures against vandalism, stray dogs, riders, motor bicycles, etc. On the other hand, investments are needed to provide recreational facilities such as forest walks, forest museums, playgrounds and resting places.

In the Walloon Region, forest and water constitute the main resources. The economic function of timber production is therefore the main management objective. This has led to some increases in the proportion of conifers, but sufficient broadleaves must be maintained to prevent soil degradation. Silviculture aims at a mixed forest in which conifers and broadleaved species each occur in sufficiently large groups or stands to permit economic management.

The second management objective is the maintenance of the natural equilibrium (protection against pollution, conservation of flora and fauna). In this context, the balance between forest and game is important and requires constant attention.

The third objective is to develop the social function of the forest. As a result of increased mobility and leisure, more and more people visit forests. This social function is not incompatible with the productive and protective functions; in fact, a well-managed and varied forest is preferred by the public.

In the Brussels Region, the objective of producing wood from the broadleaved species has to be reconciled with meeting the demand for recreational opportunities by a very large urban population. The main problem is to regenerate the forest faster in order to re-equilibrate the age-distribution that was disrupted by a too long revolution. The managers have so far limited the recreational facilities to passive ones, such as footpaths.

2. ADMINISTRATION

2.1 Organization

Since the regionalization of forest matters in 1983, the forest administration has been divided between the regions. The international relations are the only matters that remain at the national level, under the responsibility of the Agronomical Research Administration (Ministry of Agriculture).

The Brussels Region has a very small "Water and Forest Service" that is part of the Department of Natural Resources and Environment.

In the Flemish Region, the forests are administered by the "Green Plan" - Water Resources and Forests, which is in the A.R.O.L. (Administration for land management and natural environment). The central office of the forest service consists of the following six sections:

- finance and administration

- legislation, private forests, scientific research

- forest planning and economics

- estate affairs (purchases) and international relations (EEC, FAO, Benelux)

- hunting and protection of birds

- freshwater fisheries.

The external services consist of:

- 5 "inspections"

- 9 "cantonnements"

- 33 "brigades"

- 120 "triages".

In the <u>Walloon Region</u>, there is a directorate general for forestry attached to the Ministry of the Walloon Region; this directorate general has a central office and external services consisting of 11 "inspections", 36 "cantonnements" 146 "brigades" and 516 "triages".

The Directorate General is charged with:

a) The management and protection of publicly owned forests;

b) The enforcement of the Forestry Code and of the other laws and regulations concerning forests, hunting and fishing;

c) Management of nature reserves;

d) The enforcement of certain special laws and regulations: rural code, pests and diseases, etc.

2.2 Legislation

The <u>Forestry Code</u> of 1854 has hitherto provided the basis for the supervision, protection and exploitation of the publicly owned forests. Private forests are not subject to this Code, but under a law of 1931 the authorities are entitled to oppose abnormal or excessive fellings. Under a law of 1962, private forests are also subject to some restrictions concerning deforestation.

The revision of the Forestry Code is now being envisaged to meet the needs of regionalization and to take account of modern concepts of forest policy.

In the <u>Flemish Region</u>, the main objectives of the forthcoming forestry decree are:

- a clearer definition of "forest" and "non-forest" land;

- recognition of the multi-purpose role of forests;

- fundamental rules for the management of all forests in the Region;

- improvement of the productivity and services of all forests, including those in private ownership.

The measures by which these objectives are to be achieved include, among others: forest inventory, supervision of all fellings, technical assistance to woodland owners, subsidies for afforestation and encouragement of forest property consolidation.

The basis of land use planning is provided in regional development plans.

In the <u>Walloon Region</u>, the revision of the Forestry Code which is now being envisaged aims mainly at eliminating practices which have fallen into disuse and including new prescriptions which take account of modern technology. The recognition of the multi-functional nature of forests and the problems of improving the private forests will also be included in the revision.

2.3 The General Framework of Forest Management

Wood production is of great importance to the national economy: 47,500 salaried personnel and 12,700 independent persons work in the sector, which is responsible for a gross value added of 56 bn BFr per year.

In the Flemish Region, the emphasis in management is on conservation and protection of the forest resource. Particular attention is paid to possible forest decline through atmospheric pollution.

In the Walloon Region, some priorities have been defined. These include, among others:

- forest research

- information and public relations

- forestry training

- encouragement of forest nurseries

- better knowledge of the market

- quality of sawn timber

- adaptation of administration to regionalization.

In the Brussels Region, the main management priorities are:

- the regeneration of over-mature beech stands over the next 18-24 years;

- improving the facilities for the public;

- a study of water resources in the perimeter of the forest.

2.4 Budget

In the Flemish Region, 250 million BFr were provided in the 1986 budget for hunting, fishery, forests and conservation of nature, i.e. 2.98% of the total budget. An additional 90 million BFr were provided for the purchase of forests, reserves and ponds.

In the Walloon Region, 389 million BFr were provided for the above purposes (including 66 million BFr for acquisitions) in 1986.

3. <u>MONETARY AND FISCAL POLICY</u>

3.1 <u>Incentives</u>

In the <u>Flemish Region</u>, the only existing public financial intervention
is based on a royal decree of 1981 by which limited silvicultural
operations undertaken by publicly administered forests (e.g. Communes) may
be subsidized to the extent of 66% of the cost. Private forests receive no
subsidies at present, but may possibly do so, subject to certain conditions
(e.g. management plans), under the new code.

In the <u>Walloon Region</u>, the Communes and other public establishments
receive subsidies of 30% for plantations of conifers, 45% for plantations
of broadleaved species, 60% for tourist facilities and 30% for forest
roads. Aid to private forestry is confined to the payment of BFr 5,000/ha.
for the first thinning in conifer stands, if certain detailed conditions
are fulfilled.

3.2 <u>Taxation</u>

There are two types of tax:

- tax on income (property tax + rates)

- succession taxes.

The first is based on the cadastral income, which is established at
360,000 BFr per 1,000 ha of forest. For this cadastral income, the property
tax is 11,000 BFr per thousand ha. of forest and the additional rates are
180,000 BFr.

The succession tax is based on the market value, for which the
national average is 220 million BFr per 1,000 ha. The first 200,000 BFr are
tax-free.

According to the system of instalments, the total remaining tax of
36.651 million BFr which is due on 1,000 ha. is payable in annual
instalments of 1.221 million BFr over 20 years.

Taking in account the price of wood, the average taxation rate is
about 30%. The private forestry sector is pressing strongly for a reduction
of these taxes.

4. <u>FOREST PROTECTION</u>

Forest fires pose a problem only in the east of the country. Most
fires are caused by man and the months of greatest fire risk are March,
April and May. The problem of wind-thrown wood requires special attention
in some parts of the country.

In the Flemish Region, there is an active policy of purchasing and managing mostly non-forested areas for the conservation of nature. Some of these areas are managed by the forest personnel, others by private associations which may receive subsidies for the purchase and management of areas of conservation interest.

In some forest reserves, there is no management at all, while others are managed so as to achieve a specific conservation objective. Management in many forests outside the reserves is also based on bio-ecological principles so as to maintain the natural value of the forest.

In the Walloon Region, State nature reserves total 4,693 ha. and private reserves about another 5,000 ha. Within the State-owned reserves, there are three forest reserves with a total area of 152 ha.

Recreation

The forests subject to public administration are, in principle, open to the public. Exceptions can be made for technical reasons (protection of regeneration, fire risk, etc.). Demand for recreational opportunities in forests are particularly great near towns. Facilities are planned so as to avoid excessive pressures.

There are no special rules for private forests, but arrangements are sometimes made between local administrations (e.g. Communes) and private owners whereby, in return for opening a property to the public, the owner receives some compensation per metre of opened track.

With regard to hunting, ministerial decrees establish each year which species of game may be hunted and during which period. There are also species which are protected under national legislation.

Relations with Agriculture

Before regionalization, forestry had been under the Ministry of Agriculture. Now the two activities are strictly separate. Conversion of farmland to forestry requires special permission which, in practice, has only been granted sporadically as there are few marginal agricultural areas. A certain interest in afforestation has, however, developed as a result of the EC Directive 797/85 concerning the improvement of agricultural structures. The matter will be debated between foresters and agriculturists in the near future.

5. UTILIZATION

A distinction must be made between private and public forests. There are no specific regulations governing the harvest and transport of timber in the private forests; these aspects are better regulated in the forests under public administration. In these, the timber is sold standing and the felling rules are the same for each region. The rules are specifically designed to prevent damage and protect regeneration and more generally to protect the ecology of the forests. Forest industry is completely separate from forestry and comes under the Ministry of Economic Affairs.

Wages of forest workers are low, the work is hard and has often to be done under unfavourable conditions.

The degree of mechanization of forest operations is still relatively modest. The reasons are economic, structural and physical.

1,200 persons are employed in silviculture and harvesting, spread among 216 enterprises. There is only one enterprise that employs more than 50 people. In addition, there are 955 independent harvesting contractors; for most of these, harvesting is their principal occupation.

6. TIMBER MARKET

The total volume felled in 1984 was as follows:

Ownership	Conifers	Broadleaves (in 1,000 m3)	Total
State forests	180	140	320
Other public forests	563	358	921
Private forests	1,059	657	1,716
Total	1,802	1,155	2,957

The balance of trade of roundwood was as follows in 1981:

	Imports	Exports	Balance
Sawlogs	301	542	+ 241
Small roundwood	3,301	393	- 2,908
Total	3,602	935	- 2,667

7. EMPLOYMENT

The general social legislation applies also to the persons employed in the forestry sector. For forest workers, there is also a separate committee on which both sides are equally represented.

8. EDUCATION AND TRAINING

8.1 Forestry Personnel

Forestry education is available in the Faculties of Agronomy at two universities in the Dutch language and at another two in the French language. Forestry tends to be in a minority position in these faculties.

Training at technical level is more developed in the Walloon Region than in the Flemish Region where there are no specific schools for such training but only some week-end courses. The whole question of training forestry technicians is under review.

8.2 General Public

Information about forestry is published in brochures, many copies of which are distributed to schools.

In the Flemish Region, a "Week of the Forest" is organized every year.

In the Walloon Region, a "day of the tree" is organized each year at the end of November and forest museums have been established in the most frequented forests.

9. SCIENTIFIC RESEARCH

At national level, forestry research is undertaken at:

- the Research Station for Forestry and Water Resources at Groenendaal;

- the Poplar Research Station of the Centre for Agronomic Research of Gent;

- the Station of Forest Technology of the Centre for Agronomic Research at Gembloux.

At regional level, some forestry research projects are financed in collaboration with universities.

10. INTERNATIONAL COOPERATION

Belgium, through its General Administration for Cooperation and Development, provides direct bilateral aid to projects in forestry and forest research in Africa and in South America. It also finances forestry projects of universities and non-governmental organizations and contributes to the activities of international organizations through multilateral aid.

BULGARIA

1. INTRODUCTION

Of the total land surface of 110,000 km2, areas classed as forest account for 3,744,000 ha, or about 34%. All forests in the People's Republic of Bulgaria belong to the nation. An insignificant portion (0.3%) is put at the disposal of agricultural complexes to provide firewood and building material and another 3% is forest pasture on sites which are suitable for the purpose. Some forests (2.3%) are put at the disposal of other public establishments, including forest research institutes.

Before the Second World War, the position had been as follows:

Communal forests	55%
State forests	26%
Private forests	17%
Other forests (cooperatives, religious bodies, etc.)	2%

The socialist revolution of 1944 made it possible to nationalize all forests in 1947/48; by this revolutionary act, all forests have become State forests, which means that they belong to the people. The conditions have thus been created which permit the reasonable utilization of the forest resource and a new approach to the solution of the many problems confronting forestry.

Since nationalization, the country's forestry priorities have been:

- The rapid and categoric realization of a complex series of measures to rehabilitate and protect the forests, to raise their productivity and to ensure that forests play their full part in the conservation of the natural environment;

- The economic and effective use of wood;

- Collaboration, especially with the USSR, but also with other countries in the socialist camp, as well as in Western Europe, Africa and elsewhere.

2. ADMINISTRATION

Forest ownership remains unaltered in the sense that all forests will continue to belong to the State. The fact that forests may be put at the disposal of other establishments does not alter their ownership.

The direction and management of forests is the responsibility of the Association of Forestry and Forest Industry (AFIF) which has its seat in Sofia.

The Department of Forestry at the Ministry of Agriculture is concerned mainly with the direction of policy and it also provides a link between the Government and the AFIF.

Modern multiple use management is of extreme importance to the economy of the country. The forestry sector complex comprises three production systems:

a) Silviculture and wood production, which also includes the administration of accessory activities such as hunting and fresh water fisheries;

b) Mechanical wood processing, including the furniture industry and carpentry;

c) Chemical wood processing, which includes the pulp, paper and board and packaging industries.

Silviculture and wood production is organized into 15 "forestry combinats", the headquarters of which are situated in some major towns in northern and southern Bulgaria. Each combinat has between 5 and 20 forest districts which manage forest operations in the territory of one or more communes.

Forest policy is directed by AFIF in close collaboration with the Ministry of Agriculture and Forestry in accordance with the directives of the Central Committee of the Communist Party of Bulgaria and of the People's Government. Forestry is financed via the budget out of the income from the sale of forest produce, hunting and various other accessory activities. At present, a study is in progress to consider a system of self-financing for districts where there is much production, while the present system of centralized financing would continue for districts with a preponderance of cultural operations (reforestation, erosion control measures, etc.).

3. <u>MONETARY AND FISCAL POLICY</u>

There are financial accounts departments in every forest district as well as in every forestry combinat and in the AFIF. In these accounts offices, all revenues and outgoings, except wages and salaries, are accounted for. Taxation policy is designed to facilitate forestry operations.

All proceeds from the sale of standing timber are remitted to the State budget and credited to the account of a fund entitled "fund for silvicultural operations". As there are no private forests, there is no financial policy regarding these. Agricultural cooperatives, however, receive plants free of charge as well as other aid from the forest districts for erosion control measures or to create new forests on their territory.

4. <u>FOREST MANAGEMENT AND PROTECTION</u>

All the forests of the People's Republic are inventoried and managed. The scientifically motivated and highly efficient silvicultural operations are based on forest management plans which are prepared for all forest districts and represent a point of reference for all silvicultural operations.

In the People's Republic of Bulgaria, the above-mentioned activities are undertaken by the institute "Agrolesprojekt" (Institute for Agricultural and Forestry Studies) which forms part of the organization "Lescomplekt".

The institute Agrolesprojekt, which was founded in 1901, apart from its core forestry planning activity, also plans projects in a variety of specialized activities including erosion control, landscaping near conurbations, wild life management, regional planning, etc.

Forest management plans are reviewed every ten years. There are over 60 erosion control projects within the framework of a national plan for erosion control, 30 projects for river and torrent control, over 150 projects for town parks and forest parks, roadside landscaping, etc. There are also projects for 3,000 km of forest roads. In addition, two maps of Bulgaria's forest have been drawn up.

The forest management plans serve as a basis for forecasting and planning the development of the forest resources and the forest economy up to the end of the 20th century.

In accordance with Article 5 of the Forest Law of 1958, the forests are divided into two groups: forest with economic objectives, and forest with special objectives. The main economic objective is the production of timber but, given the mountainous character of the country, the protective functions are not neglected. The forests with special objectives (where any necessary production is a secondary consideration) are classed as follows:

a) Protection forests, which comprise 18% of the forest area. These include, for example, strips around lakes, along rivers and the shore of the Back Sea, below the tree line in mountains, seed stands, etc.;

b) Forests used for health and recreational purposes (4%);

c) Green belts around towns and industrial centres (2%);

d) Reserves of natural ecosystems which have been subjected to little or no economic activity (1%);

e) Other protected areas, such as national parks and historic sites (1.5%);

f) National shelter belts, mainly in the North-East of the country (0.5%);

g) Eroded forest land (0.3%).

The proportion of forest with special objectives is likely to be increased to about 35% of the total forest area in order to meet the rising demands of the workers and of tourism.

For the protection of forest fauna, thirty districts have been organized; they are partly located in the forest with special objectives. A variety of organizations, including the AFIF, have collaborated in the introduction of planning and controlling the various activities involved: reduction of harmful animals, supplementary feeding of useful game during the winter, etc. These measures have on the whole had a beneficial effect. A rapid increase in game has been achieved through artificial dispersal of animals raised at breeding stations.

Good results have also been achieved with the raising of various species of game birds (partridge, grouse, quail, pheasant, etc.).

The game population includes over 15,000 red deer, 2,700 fallow deer, over 120,000 roe deer, 31,000 wild boar, 1,500 chamois, over 750 bears, etc.

Apart from the increase in the numbers of game, there has also been a considerable improvement in the quality of the trophies. The indications are that substantial further increases in game populations could be achieved without significant damage to forestry or agriculture, and measures to bring about this increase are envisaged.

Although not richly endowed with water resources, there are in Bulgarian waters 86 species of sea fish, 65 species of fresh water fish and 36 migratory species. Fish culture (trout, carp, etc.) is being developed on a considerable scale.

The policy concerning the afforestation of land abandoned by agriculture is implemented by specialized services for land improvement and erosion control, which collaborate with the AFIF, local communities and the forest districts. These services, in addition to afforesting abandoned agricultural land, also plant poplars along the banks of water courses.

The public has access to forests except where such access would interfere with silviculture (e.g.. regeneration) or with the conservation of nature.

Deforestation has virtually been eliminated and illegal fellings, which are severely punished under the Forest Law, are now very rare, as are forest fires.

5. UTILIZATION

The forest districts are responsible for harvesting timber and transporting it to temporary depots. During the past 15-20 years, very large areas of young stands have been thinned as part of a programme to raise productivity. About 125,000 ha. are thinned annually, of which at least 115,000 ha. are stands less than 40 years old. Stands under that age resulting from afforestation already constitute 60% of the country's total forest area. That means that the annual area to be thinned will soon have to be doubled.

Crown thinnings, low thinnings, combined crown and low thinnings as well as line thinnings are employed. The choice depends on species and their biological characteristics.

About 60% of all coniferous stands and 70% of the broadleaved stands are regenerated naturally. In the forests with special objectives, the fellings are conducted not only with a view to ensuring regeneration, but also with a view to safeguarding the special function; that is why the shelterwood system and the selection system are preferred.

The conversion of forests of low productivity and afforestation have led to an increase in the proportion of conifers from 12.3% of the total forest area in 1950 to 33.1% in 1980; a further increase to 40% is expected by the year 2000. Afforestation reached a peak of 80,000 ha. per year during part of the 1960s and now continues at about 40,000 ha. per year.

The combined effect of the above measures will be that the forest resources of the People's Republic of Bulgaria will have more than doubled between 1940 and the year 2000.

There was little development of forest industry before the repurchase by the State of the wood processing plants from cooperatives in 1948. By enlarging and modernizing the small, old fashioned mills, 50 enterprises were created within a short space of time. Improved technology and better organization enabled these to increase production significantly. The wood processing industry has always received assistance from the USSR; the most effective aid has been the participation of Bulgarian workers and specialists in the joint exploitation of forests within the Soviet Union. At present, a considerable number of our enterprises process logs imported from the USSR because the volume of large logs available in Bulgaria's forests has been getting less year by year because of the reduction of old stands.

6. TRADE AND COMMERCE

Wholesale and retail trade in timber is entirely a privilege of the State right from the point when the logs are harvested by each forest district. That privilege also applies to imports and exports of wood and wood products. Exports are kept to a minimum because of the shortage of wood to meet domestic requirements.

A very small amount of tropical wood is imported, mainly from Africa, in order to supply the needs of the furniture industry. For this purpose, a joint enterprise was created in the Republic of Guinea in the 1970s, but this enterprise has since been transferred entirely to the State of Guinea.

7. EMPLOYMENT

The labour code passed by the National Assembly three years ago regulates the relations between workers, employees and employers in forestry and forest industry. The workers and employees are organized by forest districts and forest industrial enterprises in an independent trade union. This union looks after their interests and regulates the relations among the employees themselves as well as with their respective employers and the State. Salaries and social insurance benefits are regulated in accordance with the labour code. Special provisions for safety at work have been issued and are rigorously applied. The proper nutrition of workers and employees is assured on a scientific basis; also the amount of time allowed for eating is assured. Mobile kitchens have been organized, but at some projects in remote areas a hot meal at midday cannot be provided.

In all industrial enterprises, all facilities for personal hygiene (washrooms with hot and cold running water, dressing rooms, etc.) have been installed. This has, however, not yet been possible everywhere in the forest districts for forest workers because of the dispersion of the activities.

There is almost no unemployment at all in forestry and forest industry. On the contrary, there is a shortage of labour because of a migration to other industries where the salaries and working conditions tend to be better.

8. EDUCATION AND TRAINING

Engineers specialized in forestry and wood processing receive their training at the Higher Institute of Silviculture, which also has a department of landscape architecture. For chemical wood processing, engineers are trained at the Institute of Chemical Technology. Both institutes are located in Sofia. The courses at each institute last for 4-5 years.

To meet the demand for technicians and skilled workers, there are 9 intermediate technical schools ("Technicum") and 10 vocational technical schools; there are also 30 professional centres with 18 sub-units for the training of qualified workers. A special centre for refresher courses for managers has been established in order to raise standards. About 200 engineers from the various branches of forestry and forest industry participate each year in the courses, which normally last for 45 days.

Each forest district and industrial enterprise has the right to provide bursaries to its nominees and to send the recipients to the appropriate institutions for training at intermediate or superior level, subject to the requirement that these holders of bursaries subsequently work in the enterprise that has sponsored them.

As work becomes more sophisticated, special attention must be paid to the training facilities at intermediate and superior level in order to meet future staff requirements both in terms of quality and numbers.

9. RESEARCH AND DISSEMINATION OF INFORMATION

Forestry research in Bulgaria began in 1928 when an experimental station was opened with the objective to undertake a "multilateral study of the natural and economic conditions of the Bulgarian forest". Despite difficulties, useful results were achieved. In 1942, the station was converted into the Institute of Forest Research and Experimentation. An enormous increase in forest research personnel and activity was initiated immediately after 1944.

The Institute is an independent body for scientific research within the system of the Academy of Sciences. It continues the traditions of its predecessors in forestry research. Apart from the Central Institute in Sofia, there are outstations in five towns as well as hydrological and anti-erosion observation stations.

Recently, particular attention has been devoted to questions of protecting the environment in collaboration with the Permanent Commission for Nature Conservation and other relevant bodies. The love of nature of the Bulgarian people is reflected in the great support by the public for the activities organized by the National Committee for the Protection of Nature.

For several decades, the first week in April has been dedicated to forestry problems, and during the whole of May, forest ecosystems enjoy privileged attention. A number of laws and guidelines deal with various aspects of protection: against pollution of air, soil and water, etc. The basic document in these matters is the fundamental Normative Document on the conservation, improvement and rehabilitation of the environment, which was promulgated by the Council of State in 1975.

After the USA, the People's Republic of Bulgaria occupies second place with regard to the number of biosphere reserves. Unesco has listed 17 such reserves and more are being planned.

Several journals disseminate information about the protection of forests and of the environment as a whole.

Scientific organizations, schools, universities, the agencies of the Ministry of Agriculture and Forestry, AFIF, and the Committee for the Protection of the Environment all play their part in promoting a better understanding of forestry problems.

10. INTERNATIONAL COOPERATION

Apart from its cooperation with the USSR, which has already been mentioned, the People's Republic of Bulgaria cooperates actively with several countries and international organizations, especially with FAO and the bodies under its patronage which are concerned with Europe and the Mediterranean region, i.e. Silva Mediterranea and the European Forestry Commission, but also with other organizations such as IUFRO.

The organization "Lescomplekt" undertakes consultant assignments as well as projects in forest and forest industrial engineering not only at home but also abroad in a number of countries in Asia, Africa and Latin America. "Lescomplekt" has working contacts throughout the world with similar organizations and with scientific institutions in the fields of forestry and forest industry. It is registered with various international organizations including FAO, UNDP, UNIDO, the Arabian Fund for Social Development and the Development Fund of Kuwait.

CYPRUS

1. INTRODUCTION

The main forests of Cyprus are natural forests which today occupy the two mountain ranges - the Northern Range and the Central Massif - and cover an area of 145,900 ha. There are in addition about 14,300 ha. of lowland State forests, most of which are practically non-existent having been encroached upon and cultivated. Communal forests occupy 1,600 ha. and private forests and plantations about 13,600 ha. The small private forests, which exist in Cyprus mostly on very poor marginal agricultural land, do not usually receive any management from their owners. Limited funds in the Forestry Department are the only obstacle to a radical increase in the area of the State Forests by purchase of abandoned hilly land which has become sub-marginal for agriculture.

The total forest area of all categories is 175,400 ha., which is 19% of the total land area of Cyprus.

2. ADMINISTRATION

Organization of Forestry Administration

Forestry administration in Cyprus at national, district and local levels is the responsibility of the Department of Forests, which is a government department under the Ministry of Agriculture and Natural Resources. The Department has its headquarters in Nicosia, the capital of Cyprus. It is headed by a Director, who is assisted by four Senior Conservators of Forests, who are in charge of the various functions into which the Department is divided. The functions consist of nine Territorial and eight Specialist Divisions.

The Forestry Department is responsible for all matters pertaining to forestry. The formulation of policy is the responsibility of the Minister, the Undersecretary or the Director of the Department, according to the nature of the subject. The formulation of law is the ultimate responsibility of the House of Representatives. Other institutions influence the implementation of the national forest policy in that they influence the allocation of money in the budgets for the execution of projects under the policy.

In Cyprus so far there have been no legal or political constraints in the implementation of the national forest policy, only financial constraints.

National Forestry Policy and National Development

The top priority goal that has always been at the centre of development activities is the increase of water supplies for domestic use and for irrigation. With a view to ensuring rational use of underground water resources, very strict legislation and restrictions on the opening of wells/boreholes have been introduced. Another goal of the Ministry of Agriculture and Natural Resources is the adoption by the farmers of improved methods and techniques of irrigation.

In order to solve the big problems of fragmentation and dispersal of rural holdings, the Ministry of Agriculture and Natural Resources initiated in 1970 the implementation of a Land Consolidation scheme which has appealed to farmers and is advancing at a fast rate.

It can be said that the natural resources sector which had suffered a fatal calamity in the summer of 1974 had revived as if by a miracle by 1984.

The overall environmental objectives of the Government are:

- To preserve the heritage resources of the country;

- To guide and control physical development within desirable limits and mitigate undesirable side-effects;

- To achieve rational development of the resource potential of the island;

- To upgrade the leisure and recreation perspectives;

- In general to improve the overall environmental image within the economic capabilities of the country.

In 1986, an Environmental Conservation Service under the Ministry of Agriculture and Natural Resources was established. There is also a high-level Environmental Committee, comprised of the Permanent Undersecretaries of the Ministries concerned with the environment.

Forestry and National Development

The role of forestry in the Cyprus economy is multi-dimensional and is not reflected by the small contribution to the value added to the economy, which was only 0.1% in 1984.

The forestry development goals for the 1987-1991 Development Plan can be summarized as follows:

- Protection of existing forests;

- Reforestation of gaps in the forests created either by forest fires or fellings and afforestation of newly-declared forest areas;

- Supply of raw materials to forest industries;

- Implementation of the provisions of the Forest Law regarding National Forest Parks and Nature Reserves;

- Increase in productivity and reduction in costs;

- Improvement of newly-established forest plantations through silvicultural treatment;

- Rational management of the forest resources with special emphasis on the preservation and improvement of the environment (flora and fauna).

The percentage of the total public budget (including salaries) allocated to the forestry sector during 1986 (a typical year) was 0.7%.

3. MONETARY AND FISCAL POLICIES

Private Forests

As mentioned earlier, private forestry as a business is non-existent in Cyprus, as is a specific monetary and fiscal policy on private forestry; nor is there a scheme for fiscal incentives. However, the Department of Forests issues forest plants free of charge to public institutions and to private individuals for planting on their land. There are no incentives for the setting up of private owners' associations or cooperatives for the management or marketing of forest products.

Forest Taxation Systems

State forestry is not affected by taxation. As regards private forestry, there are no fiscal measures in the taxation system. The Forest Policy specifies that private forests should be properly protected and managed but there is no legislation to oblige the owners to improve their forests and make them more productive.

4.   FOREST MANAGEMENT AND PROTECTION

The land use provisions in the Forest Policy are as follows:

"Forest Reservation

To reserve in perpetuity as protection forests as much as possible of the high level catchment areas and sufficient other lands, whose cultivation cannot economically be justified, to ensure a prudent balance of agricultural and forest products.

Water Conservation

To prevent flooding and waste, and to regulate the flow of waters by protecting the catchments of streams and other waters.

Soil Conservation

To prevent desiccation of the soil and to arrest soil movement caused by water or wind erosion.

Agricultural Protection

To provide where possible protection for agriculture.

Forest Management and Protection

To apply the principle of the sustained yield to the management of all forests. "

The major destructive agents of the forest resources used to be free-range goat grazing and forest fires. The Forest Policy contains specific provisions for the combating of these agents. The problem of free-range goat grazing in the forests of Cyprus is now past history. The action taken for the solution of the problem included:

- Giving cash payments to graziers who agreed to give up grazing and adopt other means of livelihood;

- Providing employment for the graziers in the forests, e.g. as labourers, fireguards, Forest Guards;

- Allowing sheep grazing in certain areas of the forests and encouraging graziers to change their goats for sheep;

- Removing (with their consent) whole grazing communities from the forests and paying them compensation to settle where they wished or settling them in new villages built for them outside the forests and giving them land to become farmers;

- Introduction and issuing of improved goat breeds, so that the numbers of animals per household could be reduced but incomes remain the same or even increase;

- Experimentation and improvement of pastures and fodder production on arable land;

- Introduction of an adoptive Law - the Goats Law of 1913 - through which villages decided by ballot whether to exclude free-range grazing from the area of their village.

The measures to combat fires have included:

- Publicity and education of the public through the mass media;

- Talks to schools, clubs, the Police and the National Guard;

- Distribution of suitable posters, stickers, etc.

- Establishment/extension of picnic sites in forest areas;

- Organization of patrols to advise and warn the public;

- Manning of fire look-out stations at strategic points;

- Development of an effective telecommunications system (radio and telephone) in the Forestry Department both for reporting and fighting forest fires;

- Establishing a Fire Fighting Task Force;

- Introduction of the use of water and foam in fire fighting;

- Construction of a good network of fire traces/forest roads;

- Use of the Police and the National Guard in fire suppression;

- Placing of all Forestry Department staff (by rotation) on a 24-hour duty roster throughout the fire-hazard season.

The above measures proved very effective and contributed to a reduction of the percentage area of forests burnt annually from 0.31 in the period 1962-73 to 0.13 in the period 1975-86.

In 1967, provision was made for the declaration of certain parts of the main State forests as Nature Reserves in order to provide effective protection for fauna and flora. In addition to what is provided for in the Forest Law and Regulations, there are also provisions for the establishment of protected areas under the Game and Wild Birds (Protection and Development) Law, the Town and Country Planning Law, the Antiquities Law, the Foreshore Protection Law and the Fisheries Law. Responsibility for the management of protected areas lies with the institution that declares the area protected.

Policy Related to the Establishment of Recreational Areas

There is provision in the Forest Policy for the development of recreational areas as follows:

" Public Amenity

To exploit the value of the forests as areas of scenic beauty and amenity for the development of recreation and the expansion of the tourist industry. "

Policies on the participation of the rural organizations in forest management and protection.

Rural organizations, trade unions, youth movements, Boy Scouts, Girl Guides, school children and students, the National Guard and the police and many other institutions participate actively in tree planting and fire fighting, but are not involved to any degree in forest management.

Development of the Mountain Economy, including infrastructure and Services

As regards infrastructural socio-economic development and services, the Pitsilia Integrated Rural Development Project may be regarded as a very successful model in the field of rural development of low-income mountain communities. This project, which was initiated in 1978 and completed in 1984, was the first of its kind in Cyprus. Its basic objective was the improvement of living standards of the people residing in 49 villages in the Pitsilia area. The total cost of the project was CY# 8,750,000 and included a World Bank loan of US$ 10 million.

5.   FOREST UTILIZATION

The Cyprus forests are natural forests, and more than 90% by volume of the growing stock and hence of the yield is Pine (Pinus brutia). The forests are managed using a form of Group Selection System relying on natural regeneration, but augmented with artificial regeneration where natural regeneration is problematic.

The Forestry Department sells all the harvest from the forests in the form of standing trees. Marking of the trees for felling is carried out solely on the basis of silvicultural considerations.

The main institutions involved in logging and transport are:

- Timber buying contractors;

- Timber felling and logging contractors;

- Timber transport contractors.

The forests are in an understocked condition and are not yet able to produce sufficient timber to supply local demand. Woodfuel for heating - usually in open hearths in mountain villages and in the towns - is also in short supply. Gas, oil and electricity are in most cases cheaper than woodfuel, but the latter is preferred. The potential of fuelwood for energy purposes is not likely to be much higher in the near future than the present 0.5% of the total energy requirements in Cyprus.

Until 1974, all the wood industry was in the hands of small private sawmill owners who owned very old-fashioned sawmills and ran them mostly on a cottage-industry basis. In 1974, Cyprus Forest Industries Ltd was established, a public company with 40% of the shares distributed to the general public and 60% owned by the Government, and having a modern, fully automatic sawmill, a very efficient particle board plant with a capacity of 30,000 m3 of particle board per year and a plywood factory with a capacity of around 2,300 m3 of plywood per year using imported logs.

Government policy has been to assist the company mainly by guaranteeing supplies of raw materials at pre-agreed prices and on a long-term basis.

The Government also protects locally-produced timber products by means of import duties and occasionally import restrictions.

Wood utilization in Cyprus is now very efficient and effective, and recovery is almost 100%.

Environmental Restrictions in Forest Utilization

In 1967, provision was made for the classification of the main State Forests into:

- Permanent Forest Reserves to be managed intensively for production of timber;

- National Forest Parks to be used for the provision of amenity and recreation for the public in general;

- Nature Reserves to provide protection to flora and fauna.

There are also restrictions on felling in areas adjoining tourist routes, trunk roads, popular paths and nature trails, and prohibition of felling in rocky areas which are difficult to regenerate; in addition, the felling of Cedars is completely prohibited.

6.   TIMBER TRADE AND MARKETING

The local production of timber and wood products is only about 60,000 m^3 R.U.B. per annum,, whilst the volume of imports is about five times higher, i.e. about 285,000 m^3 R.U.B. equivalent, representing a C.I.F. value of CY£ 41 million. The importation of sawn timber and other wood products is in the hands of timber merchants who have to obtain a licence from the Government before they can import.

7.   EMPLOYMENT

In the 1950s the threat to the forests from certain villages in and near the forests was so grave as to render imperative the almost continuous employment by the Forestry Department of their inhabitants, for whom there was rarely any other work. The arrangement of work which benefits the forests as well as these villagers is still a constant concern of the Forestry Department.

There is no specific industrial legislation relevant to employment in the forestry and forest industry sectors. Recruitment, minimum wages, wage increases, leave regulations and other conditions of employment are determined by free collective bargaining.

The Social Security Scheme in Cyprus covers compulsorily every person gainfully occupied either as an employed person or as a self-employed person.

The creation of conditions of full employment is one of the foremost objectives of the Cyprus Government; unemployment at the time of writing is equal to 3.6% of the economically active population.

8.   FORESTRY EDUCATION AND TRAINING

At professional level, all senior management staff recruited to the Forestry Department must hold a University Degree in Forestry.

At technical level, as early as 1951 the Cyprus Forestry College was established, which provides a two-year Diploma course in basic sciences and the various subjects of Forestry. The language of instruction is English as the course is open to students from other countries.

Vocational training is not organized on a permanent basis and is given in short courses as and when required.

Present trends indicate that by the 21st century there will exist a large pool of personnel professionally qualified in forestry but no jobs to absorb them. There is already some unemployment today.

9. FORESTRY RESEARCH, EXTENSION AND INFORMATION

Forestry Research in Cyprus is carried out by the Research Division of the Forestry Department, which was established in 1954.

During the last ten years, the work of the Research Division has centred on the improvement of the Brutia Pine (Pinus brutia), which is virtually the only economically significant tree of the Cyprus forests. The following projects are currently under way:

- Artificial selection and propagation of selected individuals, namely selection of "Plus" trees, establishment of seed orchards, tree banks, provenance trials, progeny trials.

- Hybridization, namely experimental cross pollination of Pine species.

The responsibility for implementing the extension programme rests with all the staff of the Forestry Department. However, other institutions, like the Government Press and Information Office, the Cyprus Broadcasting Corporation (Radio and T.V.), the press, schools, the Interministerial Committee for Youth Activities, various environmental organizations (NGOs) and the Extension Service of the Department of Agriculture, play an important role in forestry extension and public education. Perhaps the most significant role has been played by the Cyprus Forestry Association, in existence since 1920.

10. INTERNATIONAL COOPERATION

The Cyprus Forestry Department has developed a policy of extensive international relations and cooperation. Institutions with which good relations and cooperation are maintained include:

- The Governments and Forestry Services of many countries of the world;

- Universities, Research Centres and other forestry institutions in many countries;

- FAO of the United Nations and all its associated departments and commissions;

- UNDP and related institutions;

- IUFRO and related institutions;

- The European Forestry Commission;

- The ECE - Timber Committee;

- The EEC - on forestry matters;

- Unesco;

- UNEP;

- IUCN;

- ICRAF;

- the Commonwealth Secretariat and the Commmonwealth Fund for Technical Cooperation;

- The Oxford Forestry Institute;

- The Commonwealth Agricultural Bureau;

- The Commmonwealth Forestry Association.

CZECHOSLOVAKIA

1. INTRODUCTION

1.1 The Czechoslovak forests

The Czechoslovak Socialist Republic (CSSR) consists of the Czech Socialist Republic (CSR) and the Slovak Socialist Republic (SSR).

Forests occupy an area of 4,582,000 ha., which corresponds to 35.8% of the total surface area of 12,800,000 ha.

The afforestation of land unsuitable for rational agriculture has increased the forest area by about 10% since 1945.

97.27% of the forests belong to the State, 2.69% are in the hands of uniform agricultural cooperatives and 0.05% are private.

Socialization of the forest resource has created the basic prerequisites for benefitting from the advantages of socialist production ways and relations. The forestry policy of the CSSR is directed towards a goal-oriented and planned development of forestry and uniform control of the entire sector.

A very significant role is played by genetics and selection. These two disciplines have a long-standing tradition in the CSSR and are developed to a very high level.

The Forest Act distinguishes between economic forests, protective forests and special purpose forests, but all CSSR forests have a multi-purpose function. This means that even the economic forests have to fulfil all the other useful functions of the forest. The protective, and even more, the special purpose forests also fulfil, though to a limited extent, the production function.

Generally speaking, the forest has an irreplaceable role in the protection and creation of the living environment as well as being an irreplaceable constituent of the landscape.

Forestry policy provides for constant improvement of work safety and the social status of the foresters, upgrading of their qualifications, improvement of their working and living conditions.

1.2 Forest Law

The principles of the forestry policy are all included in the Forest Law and the accompanying legal measures. The present-day Forest Law, passed in 1977, consists of a set of individual laws and decrees: the federal law on forests, the Czech and Slovak national laws on forest and State forest administration economy, the Czech and Slovak decrees concerning specialized forest administration, the forest rangers, protection of the forest land fund, classification of forests and forest planning.

2. STATE ADMINISTRATION

2.1 Administration of national forest wealth

Following the federal constitution of the Czechoslovak Socialist Republic, ministries of forest and water economy were established in the two national republics. They represented the supreme bodies of the State forest and water economy administration as well as of anti-pollution protection.

Forest economy administration is carried out by specialized departments in the ministries and by departments of water, forest and agricultural economy in regional and district national committees.

2.2 Organization of the forest economy

The already completed process of forest socialization resulted in the corresponding management and organisation of the national forests. The national Ministries of Forest and Water Economy control directly, without any intermediates, the State forest enterprises and other forestry organizations. Furthermore, each ministry controls within its territorial competence the Research Institute of Forest Economy, the Lesprojekt (Institute of Engineering), the Enterprise of Technical Development and the Administration of Forest and Water Economy Staff Training and Education.

Other State organizations may utilize the national forests, thanks to an exception from the Forest Law in cases where they need the forest to accomplish their tasks.

A totally uniform specialized economy of all CSSR forests is guaranteed. State forest enterprises are state economy organizations whose territorial competence corresponds approximately to the regional borders of the Republic. Individual enterprises, which average about 25,000 ha., constitute the basic organizational units. They are subdivided into forest administrations of about 2,500 ha. and forest districts of 800 ha.

The Ministries of Forest and Water Economy are responsible for elaborating forest policies, which have to meet the societal needs of the national economy. They communicate with the central administration, political and trade union bodies of the national republics, as well as federal bodies. They cooperate with the Czechoslovak Academy of Sciences, with university-level forestry faculties, with a national office for press and information, radio and TV.

The research institutes of forestry, the Lesprojekts and the Institutes for forestry education and training are directly controlled by the Ministry of Forest and Water Economy.

2.3 State forestry policy and the development of the State

In its initial stipulations, the Law on Forests states:

"The forests are one of the major wealths of this country; they are one of the basic environmental components yielding at the same time a permanent timber for the national economy. The forests improve and influence the atmosphere, water and soil; they create natural environments for numerous plant and animal species and their communities; they maintain natural beauties while being the source of health and refreshment of the population".

The Forest Law deals with all production and service functions concerning the forest and forestry.

Apart from the Ministry of Forestry, the following bodies influence State forestry policy: the Ministry of Culture, the Ministry of Agriculture and Nutrition, the Ministry of Industry, the Ministry of Education, the Ministry of Finance, the Ministry of National Defence, the National Commission for Scientific, Technical and Investment Development, the National Planning Commission and national committees at all levels.

In the Czechoslovakian planned economy, the connection between forestry plans and the entire national economy development plans is of utmost importance. The national economic plans can be divided into long-term development plans (10-20 years), medium-term plans (5-10 years) and one-year annual operating plans. The generally valid legal measures are compulsory and binding on forestry planning.

It is necessary in long-term planning for the national economy plan to be adapted to the possibilities and prerequisites of forestry, while in short-term planning, five-year plans and annual executive plans, it is necessary that forestry planning fully covers accomplishment of the national economy plan.

The proportion of forestry in the national income of Czechoslovakia is only 1%. Production equipment costs represent only 0.43%, however, wages represent 1.56%. Thus is can be seen that forest production is highly labour-intensive with rather low levels of technical equipment, compared to the average of other branches of the national economy.

Current operating costs and capital investments in forestry are covered by the forest economy from its own activities. The Government does not grant any investment credits to forestry.

3.   FINANCE AND TAXES POLICY

Since there are practically no private forests in the CSSR, the State finance policy has an impact only on State forestry organizations. Wood prices are based on production costs, taking into account at the same time the utility value of individual species. Prices are not determined by the market mechanism and are adjusted periodically. Other service functions of the forest are not reflected in the prices.

4.   FOREST ECONOMY AND PROTECTION

4.1 Forest economy modifications

In order to guarantee permanently the forest's production and other useful functions, individual forest units elaborate at regular 10-year intervals, forestry economic plans connected with and based on annual national forest inventories.

Since 1960, all the forests in the CSSR have been economically adapted regardless of their size and utilization. The forests have also been analyzed with regard to natural conditions and mapped according to individual forest types. Terrain classification has been carried out according to slope, bearing capacity of the soil and transport obstacles.

4.2 Forest Protection

Unplanned production necessitated by calamities has reached at the present time about one half of all production. The cause of this situation can be traced back to the historical development of forests in Czechoslovakia where most of the natural, mainly mixed, woods were transformed into monocultures of spruce or pine.

In the last 40 years, the state of health of the forests has been considerably impaired by atmospheric pollution and its impact on forest soils. Mainly affected are the mountain areas in the entire northern part of the CSR (Czech Socialist Republic). Recently, damage has been discovered in other exposed localities of the CSR and SSR (Slovak Socialist Republic). Analyses of damage caused by emissions have shown that the damage intensity is closely related to weather extremes (frost, cold, drought) weakening the resistance of the trees or enhancing concentrations of noxious substances in the atmosphere. Weakened trees then represent a favourable environment for the proliferation of leaf- and bark-eating insects.

Measures against damage caused by industrial emissions have a long-standing tradition in the CSSR. Depending on emission concentrations, all forests were classified into four risk zones. Investigations carried out in 1968 established that approximately one-third of all forests are exposed to noxious emissions.

Economy and management in emission-affected forests differs considerably from that in unaffected forests. In the most threatened areas, the production aspect is pushed into the background in favour of the remaining functions. In mountain areas, the water economy and land protection functions are of primary importance. In many cases, it is no longer possible to work with the original coniferous species, and less productive but more resistant broadleaved species must be planted. Moreover, the preservation of the gene fund of threatened woodlands is extremely important so as to enable their reintroduction to the affected zones after the foreseen cessation of emissions.

Other significant causes of damage are snow and wind. Considerable damage is also caused by game, especially deer.

4.3 Water economy and land protection forest function

The Czechoslovak Socialist Republic is located on the watershed of three seas - the Atlantic, the Baltic and the Black Sea. That is why its forests have exceptional water economy importance. Czechoslovakia depends totally on precipitations for its water supplies, more than 50% of which fall on forests. For these reasons, forests must guarantee both the quantity and quality of water supplies. These requirements are stipulated by the Water Law of 1973 in all areas important from the water economy point of view.

4.4 Protection and improvement of the environment

In highly industrialized Czechoslavakia, the forest and forestry have an irreplaceable role in the protection and improvement of the environment. In compliance with the Law on Nature Protection, national parks, protected regional areas, State natural reservations and protected natural formations are established and officially proclaimed. The national parks are established by the governments of the national republics. Protected landscape areas and State natural reservations are established by the Ministry of Culture.

It is assumed that the protected landscape zones, together with the national parks, will cover in a very short time approximately 10% of the total forest surface area in Czechoslovakia.

The State natural reservations are mostly established in forests preserved in their original and natural state. At present, there are about 3,000 State natural reservations officially established and others are to follow. The oldest reservations were officially established more than 120 years ago - the Zofin primeval forest in the Novohradske Mountains, the Boubin primeval forest in the Sumava Mountains and the Dobroc primeval forest in Slovakia.

In Czechoslovakia, about 70% of all forests are used for recreation purposes. Forest management has to be modified, however, only in forests with an important recreation function in close proximity to big cities and industrial agglomerations and in areas of concentrated summer and winter sports. The spa forests established in close proximity to spa centres have a special health function.

4.5 Game keeping and hunting

Game keeping and hunting have a long-standing tradition in Czechoslovakia and are very popular with all walks of life. Hunters must have a hunting permit and must be members of the Czech or Slovak hunters' associations. Forest enterprises have the right to hunt on only 20% of their forest area, while the remaining hunting areas are leased to hunters' associations. The hunting permit entitles the owner, at the same time, to own and use listed hunting arms. The hunting permit may be acquired only by graduates of forestry schools or inhabitants who have passed special examinations as determined by the Hunting Law.

The production of one hectare of hunting area is on average 0.8 kg of game per year. There are, however, numerous problems in game keeping. The intensive application of chemicals and the mechanization of agriculture have drastically reduced the numbers of small game, especially hares, partridges and pheasants. On the other hand, deer and boars exceed permissible numbers and are penetrating into areas where they have never lived before. The excessive populations cause damage not just in forests but also on agricultural land.

In order to reduce the damage caused by deer, some intensive breeding areas have been established. To preserve rare animal species, reservations with special statutes have been established.

4.6 Development of the mountain economy

In mountainous areas, the protection of land and water is exceptionally important. In the most threatened areas, biological or technical amelioration is carried out to prevent land erosion and control run-off.

Mountain streams, and indeed all streams in the CSSR, are administered by State water economy organizations in compliance with the Water Law. Forestry organizations administer most of the brooks and torrents.

5. UTILIZATION OF FORESTS

5.1 Wood production and transport

In the Czechoslovak forests, wood production is highly mechanized. Because of the distribution of the woodworking industry, most of the timber is transported by road to the processing plants, whilst only a minor part is shipped to the consumer by rail.

Technical developments and rationalization of labour have resulted in the systematic reduction in the time needed for the production of 1 m3 of wood. The current production time is 2.21 hours.

The ever-increasing pressure to obtain timber for processing has resulted in the greater utilization of wood of small dimensions obtained from young stands, and of lower quality wood from broadleaved species and residues. Such measures are evaluated not only economically - from the point of view of energy and cost requirements - but also ecologically.

5.2 Wood and timber processing

Wood processing in Czechoslovakia is carried out mainly by State organizations controlled by the national ministries of industry. Only a small proportion of the wood is processed by forestry organizations as associated secondary production as well as by specialized production cooperatives.

About 25-30% of wood products are intended for export.

Because of industrial emissions, forestry production will be
stagnating or even decreasing while the social demand for wood products
will continue to grow and the pressure to utilize all residues will
increase. Bark and sawdust are used mainly as energy sources in the timber
industry but a considerable amount of bark is also used for fertilization
in agriculture and in forest nurseries.

Investment financing of the wood processing industry development is
covered by the industry's own resources and from the State budget. The wood
processing industry - like all other branches of the national economy - is
controlled by the State plan.

The development of the wood processing industry is studied together
with its impact on the environment, and especially on water pollution. The
highest waste water pollution occurs in pulping and the manufacture of
agglomerated and chip boards. In the newly-built plants, chemical raw
materials for further processing and production are recovered from the
waste water to maximum extent. In compliance with existing legal measures,
efficient cleaning and treatment equipment is installed in all works.

5.3 Energy from wood

Recently, great attention has been paid to the utilization of
low-quality wood for energy, but special forest plantations for energy
purposes are not being considered.

Special boilers are manufactured in the CSSR to heat forestry and
wood-working plants or smaller housing blocks and units. Compared to
conventional energy sources, wood costs are about 40% higher than lignite
but substantially lower than fuel oil or natural gas. Wood will always
remain only a marginal energy source since most of it will be utilized for
industrial processing.

6. TIMBER BUSINESS

The domestic and foreign timber exchanges are governed by the State
plan. All wood raw material, including chips, is traded by the national
Ministries of Forestry and Water Economy. Foreign trade is carried out by
specialized foreign trade corporations.

Raw wood prices on the home market are not influenced by the market
but the prices of exported timber are determined by world market prices.

7. EMPLOYMENT

7.1 Forestry workers

The rights and duties of all branches of the Czechoslovak national
economy are governed by the unified labour code and the regulations issued
to execute it. Another generally valid legal measure is the National
Insurance Law guaranteeing to every worker free health care in case of
illness and sickness fees in case of work disability. In compliance with

the Retirement Law, every citizen has the right to an old-age pension after the age limit of 60 years in the case of men and 57 years in the case of women. In the case of women, the age limit is further decreased, depending on the number of children borne.

Of the total Czechoslovak manpower, forestry labour represents 1.23% and the wood processing industry 2.34%.

Staff numbers in individual branches of the national economy are determined by the central planning body.

The wages of forestry workers are 3% higher than average wages in the national economy, while those of the wood processing industry are 7% lower.

7.2 Care for workers

Exceptional attention to be paid to the welfare of workers through skill upgrading, health care, housing construction, greater work hygiene, better working conditions, etc. Housing construction has had a decisive impact on the stabilization of skilled labour. During the last ten years, about 20% of all forestry workers went to live in new apartments.

A significant role is played by trade unions in the care for workers. Workers in the forestry and wood processing industry have one united trade union organization: the Trade Union of Workers of the Wood Industry, Forestry and Water Economy. Unions are represented at each enterprise and plant. The trade unions are involved in decisions concerning remuneration, performance standards, wage regulations, health insurance, etc.

7.3 Health protection and work safety

Health protection and safety at work have an exceptional priority. The relevant rules, instructions and measures are broken down in individual forestry organizations to correspond to local specific conditions. Their implementation is furthered by training, schooling and a system of regular checks. Training of forest workers and forest administrators is carried out every year.

8. EDUCATION AND TRAINING IN FORESTRY

8.1 School system in forestry

Forestry training and instruction is provided by secondary-level vocational schools and forestry faculties controlled by the national ministries of education. Vocational forestry schools provide a complete secondary level education. Only boys who have completed an eight-year elementary education are accepted. The studies last four years and culminate in a school-leaving examination. Graduates from the secondary level vocational forestry schools are then sent to manage basic forestry organizations - forestry districts - or are called upon to carry out some special functions in higher level units - forestry administrations or forestry enterprises. The two national republics have their own forestry faculties. In the Czech Socialist Republic (CSR), the forestry faculty is part of the University of Agriculture, while in the Slovak Socialist Republic (SSR), the forestry faculty is part of the Forestry and Wood Industry University.

University-level education in wood processing is provided for the whole of Czechoslovakia by one single wood processing faculty in the SSR.

The education and training of forest workers, as well as of other technicians, are provided by specialist bodies in the Ministries of Forest and Water Economy - the Administrations of Forestry and Water Economy Education controlled by forestry and enterprise schools. The three-year vocational course is open to boys who have completed their eight-year elementary school education.

Forestry faculties offer postgraduate courses with specialized professional orientation. Vocational forestry schools offer post-secondary school studies. There are centres at all State forest enterprises offering various courses for workers and technicians.

General education schools deal with forestry only in terms of its general position within the national economy and community development. The public is informed about the role of forests as an irreplaceable factor in the creation and protection of the environment.

8.2 Specialized press

In the two Republics each month one specialized magazine is issued dealing with operating practice as well as one review based mainly on theory and science.

The forestry and hunting literature is published mainly by the State Agricultural Publishing Houses, which also publish textbooks for forestry faculties, forestry vocational schools and forestry training centres.

Forestry research institutes issue Study Proceedings, Forestry Research Information, Technical and Economic Information, Study Information, etc. Forestry faculties publish their own Study Proceedings.

All State forest enterprises publish their own magazine.

9. RESEARCH, DEVELOPMENT AND INFORMATION

In the CSSR, forestry research has both a general and applied character. Basic research is centred mainly in specialized institutes of the Czechoslovak Academy of Sciences and in forestry faculties. Applied research is carried out and provided for by the Czech and Slovak Forestry Research Institutes controlled by the national forest and water economy ministries. The division between basic and applied research appears to be disadvantageous because mutual coordination is very difficult. Very often, the basic research does not solve the problems and tasks indispensable for applied research.

Completed research tasks are always described in a final report open to opposing views. The results are applied by the Ministries of Forest and Water Economy and by the organizations controlled by them. In more complex cases, the researchers themselves participate in practical implementation.

9.2 Publicity

Exceptional attention is paid to forestry publicity and its close connection with the environment. Top scientific and practical foresters regularly publish articles in dailies and other periodicals; they often speak on radio and TV and participate in press discussions; they are active in the Scientific and Technical Association, the Union of Nature Protection and other social and youth organizations.

10. INTERNATIONAL COOPERATION

The most important Czechoslovak participation in international organizations is in the Council of Mutual Economic Assistance - the international organization of socialist countries where forestry problems are dealt with by the Permanent Commission on Agriculture with its specialized forestry section.

Cooperation is centred on science and practice, on biological, technical and economic issues. The cooperation is implemented in the form of coordination consultations and symposia, transfer of information, consultations of specialists, exchange of scientists and men of practice, etc.

In addition, annual forestry section meetings are organized in individual member countries; these meetings deal with a predetermined range of selected problems.

Because of its acquired knowledge and experience, the participation of the CSSR is extremely important in questions connected with the forest dying due to atmospheric pollution and unfavourable changes in the development of forest soils.

Since 1969, the CSSR has been a member of FAO.

Within the Economic Commission for Europe (ECE), the Czechoslovak forestry representatives are active in the Wood Committee and the Committee for Trade Development.

The number of Czechoslovak IUFRO members is quite impressive.

The selection station of the Czech Forestry Research Institute is a member of the International Seed Testing Association (ISTA) and has acquired the right to issue international certificates for seeds exported from the CSSR.

The Czechoslovak Socialist Republic is an active member of the ISO - International Organization of Standardization.

10.2 Technical assistance to developing countries

The technical assistance provided by Czechoslovakia to forestry in the developing countries of Africa, East Asia and South America is quite advanced. The technical assistance is mediated through FAO or on the basis of bilateral international agreements.

DENMARK

1. INTRODUCTION

Forest area

Denmark's total forest area (1976) comprises 493,000 ha., i.e. about 11.5% of Denmark's total area (43,080 sq. kms); 406,000 are forest-clad. Almost all Danish forests are high forests.

One-third of the forests are broadleaved (mainly beech and some oak, ash and sycamore) and two-thirds are coniferous (mainly spruces and firs). Between 1965 and 1976 there was an increase of 19,000 ha. in "non-forest-clad" areas and 2,000 ha. in actual forest. This reflects the policy of the Government to buy land for outdoor recreation; in most cases non-forest-clad areas are preferred.

The area with broadleaved trees, notably with beech, is shrinking, mostly being replaced by spruce.

Forest area by ownership

Owners	Total forest area (ha.)	
	1965	1976
Central Government)		149,531)
Parishes)	147,630	1,060) 169,923
Municipalities)		19,332)
D. Heath Society	12,058	12,214
Foundations	24,152	27,162
Companies,		
enterprises, etc.	31,536	58,665
Individuals	257,074	225,330
	472,450	493,294

Seventy-six percent of Denmark's forest area is made up of forest properties above 50 ha., and 9% of forest properties under 5 ha. But the latter very small properties constitute 79% of the total number of forest properties. Eighty-nine percent of the number of these "small woods" are parts of farms.

Production

Denmark's total annual "allowable cut" can be set at 2 million cu.m. with bark at present (after heavy storm-fellings), i.e. about 5 cu.m. per forest-clad hectare. The allowable cut is expected to increase to 2.3 million cu.m. by the year 2000, and to 2.9 million cu.m. by 2010. The total present annual increment is estimated to be 2.2 million cu.m. with bark. Denmark is at present only 25% self sufficient in forest products.

2. THE PRESENT FOREST ACT

The basic goal of the present Forest Act of 1935 is to ensure a large and valuable wood production. This is done mainly by imposing a special forest maintenance obligation on the greater part of the forests in the country.

The obligatory forest areas must be kept covered with trees of such kind, quality and quantity that they form closed high forest (or by continuous growth will be able to form closed high forest within a reasonable period of time). In the Act, this is called "good forestry".

The forest maintenance obligation is an area-reservation for silviculture. This means that these areas cannot be taken over for other uses, such as building, urbanizing, sport and leisure constructions, etc., without special permission from the forest authorities.

These rules have always been administered in a very strict way. Permission for other use of a forest area is almost without exception given only on condition of afforesting another area.

This strict administration has, inter alia, given the result that the forest area in Denmark within the last 150 years has increased from about 2% to about 11% of the country today.

The forest authorities are guided by the National Forest Council, which consists of government officials and representatives of forestry organizations.

The Act further contains various regulations concerned with nature conservation, e.g. the prevention of clearing broadleaved forests.

Additional laws supplementing the Forestry Act include the provision that a coherent obligatory forest of less than 50 ha. cannot be divided without a special licence.

3. ADMINISTRATION

Organizational pattern of forestry administration, etc.

Until 1973 practically all public forest administration came under the Ministry of Agriculture. After long consideration in government circles a new Ministry of the Environment was established in 1973/74 with responsibility, inter alia, for:

- the management of the national forests by the National Forest Service;

- the administration of the Forestry Act and other Acts such as the Sand Drifts Act which apply to private forests as well as to State forests;

- the protection of Nature, Monuments and Sites (transferred from the Ministry of Culture).

The Ministry of Agriculture retained responsibility for:

- support of private forestry
- forestry research
- vocational and technical level education.

As from January 1987 the National Forest Service and the National Agency for the Protection of Nature, Monuments and Sites have been combined to form the National Forest and Nature Agency. The new agency has the task of strengthening the integrated policy concerning forest production and nature conservation. The tasks of the agency are management of the State forests, outdoor recreation, administration of legislation concerning private forestry, dunes, nature conservation, utilization of soil-materials, buried relics of the past, trade in forest products, and mapping of the sea bed.

The headquarters of the new Forest and Nature Agency comprises 13 divisions and employs 258 persons, 120 of whom are academic professionals. Local units, which consist of 33 districts and one seed and plant station, employ 1,818 persons broken down as follows:

academic forestry professionals	43
forest technicians, etc.	196
clerks, apprentices, etc.	57
workers, wardens, etc.	1,522
Total:	1,818

Degree of centralization or decentralization; functions and responsibilities

So far the Forest Service has been rather decentralized, i.e. the heads of forest districts (skovridere) have considerable freedom of action within the limits set by the 15-year working plans, annual net budgets and regulations on such matters as the use of herbicides.

Concerning the exercise of authority in private forests, much is also delegated to the heads of government forest districts, but exemptions from legal regulations must normally be submitted to the headquarters of the Forest Service for decision.

The Agency for the Protection of Nature has neither regional nor local branches, but works in a rather centralized way. The County Councils are in fact the regional authorities for the enforcement of the relevant legislation, but they are rather independent. This status of the County Councils will probably be maintained, but the districts of the new Forest and Nature Agency are expected to become the links with the County Councils and be entrusted with a good deal of decision making. Many of the problems that they will in future meet outside their own boundaries will be similar to the problems they already know from inside.

The Ministry of Agriculture is also responsible for hunting and wildlife management, a museum for hunting and forestry, and forest research and education at the level of forest technicians and workers (skilled workers, though, come under the Ministry of Educ

Technological forest research is maintained by the Ministry of Industry, as are also forest industry and trade. Professional forestry education and some research, particularly on genetics, come under the Ministry of Education, which is also responsible for the training of skilled forest workers, though part of it takes place at the School of Forestry (Ministry of Agriculture). Forest development aid to non-industrialized countries is maintained by the organization DANIDA in the Ministry of Foreign Affairs.

4. POLITICAL INITIATIVES FOR FOREST POLICY

Recently, the following initiatives of relevance to the formulation of policy for the forest sector have been taken in Denmark:

(a) A number of studies on the community and social impacts of forestry and the timber industry have been carried out, among them a study on the macro-economic impact of the forest sector in Denmark and studies on the use of the forests for recreation and on the population's forest preferences.

(b) The Minister of Agriculture has set up a Committee on Forest Policy. This committee reported in November 1986. A number of the conclusions of the committee will be mentioned in this paper.

(c) In January 1987, the National Forest and Nature Agency was established as an aggregation of the National Forest Agency and most of the National Agency of Nature Conservation.

(d) In March 1987, the Minister of the Environment presented a statement to the Environmental and Planning Council of Parliament concerning nature conservation and outdoor recreation. The statement underlines, inter alia, that forestry and afforestation of marginal agricultural land has a major influence on nature conservation and recreation now and in the future.

(e) In June 1987, Parliament presented a statement on an aggregated strategy for marginal agricultural land. The statement concentrates on four major fields:

- conservation of peatland and agricultural land around lakes and streams;
- re-establishment of the so-called small biotopes in open, intensively-cultivated agricultural land;
- afforestation of poorer, marginal agricultural land; and
- improvement of the possibilities for recreation and tourism in the open land.

The statement is connected with the activities concerning the discussions on future agricultural policy in the European Common Market.

(f) In April 1987, Parliament adopted a plan concerning environmental improvement of the sea around Denmark. Part of the pollution of the sea originates from intensive agriculture and this plan also emphasizes the importance of forestry as a "cleaning" factor to the environment.

(g) In April 1987, the Minister of Agriculture presented a statement on future forest policy in Denmark. It is stated that forest policy in Denmark has four main objectives:

- to ensure an increased production in forestry and in the timber industry, and less dependence on import of timber products;
- to ensure the existence of a private forest sector with profitable companies;

- to increase the environmental and recreational values of the
  forests; and
- to improve the utilization of resources in forestry and
  profitability.

(h) A bill of a new Forest Act was presented to Parliament on 28
January 1988 by the Minister of the Environment. The bill will
give a more explicit formulation of the balance between the
economic yield and the recreational benefits of the forests.
Also, the bill will emphasize the importance of governmental
supervision of private forest owners.

(i) A bill of a new Act concerning the structure and efficiency of
agriculture was presented to Parliament on 18 February 1988. The
bill is a follow-up of initiatives in the European Common Market
with the purpose of strengthening the common policy of
agriculture. The proposal has three means:

- subsidies to afforestation;
- subsidies to farming that protects the environment; and
- subsidies to suspend intensive agriculture (set-aside).

(j) A bill of a new Act concerning the preservation of nature,
afforestation by the State, etc. was presented to Parliament on 18
February 1988.

It is the perception of the Danish Government that it should
regulate the development in forestry mainly in the following
fields:

- increase of timber production;
- improvement of nature, environmental and recreational
  considerations in forestry; and
- research and education in forestry.

In the following, other statements by the Government are referred
to.

5.   OTHER ISSUES CONCERNING FOREST POLICY

Of the total national budget, about 1.4 billion Danish kr. are
allocated to forestry.

There is not much special monetary and fiscal legislation for forests.
This is notably true of income taxes. It should be mentioned, though, that
it is the practice of the tax authorities in case of serious storm-fellings
to consider half of the value of the storm-felled trees as capital
withdrawal and thus tax-free.

As to tax on real property including land tax, the assessment of the
rateable property value and land value presents a problem in forestry.
This is firstly due to the fact that the statistics for forest sales prices
are mostly based upon small forests, since they dominate the market and on
average can fetch higher (fancy) prices per hectare than big forests, which
are usually commercial properties. Secondly, it is decisive which rate of
interest is chosen for the calculation (capitalizing) - a low rate will

lead to a high value and _vice versa_: 4-5% has been used in recent years; thirdly, the conversion from property value to land value is somewhat questionable; fourthly, the property value affects the fortune value directly, and indirectly the fortune levy and the gift or death duty.

Monetary incentives (e.g. grants and loans) include the following:

- for afforestation on bare lands the Ministry of Agriculture pays part of the investment costs, other than land acquisition, subject to forest maintenance obligation;

- coverage by the Ministry of Agriculture of about 70% of the advisers' salaries and some allowances;

- grants may be paid to owners of small private woods with the dual purpose of promoting employment and improving future production and environment. Most of this money has been spent on much-needed thinnings;

- loans and grants to woodland owners and forest industries after storm fellings.

Forests over 50 ha. are granted an extra reduction of 20% of the appraised property value before computation of taxes.

The fiscal measures mentioned above unfortunately leave a meagre result, notably for big properties with big buildings, so that owners, with the generally unfavourable development of wages as against prices for wood, may be tempted to neglect good forestry measures and resort to ruthless exploitation.

It has not been possible so far to achieve fiscal legislation that is suitable for forestry. This applies particularly to the provisions covering inheritance.

6. THE BILL FOR A NEW FOREST ACT

On 28 January 1988, the Minister of the Environment presented a bill for a new Forest Act to the Danish Parliament.

Like the present Act the bill has as an essential goal a large and valuable wood production, but in a way that differs from the present Act on several points.

The bill emphasizes the importance of multiple-use forestry. At the same time measures should be taken to maintain the interests of wood production as well as the interests of environmental matters and recreational benefits.

This multiple-use forestry is to be realized through several different rules.

(a) As with the present Act the forest maintenance obligation is imposed on the greater part of the forests.

(b) The bill contains the basic rules for what is called good forestry.

(c) There are special rules to ensure better protection of forest boundaries with broadleaved species and bushes, of small biotopes in the forest, etc.

(d) There are rules on economic subsidies to private forest owners for establishing new stands of broadleaved trees, especially beech and oak.

(e) The State Forestry, who locally is the supervisor of the private forest owners, should in a higher degree than at present be a consultative and informative authority rather than a traditional supervisor.

(f) A new Forest Council will be appointed. It will consist of government officials and representatives of forestry organizations, the Danish Nature Conservation Association, the Leisure Council and forestry science.

It has finally to be emphasized that although the bill of a new Forest Act contains rules on environmental matters and recreational benefits, the main point of the bill is still to ensure a large and valuable wood production.

7. FOREST MANAGEMENT AND PROTECTION

The idea is spreading of having groves or woods as shelter against wind, smoke and noise.

In the national forests the management is a multiple-use one with a broad pattern varying from place to place. Increasing stress is laid on recreation. The same applies to most communal forests.

Problems of storm and sea water are of great importance in Denmark. Precautions include careful choice of species and provenances, shelterbelts and proper thinning systems. Forest fires are prevented by restrictions and fought by fire brigades.

The work on the privately-owned dunes along the North Sea is directed by the local Forest Service district, the chief of which is chairman of a so-called Sand Drift Commission in which there are two further members: one .chosen by the regional county council and one by the local commune. The detailed continual inspection and the detailed direction of the practical work is performed by the communal member, assisted by one or more appointed dune wardens (klitfogeder). The expenditure is divided according to detailed rules between the Government (Forest Service), the County Council, the Commune and the owners. There are heavy constraints on building, digging, etc. in the dunes. Because of the greatly increased use of the dunes by tourists it has also become necessary to restrict the traffic therein.

Nature reserves and game reserves are other protected areas, with access restrictions even to those on foot, at least during parts of the year. The Forest Service is usually responsible for their management.

- 62 -

There is free access on foot, on horseback and on bicycle round the clock in public forests. Closures and explicitly forbidden areas are exceptions.

Private forests larger than 5 ha., served by a public road or path, or which are legally accessible in some other way, are open to the public, but only on foot and on existing roads, and not at night, nor within 50 m. of habitations or with loose dogs. The owner, however, can forbid access on hunting days, and where intensive forest work is taking place.

With Denmark's small forests and uncultivated areas, its intensive agriculture and increasing traffic, various animal and plant species are becoming rarer. Old-fashioned exercises by scouts mostly cause little damage, but a special threat is presented by orienteering sportsmen, who in principle want to go or run anywhere and seem in some cases, when they pass one by one at 5-15 minute intervals, to cause stress, e.g. to roe deer, and long wanderings by red deer. The Danish Forest Service has found it necessary in the public forests to establish two classes of area: A, where orienteering outside the breeding season is normally permitted (though with some constraints as to the number of participants, etc.) and B, where orienteering is normally forbidden. Even motor-orienteering is permitted now and then in the A forests. Some private forest owners have also made agreements with sporting clubs.

The Forest Service publishes folders describing walks with marked routes in the Government forests and providing information abut the forest and its plants, animals and geological history.

The Forest Service as well as some private forest owners have also established many parking spaces, and other amenities for day visitors as well as a considerable number of camping sites which are generally managed by tenants. Norms are set up in most cases by agreement with the Danish Camping Union.

The National Forest and Nature Agency will pay compensation for forest fires and wanton destruction of private property, caused by visitors, and it also pays for litter baskets and signposts.

The implementation of the Act of Hunting, No. 21, 3.6.1967 (latest amendment No. 294, 9.6.1982) comes under the Ministry of Agriculture and vests the landowner with the hunting rights and thus with the management of his wildlife resources in accordance with the Act. It deals with what, how, when and where it is permitted or forbidden to hunt as well as with reserves for wildlife, damage by animals, hunting licences and the hunting fund.

With money from that fund the Wildlife Administration pays for third party liability insurance (connected with the game licence), general administration, investigations on game biology, the establishment and running of game reserves, etc. Various groups of sportsmen, landowners and biologists are represented on advisory or governing committees.

8.   FOREST UTILIZATION

There is in Denmark a tradition for logging by the forest owner or his people and sale either by the side of lorry-carrying roads or at the sawmills. The development of big wood-harvesting machines, however, is in many cases changing the pattern to logging by contractors.

The Danish Institute for Forest Technology (Skovteknisk Institut), which has a close relationship with forest owners but enjoys public support, gives advice and carries out research on all forest operations.

There is no general national policy for the development of the wood processing industry, but the Danish Wood Council, which is composed of representatives from employers' and workers' organizations in the industry, from forestry organizations, public academies, etc. and enjoys public support, renders advisory services as also does the Informative Council of the Wood Line (Traebranchens Oplysningsrad = TOP).

Participation by forest owners in forest industry has taken place in various cases and forms. Unfortunately, forest owners are sometimes apt to delivery their lowest quality wood, which they cannot get rid of elsewhere, to their "own mill". This, of course, is a handicap for the "own mill". Their problem seems easier to solve when there are some outside businessmen on the board.

The generation of energy from sawmill residues for the mill's own use or for heating neighbouring houses is nothing new.

In 1983, however, the Danish Forest Service obtained the approval of Parliament to launch a project with a broader production and application of wood chips, in the first instance in public institutions, such as schools, barracks, old people's homes, etc. Each institution was offered:

(1) a long-term contract comprising guarantee of a continuous supply
    of a certain quantity of well-dried wood chips, and
(2) an automatic heating plant of high quality.

Most of the expected advantages from the project have come about: early thinnings as well as removal of total unwanted stands are made economically possible. Ecological damage to the soil can be avoided either by felling 3-4 months before chipping so that needles and twigs are left on the ground or by fertilizing.

9.   TIMBER TRADE AND MARKETING

Denmark is a timber-deficit country with a low self-sufficiency of between 25 and 30%. Most imports come from Sweden and Finland. Domestic and international timber trade is virtually free of restrictions.

It may, though, be worth mentioning that after heavy and widespread storm-fellings, the National Forest Service has a tradition of stopping fellings in the national forests for some time.

There are no compulsory legal regulations concerning standardization and grading systems, but for round timber grown in Denmark there are agreements between the trading organizations of the forest owners and of the forest industry on measuring and visual grading, based on the recommendations of the Meter-Commission of 1910-12.

The dominance in Denmark of Swedish sawn softwood for construction has led to the general adoption, at least for bulk supply, of Sweden's major uniform grading system ("Gröna Boken").

Sawmillers, etc. are supplied with roundwood from the national forests almost proportionally to their previous consumption, as long as they comply with the general prescriptions and agreements, and can be relied upon to pay.

10. EMPLOYMENT

Act No. 681, 23.12.1975 (with later amendments) on Labour Environment is valid for all industry including the forestry and wood industry.

The employment in Danish forestry plus all wood industry amounts to 7% of the total number of workers in Danish industry.

During the period 1961-84 the number of supervisors on private estates decreased but the two big advisory groups: Associations of Small Wood Owners and the Danish Heath Society both increased their forestry staffs.

The Commission believes that the different property structures need different management structures, but that lasting solutions must be founded on organizations, which are big enough themselves or have access to big organizations, and service bodies, so that:

  - an internal professional, creative, environment can grow and be maintained;
  - an efficient office environment can be made and maintained;
  - communications between owners, customers, and providers of services can be created and maintained;
  - the organization can make sure that all staff members get adequate in-service and continued training.

As to pay and other conditions for forest professionals and forest technicians, agreements are negotiated with their trade unions.

It is a general principle either to recruit workers who have had basic vocational training or to send them to a training course as soon as possible. Most forest workers are members of the trade union for so-called "special workers".

11. FORESTRY EDUCATION AND TRAINING INCLUDING FOREST INDUSTRIES AND WILDLIFE AND NATIONAL PARKS MANAGEMENT

Almost all initial education and training under this heading comes under public institutions.

Professional forestry education takes place at the Forestry Institute and other institutes of the Veterinary and Agricultural University in Copenhagen. The duration is six years, including two years in forest districts, covering basic disciplines and special forestry disciplines. This education qualifies the candidate for leading posts within forestry, forest research, forestry industry and management of national parks.

Forest technicians must follow a course of four years and three months, about half of which takes place in the Danish School of Forestry (Skovskolen i Nodebo), Ministry of Agriculture, and the other half in the field in various forest districts. Most students become foresters: rangers (skovfogeder), but a number are employed as work leaders in forest industries, enterprises, etc.

Skilled forest workers (EFGs) get a training of three years' duration. Those who qualify can either be employed as forest workers or pass upwards in the educational system, heading for the examinations of forest technicians.

At the Danish School of Forestry, there is also vocational training for ordinary forest workers without the EFG-base. The courses have a duration of 1 to 4 weeks; there are basic courses for beginners, and special in-service training for more experienced workers.

At the Danish School of Forestry, special courses are arranged for drivers of tractors and of other forest machines; there are also mixed courses for small forest owners.

So-called "Nature Schools" (Ministry of the Environment and Ministry of Education) are run in different ways, one of which is the model used in the State forests, and which is designed for children in the fifth primary school class who, as part of their schooling in biology, ideally pay two to four whole-day visits to the school, under the guidance of their biology teacher; but they should also get information from a local forester on various aspects of forestry.

Nature schools are normally managed by a joint Communal School/Forest Service Commission.

12. FORESTRY RESEARCH, EXTENSION AND INFORMATION

Denmark's main achievements in forestry research have probably been in production, thinning, genetics and recreation.

In the Danish Veterinary and Agricultural University, Ministry of Education, there is some research in all fields of forestry, mostly in the Forestry Institute. An arboretum deals with dendrology and forest genetics.

The Government Forest Research Institute (Statens forstlige Forsogsvasen), Ministry of Agriculture, deals mainly with traditional biological research.

The Danish Institute for Forest Technology, which is semi-public and comes under the Ministry of Industry, provides an advisory service and undertakes some research in machine techniques, working environment and safety, working and transport systems, regeneration and tending of young stands, wood for energy, and measuring methods for felled roundwood.

The Danish Institute for Game Biology (Vildtbiologisk Station),
Ministry of Agriculture, carries out research on game populations, care and
damage.

Research on transboundary pollution and acid precipitation takes place
at several research centres and the Commission on Forest Research (Ministry
of Agriculture) has established a new Coordination Group on Pollution and
Acidification in Forests.

Denmark is happy that it is a member both of the EEC and SNS (Comm.
for Nordic Collaboration).

Research results are disseminated through:

- articles in journals and periodicals
- lectures
- application to practice is either by forest managers or advisers.

The Danish Forest Society occasionally arranges meetings with
journalists, who usually show little interest in Danish forestry. For a
number of years "acid precipitation" and "forest death" achieved
considerable publicity, though it is not very serious in Denmark and can
mostly be explained without reference to transboundary pollution. This is
the opinion of most Danish foresters, be they practitioners or scientists;
therefore they do not give appalling descriptions with the result that
journalists, who can better sell sensational horror stories, turn to other
sources.

13. INTERNATIONAL COOPERATION

Denmark has had professional forestry connections with other countries
since the last century, originally in the form of individual or group study
tours, and later as a member of big organizations which hold regular
meetings, such as FAO/EFC, FAO/COFO, ECE/TIM, OECD, various Nordic bodies
and CEC. The main idea has been, and still is, to exchange knowledge and
experience.

FINLAND

1. INTRODUCTION

About one third of Finland's total length lies north of the Arctic Circle. The land area is 305,000 sq.km, of which 201,000 sq.km or 66% comprise forest land. Most of the country lies below an altitude of 400 m.

Natural vegetation is essentially boreal coniferous forest, with a zone of treeless tundra in the north and small areas of temperate mixed forests in the south-west.

Precipitation is 700 mm per annum in the south and 400 mm in the north. Evapo-transpiration is low. Swamp peatlands account for about one-third of Finland's land area.

Ownership of the 21.6 million ha. of forests is distributed as follows:

Private	63%
State	24%
Companies	9%
Others	4%

Total	100%

The category "others" includes parishes, local authorities, etc.

Timber production constitutes the main use on 18.2 million ha., while the remaining 3.4 million ha. are devoted mainly to nature conservation and recreation.

There has been a structural change among private forest owners as more and more forests have been transferred from farmers to town residents as a result of the rural depopulation. Nowadays, almost half of the 300,000 private forest holdings are owned by other than the agricultural population.

The planning of forestry has been based on the systematic forest inventories, which started in the 1920's and which have since been carried out continuously covering the whole country. According to these inventories, there is now more wood in the forests than ever before.

Forestry was based in olden days on the concept of the sustained yield. Forestry and forestry policy were thus quite static and usually forestry was seen as a part of agriculture. Since the 1940's, the concept of progressive yield has been adopted.

Between 1975 and 1982, annual development programmes were drawn up which specified the extent of silvicultural and basic improvement operations as well as the key elements in wood production measures.

In 1985, a programme known as FOREST 2000 was presented by the Economic Council. The programme covers such key areas as prospects for increased wood production, utilization of forests, development of the forest industries and improvement in price competitiveness. The FOREST 2000 programme has given impetus to changes in forest policy, especially forest legislation.

2. ADMINISTRATION

The general structure of the administration of Finland's forestry has been as follows:

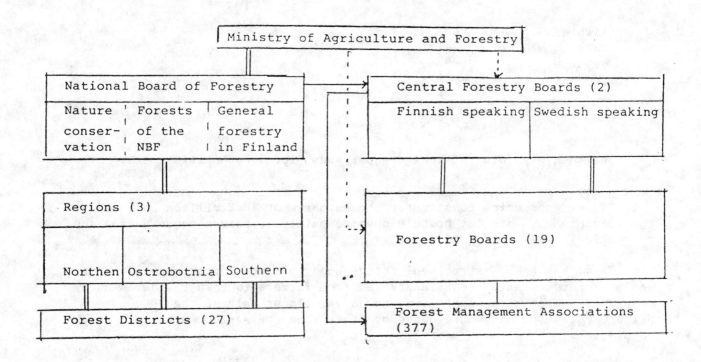

======= normal subordinate relationship

_____ inspection and/or supervision

- - - appoint members

The State forests have had an administrative system since the 1850's.
The National Board of Forestry (NBF) was founded in 1863 and has since had
a strong impact on Finnish forestry and forest policy.

The implementation of the forest law and the forest policy connected
with it is carried out through NBF and the central forestry boards. The
boards are given the task of enforcing and supervising the law.

The Ministry of the Environment, which was established in 1983, as
well as the Ministry of Finance, both also have a strong impact on forestry
policy.

General industrial policy is planned in the Ministry of Trade and
Industry. The Ministry of Labour, the Ministry for Foreign Affairs,
especially the Department for Development Cooperation (FINNIDA), and the
Ministry of Education also exert some influence. The involvement of
interest groups and major political parties in preparing the legislation
has in general guaranteed the subsequent adoption of the laws.

The relation between national forest policy and national development
can clearly be seen in the objectives of the FOREST 2000 programme drawn up
in 1985:

1)   support for the general objectives of economic policy;

2)   balanced development of the different forms of forest use;

3)   complete utilization of the productive capacity of forest land;

4)   economic viability of the measures applied;

5)   matching the timber assortment structure and volume of timber utilized
      with the cutting potential;

6)   the creation of conditions favourable for viable forest-based
      industries.

In Finnish forest policy, regional aspects have always been important.

Investments in forestry are supported by the State through the Law
Concerning Forest Improvement. The investments of the forest industries are
regulated by a committee where the role of the Bank of Finland is dominant
and the major interest groups are represented. Permission from the
committee is needed for all new investments. The objective of the committee
is to find a balance between international supply and demand for forest
products, and Finnish forest resources and industrial capacity.

3. MONETARY AND FISCAL POLICIES

Private Forestry

The economy of Finland, like that of most European countries, hit rock bottom amongst the ruins of World War II in 1945 when Finland lost 8% of her land area and 12% of her forests. People from the ceded area, 422,000 or 11% of the total population, had to be resettled.

Private forests comprise 63% of the forest land area, 71% of the growing stock and 75% of the increment of the forests. The number of private forest holdings with a minimum of 2 ha. of forest land exceeds 310,000. The average size is 32 ha.

The most important instruments of forest policy in Finland are contained in two laws. Of these, the Law on Private Forests ensures the minimum silvicultural standards in forest management by prohibiting forest devastation and by providing for compulsory reforestation. The Law Concerning Forest Improvements in turn makes it possible for woodland owners to obtain low-interest loans and direct subsidies for different measures to increase the yield.

State loans and grants for forest improvement works are directed via forestry boards to the forest management associations, and from there to the forest owners.

Forest Taxation

The forest taxation system applied in Finland is an area-based yield taxation which is not based on actual stumpage revenue but on an assessed average yield.

Income tax is paid to the State and the municipality. Income tax is calculated by adding the net yield of the forest to the value of forest work done by the owner and his wife. Evaluation of the value of net yield is based on the productivity of the land, distribution of tree species and timber assortments in the region, as well as the average costs of timber production which can be deducted from the yield. In Finland, property tax is also paid to the State. The property tax for forestry is relatively low compared to property tax in many other categories of wealth, as the taxable property is computed by capitalizing the value of the forest yield at 10% of interest. There is a limit below which property tax is not exacted.

Forest taxation has been sometimes strongly criticized. Despite this, no better system has so far been developed. One effective measure in the present situation would be for taxation to be varied according to age (or treatment) class so that old and mature stands would be taxed more heavily.

4. FORESTRY MANAGEMENT AND PROTECTION

Regular forest inventories (the first conducted in 1921-24 and the seventh in 1977-84) and continuous research into use of wood have created the preconditions for systematic forest management based on sustained and increasing yield.

It is up to the individual forest owner whether or not to prepare and follow a forest-management plan, but various incentives are given. By the end of 1987, about 64% of private forests had been included in forest management planning.

Forest owners' environmental attitudes have changed to the extent that some of them are unwilling to allow intensive forest management on their holdings.

In the new forestry legislation of 1987 the needs of multiple use are taken into account better than before.

The more detailed restrictions are expressed in the Nature Conservation Act, the Protected Forests Act and the Planning and Building Act.

Professional foresters often take the view that good forest management automatically leads to optimal multiple use.

The recreational use of forests is based in practice on traditional rights of public access to the natural environment (the right of common access, as it is known in the Nordic countries), which applies to berry and mushroom picking, as well as to walking, skiing, temporary camping, etc. That notwithstanding, only 2-3% of the berry crop and an even smaller proportion of mushrooms are picked each year, even though incentives exist in the form, for example, of turnover tax exemption on sales of berries.

Multiple-use applications are expected to decrease the annual theoretical cutting potential by a total of 2.2 million m3 (3-4%) by the year 2000. At the same time, the cutting potential is increased for some other reasons, so that the goal for total annual cut is inreased from 47 million m3 (in the 1980s) to 59 million m3 to 1995.

The stability of forests in Finland is monitored through the National Forest Inventory System, under which a total of 700 permanent test areas were created in 1985 to facilitate observations of a wide variety of types of damage. The research workers have recognized some kind of damages on about 11% of the Finnish Forest area. On about 4% of the forest area the damage is regarded as severe.

Some of the considerable increase (19%) in growth in the past ten years has been speculatively attributed to the fertilizing effect of prolonged nitrogen precipitation and a higher level of carbon dioxide in the air.

Air pollution control and energy-policy instruments, as well as silvicultural methods, are the means being used in efforts to limit the damage caused by acidification.

Forest fires are no longer a serious problem. In economic terms, the most important natural disasters in recent years have been storms.

Owners of land and water areas have the right to hunt, which they can transfer on lease to other persons or associations. The 9-10 million kilogrammes of elk meat which is the most common game produced each year corresponds to about 8% of the country's beef production.

Reindeer are herded in Lapland and parts of the province of Oulu, in a region totalling about one-third of Finland. About 800 households derive most of their income from reindeer husbandry, which also provides about 1,500 households with an important supplementary income.

The Reindeer Husbandry Act stipulates that grazing rights depend neither on the ownership nor possession of land, and that both private and State lands can be used for reindeer herds.

Since the end of the 1960's, various measures have been introduced to reduce agricultural land, for example, the Field Reservation Act (1969) and the Law Concerning Forest Improvement (1967).

5. FOREST UTILIZATION

During the past two decades, there has been a significant shift from delivery sales (harvesting done by the forest owner) to stumpage sales (harvesting carried out by the buyer). Nowadays, the amount of delivery sales is 13-14 million m3 per annum, and this is supposed to be the level in the future as well.

Removals averaged about 47 million m3 (over bark volume) per annum in the 1980's. The proportion of industrial timber in the removals has increased during the past two decades from 40 to 88%, while the proportion of fuelwood has decreased from 40 to 8% and that of household and other wood from 14 to 2%. Roundwood exports, which amounted to 6.9 million m3 in 1961, have decreased to 0.6-1.5 million m3 per annum.

The need for industrial timber grew faster than the supply of domestic timber, and in the mid-1960's the private forest owners also became less willing to utilize fully their forests as they became economically less dependent on the income from their forests.

Structural changes in the consumption and supply of wood, which also illustrate the intensified utilization of wood, are summarized as follows (in million m3 per annum):

	1947-49	1982-84	Change
Consumption of industrial wood:			
domestic roundwood	16.9	38.7	+21.8
imports	-	6.5	+ 6.5
wood residues	0.6	7.2	+ 6.6
waste paper*	-	(0.5)	(+0.5)
	----	----	-----
	17.5	52.4	+34.9
Removals:			
industrial timber	16.9	38.7	+21.8
exports	2.6	1.1	- 1.5
fuelwood	16.0	3.8	-12.2
other	5.5	0.6	- 4.9
	----	----	-----
	41.0	44.2	+ 3.2

* 1 metric tonne equals about 2.5 m3 of wood

Only the shortwood method is used in harvesting, with the exception of whole-tree chipping for fuel. Private forest owners generally use a chainsaw for logging and a farm tractor for haulage. In company operations and in State-owned forests, logging is mainly carried out by permanent forest workers using a chainsaw and partly by multi-purpose logging machines. Haulage is done with heavy-duty forwarders. The logging machines, forwarders and timber trucks are usually owned by private contractors.

As a result of various measures to increase operational efficiency, the productivity of timber harvesting and transport was tripled between 1970 and 1985.

Private forest owners, especially the farmers, have built up a strong negotiating organ, the Central Union of Agricultural Producers, which has also established wood processing plants.

During the last 10 to 15 years, the production of wood-based panels, especially fibre board, sulphite and dissolving pulp, as well as sawnwood in the 1980's, has stagnated or started to decrease. These products have lost much of their earlier competitiveness on the world markets. Production costs, especially the cost of roundwood and labour costs, are higher in Finland than in many other producer countries. Paper and paperboard products, especially writing and printing papers, have turned out to be the most profitable. Most production growth has taken place in those products which are of high value per unit volume and which are favoured by higher technology.

Developments in the reduction, recovery and utilization of waste have been promising. This has resulted in a saving of energy and a reduction in Pollution.

Finland has been applying an energy policy programme prepared by the parliamentary Energy Policy Council and approved by the Finnish Government in 1983. In order to reach the objectives set for domestic energy in the programme, it would be necessary to increase the use of wood-based energy sources from the present 4 to 5 Mtoe (million tons of oil equivalent) by 1995, an increase that is unlikely to be met by then. The simple explanation for the gap is that fuelwood is not sufficiently competitive with other energy sources and its use is still inconvenient for private consumers in their households. During the last few years, the question has been raised whether the situation could be improved by taxation, which has proved to be an effective measure at least within the industries.

Incentives are seldom used for the financing of forest industries, which have always been independent enough to take their own decisions.

Nowadays, forestry directly accounts for 3.7% and the forest industries for 4.4% of Finland's GNP.

The forest industries account for 36% of the value of total exports of Finland.

The indirect impacts of forestry and the forest industries on the development of Finland's economy are even greater than the direct ones. They were the basis for the development of the metal industry, electronics and ship building. Machines and boilers for new pulp and paper mills were needed, as were their control lines. Processors and harvesters were needed for the mechanization of harvesting, trucks and cargo vessels for the transport of wood and forest products.

6.   TIMBER TRADE AND MARKETING

The State does not interfere very much with the internal timber trade in Finland. Sellers may select the buyer as well as the time and amount of their sales as long as the quantity of the timber cut complies with the provisions of the Law Concerning Private Forestry. The buyer can choose between delivery or stumpage sales.

As far as international marketing is concerned, restrictions have been imposed on timber sales. The seller may not sell the timber at a price lower than the recommended price, but no attempt has been made to regulate the exports of manufactured forest products. All Finnish forest products are standardized and graded according to ISO-rules.

Two-thirds of Finland's forest industry exports go to Europe, excluding the Soviet Union, but other regions are gradually gaining in importance.

7. EMPLOYMENT

Employment in forestry dropped from 72,000 man years in 1966/67 to 22,000 man years in 1986/87. While the number of forest workers has diminished, there has also been a change from seasonal and temporary workers to permanent ones. This process has also decreased the number and probability of accidents in forest work.

The earnings of forest workers have been kept above average earnings and above those in the paper or woodworking industries.

There is a collective agreement for forestry made by the labour market organizations. Every second year, the various parties to the agreement meet to negotiate wages and other relevant issues such as sickness pay.

Nowadays there is an abnormal employment situation. In remote areas, there are many trained and experienced people without forestry employment. On the other hand, in the southern and western parts of Finland, there is a constant shortage of forest workers.

8. FORESTRY EDUCATION

Higher Education

Since 1924, there has been a Faculty of Agriculture and Forestry at the University of Helsinki. In 1982, forestry education was also started at the University of Joensuu.

The number of new students yearly enrolling for the Master of Science degree in Forestry has varied from 80 to 100 during the past few years. The average duration of studies for a Master's degree is about 5 years.

Vocational and Technical Forestry and Forest Industry Education

The National Board for Vocational Education is a government central agency under the jurisdiction of the Ministry of Education. The Board directs and supervises a total of 30 educational establishments serving forestry and the forest industries.

The general upper secondary schools and vocational institutions are developed as parallel educational routes to occupational competence at all levels from skilled forest worker to forest engineer.

The objectives are to provide every person with an equal opportunity to study and to enable him/her to continue studies without interruption from one type of school or level of education to another.

As forestry is increasingly connected with other parts of society and the environment, courses are arranged in the evenings and at week-ends in order to promote public awareness of forests and forestry.

In primary schools, forestry is being taught by teachers of biology.

Private enterprises organize education and training also on their own. Typical are short courses dealing with changes in production operations.

The most severe problem in the future will be a shortage of forest workers and the lack of skilled personnel in silvicultural operations.

9. a) FORESTRY RESEARCH

State Institutions

The Finnish Forest Research Institute, which accounts for 68% of all forestry research expenditure, is a State research establishment under the Ministry of Agriculture and Forestry.

Depending on the season, the number of staff varies between 700 and 1,000, approximately half of whom are located outside Helsinki and its surroundings. The academic research personnel numbers about 250.

The University of Helsinki and the University of Joensuu also carry out forest research. As the universities' annual budgets do not provide funds for research, it must be financed from other sources. The main sponsors are the National Research Council for Agriculture and Forestry, the Foundation for Research of Natural Resources in Finland and the Finnish Cultural Foundation.

Research in wood science is mainly carried out by two State-subsidised institutions: the Technical Research Centre of Finland and the Helsinki University of Technology. A few other universities of technology also deal with forest industries, mainly from a viewpoint of processing techniques.

Private Institutions

Certain private institutions make significant contributions to research in forestry and wood science in Finland. The most significant ones are:

-   The Finnish Pulp and Paper Research Institute;

-   The Forest Work Study Section of the Central Association of Finnish Forest Industries;

-   The Work Efficiency Association;

-   The Foundation for Forest Tree Breeding in Finland;

-   The Society of Forestry in Finland.

The last three institutions receive regular financial support from the State budget.

An example of a joint project is the Finnish Research Project on Acidification. The project is implemented in various research institutes and universities and is closely allied to the work of the ECE and with work carried out in various European countries.

The dissemination and application of results is always a problem. Efforts are being made but much more effort should be directed to this end.

9. b) EXTENSION AND INFORMATION

There is no national extension programme for forestry in Finland. The main principle in extension work is that almost all the major organizations dealing with forestry belong to the Finnish Forestry Association whose main task is to produce general informative material. The association is to a large extent financed by the public sector.

10. INTERNATIONAL COOPERATION

The Ministry of Agriculture and Forestry has close contacts in forestry matters with the following nations: all the Nordic countries, the Soviet Union, China, France, the German Democratic Republic, the Federal Republic of Germany, Hungary and Poland. The Ministry is also discussing the possibilities of closer cooperation with Canada, Spain and the United States.

Very often institutes have their own direct contacts with similar institutes in foreign countries. For example, the Forest Research Institute has direct contacts with Brazil, Indonesia, Malaysia and Mexico.

Too often the cooperation is based on the cultural histories and political ties of the countries and on the strength of the administration and not so much on the sharply-focused factors which are of mutual interest.

Universities and forestry schools are also active in this respect, but scarcity of financial resources is a factor which limits the scope for international cooperation.

Development cooperation has become more and more important in recent years. In the forestry sector, the main recipients are Tanzania, Zambia, Sudan and Nepal.

The major international organization in the forestry sector with which Finland has been working is FAO. Most of the money has been directed towards the forest industries, including wood procurement and training aspects and the associate professional scheme.

FRANCE

1. INTRODUCTION

The forests occupy about 14 million ha. (25%) of France's metropolitan land area of 54.9 million ha. In addition there are 1 million km of hedgerows and rows of trees along roads.

Ownership Structure

	M.ha.	%
State	1.4	10
Collectivities	2.2	16
Private	10.2	74
	13.8	100

Types of Forest by Categories of Ownership

Ownership	High Forest		Coppice with Standards	Coppice	%
	mainly broadleaved %	mainly coniferous %	%	%	
State	33	35	26	6	100
Other public	17	32	41	10	100
Private	15	31	31	23	100

Overall, about 65% of the productive forests are mainly broadleaved and 35% mainly coniferous. Noteworthy is the large area of coppice and coppice with standards.

Annual Increment (M cu.m.)

	High Forest	Coppice	Total
broadleaved M cu.m	16.9	15.3	32.2
coniferous M cu.m	26.3	–	26.3
	43.2	15.3	58.5

In 1984, 18.6 M cu.m. of sawlogs and 11.6 M cu.m. of small industrial wood and firewood were sold; about 45% of the total 30.2 M cu.m. were broadleaved and 55% coniferous.

The main principles of forest policy are as follows:

- Policy is comprehensive so as to embrace the ecological, economic and social functions of the forest;

- Policy is long-term so as to pass on to future generations an improved forest heritage;

- Policy is continuous and independent because the choice of investment follows from decisions, the logic of which is independent of economic cycles and political hazards;

- Policy is contractual and places on those involved an obligation to behave responsibly in their choice of options and investments.

Because of the above principles, forest policy in France is the responsibility of the State; this is confirmed in Article 1 of the Law of 4 December 1985.

The main objectives of forest policy are:

- To maintain the benefits to society of the living forest managed to an acceptable minimum standard;

- to ensure its role in land use;

- to produce utilizable wood, with emphasis on the production of sawlogs under optimal conditions of profitability and productivity;

- to promote the utilization of wood and to develop a strategy for forest industrial development and exports.

The application of this policy is varied according to ownership (public or private), the nature of the forest and local priorities. These factors are taken into account in the preparation of regional guidelines for forestry.

The main recent documents on forest policy are:

- 1978: Vers la forêt du 21ème siècle (B. de Jouvenel)

- 1978: La filière bois (Y. Betolaud and J. Meo)

- 1982: Propositions pour une politique globale forêt-bois (R. Duroure)

- 1986: Declarations by the Minister F. Guillaume at the Epinal Fair and A.G. FNSPFS

- 1986: Circular of 5 May 1986 of the Minister of Agriculture concerning regional guidelines on production.

2. ADMINISTRATION

The State forests (1.4 M.ha.) originate from ancient royal estates, estates nationalized during the Revolution and acquisitions made since the end of the last century. The rate of acquisition has now slowed down, partly for budgetary reasons and partly because the tendency towards decentralization has resulted in local communes acquiring land, rather than the State. There are 25,000 State forests. They are inalienable except when authorized by a law.

Of the 2.2 M.ha. of forests belonging to the collectivities, 95% are accounted for by the Communes. In most parts of France, communes are increasing their forest holdings through purchase.

The 10 million ha. of private woodlands are divided among 3.5 million owners, over 2 million of whom own less than 1 ha., and only 10,000 over 100 ha.

The administration of forests has been under the Minister of Agriculture since 1877. At national level, a directorate entrusted with forests, with a staff of 80 persons, is responsible for all matters relating to forest policy. Its tasks include:

- the definition of forest policy and the supervision of its implementation;

- national forest inventory;

- active participation in the formulation of research programmes;

- the granting of financial aid for silviculture and equipment, especially through the management of the "Fonds forestier national" (FFN) (National Forestry Fund);

- protection of the forest (forest fires, control of forest clearing, public access) and protection of the environment through forestry (rehabilitation of mountainous terrains and fixation of dunes);

- the development and organization of markets, investment aid to harvesting and sawmilling enterprises, general economic and technical monitoring of the whole wood chain (filière forêt-bois);

- tutelage of the Office National des Forêts (ONF) (National Forest Office) which manages the State forests; and

- Harmonization of the financing and development of the regional offices of forest ownership.

The Directorate also deals, within the field of its responsibilities, with foreign countries, international organizations and especially with the organs of the European Community.

At regional level, the regional forest and timber service of the regional directorates of agriculture and forestry (decree of 1985) are responsible for the implementation of forest policy in cooperation with the regional staff of national forest offices and regional offices of forest ownership.

At departmental level, the departmental directorates of agriculture and forests are responsible for implementing general directives and the regional guidelines on matters such as forest protection, control of certain felling and afforestation measures, promotion of private forestry and public relations.

Under the administrative deconcentration introduced in France in 1982, the Directorate of Forests influences and controls forestry activities of the external services of the Ministry of Agriculture via the Regional or Departmental Prefects, who carry the sole responsibility for the deconcentrated services of the State. This system, while justifiable in itself, complicates relations and makes it difficult to get things done on time.

In order to formalize consultation procedures, two councils have been established:

- The Superior Forestry and Forest Products Council

- The Regional Forestry and Forest Products Council.

The Office National des Forêts (ONF) is financially autonomous and manages the State forests on commercial lines. It also supervises policies, organizes sales, etc., in the forests of the collectivities which bear a part of the cost of these services, whereas the State bears most of it. The ONF also undertakes various other tasks, such as the maintenance of wooded areas in the Mediterranean region.

The regional centres of forestry property (centres régionaux de la proprieté forestière) are responsible for promoting the productivity and improving the structures of the private forests. There are 17 of these public administrative units which are financed partially by the FFN and partially by the State. The main tasks are to promote cooperation between forest owners, disseminate information on silvicultural methods, prepare guidelines on production, etc.

Forestry legislation is only one of several expressions of forest policy. Most previous legislation dating as far back as 1827 was consolidated in the Forestry Code of 1979 and there has been some additional legislation since then. When new forestry measures are proposed, the Council of State (Conseil d'Etat) ensures very effectively that the rights of people are not infringed.

Forestry's main contributions to general development are:

- general improvement in rural living standards through the
  introduction of improved technologies;

- a better balance in regional development;

- safeguarding and improvement of water resources;

- improvement of the natural environment.

Since 1983, forestry and forest industries have figured in the
following four national priority programmes involving a special expenditure
of over 2 bn FFrs: modernization of industries, use of wood for energy,
development of markets, prevention of forest fires in the mountains.

In 1984, annual State expenditure on the whole forestry sector was
almost 3 bn FFr; another 2.7 bn FFr were spent by the public
establishments, such as the OFN. Expenditure on forestry accounted for 1.7%
of the budget of the Ministry of Agriculture which, in turn, accounted for
13% of the national budget.

3. MONETARY AND FISCAL POLICY

Public finance for forestry is available from the State (Ministries
and special funds, forestry funds, funds for rural development, funds for
land management, etc.) and from local collectivities. The aid includes
grants ranging from 20%-60% of the costs incurred and low-interest loans
(0.25%-5.00% interest). The total level of aid has varied in recent years
between 374 M.FFr. and 271 M.FFr per annum.

Fiscal incentives are designed mainly to favour reforestation. Young
plantations (usually up to 30 years) are therefore exempt from the taxes
based on cadastral revenue. Special fiscal incentives are available to
cooperatives and other forms of association between forest owners.

The tax system is complex. Public collectivities (State and communes)
pay land tax and the additional taxes linked with it. In 1985, the land tax
for the State forests amounted to FFr. 117 M.

The Office National des Forêts (OFN) has to pay value added tax and
tax on income. The OFN does not own the forests it manages, but receives
the proceeds from the sale of wood and other forest products.

The Communes pay neither value added tax nor tax on profits.

In private forests, owners pay land tax and additional taxes linked
thereto. Capital transfer taxes on sales or gifts of forest property are
reduced to about 1/4 of the rate normally imposed on such transactions. In
certain cases, however, the introduction of regional taxation may reduce
the effect of this concession. Other taxes on private forests include taxes
on income and on expenditure, as well as others (tax on leases of hunting
rights, tax on authorized forest clearance, etc.).

It is not possible to estimate the amount of revenue foregone through
tax concessions.

4.   FOREST MANAGEMENT AND PROTECTION

The reorientation of agricultural policies in the Member States of the European Community necessitates a review of land use planning. In France, farmers now represent only 7% of the working population compared with 15% in 1962. There is a need to convert some land from agriculture to forestry. Conversely, in some areas forest land may have to be released to agriculture for the benefit of young farmers without land.

Protection forestry (torrent control and prevention of erosion) has been the responsibility of the State, but recently local collectivities have become involved in dealing with specific problems such as avalanche control in tourist centres.

The following general principles apply:

- forests must not be considered as a land reserve although some modification of forest area may be justified in particular instances;

- forest owners as holders of part of the national heritage have certain duties which vary somewhat according to location (suburban, mountainous);

Guidelines on technical questions such as the choice of species, rotation age, silvicultural systems, provisions for public access, are given in "regional guidelines for forestry". Besides special management directives for State forests and equivalent, documents for the communal forests and private ones are approved. These documents are approved by the responsible Minister. The various financial incentives which have been mentioned are subject to compliance with these requirements.

The forests need protection against six main sources of damage:

(i)   Fire poses a major threat, especially in the Mediterranean areas where climatic and site conditions are difficult and the owners somewhat indifferent because of the poor productivity of many of these forests. A major effort by the State and collectivities has, however, resulted in a decline in forest fires. Legislative and financial measures which are planned should lead to a further improvement.

(ii)   Illegal fellings and unreasonable fellings which are punishable under the Forestry Code.

(iii) Pollution damage is of great concern. The reduction of pollutants must be tackled internationally. Silvicultural solutions to the damage do not yet exist. The latest evidence suggests that the damage to silver fir has stabilized but that the yellowing of spruce persists. The situation is monitored in 1,550 sample plots established mainly by the ONF. Various ministries and research organizations are involved in monitoring the damage and undertaking relevant research.

(iv)   Game damage is serious: hunters and foresters are preparing measures to deal with the problem of excessive game populations.

(v)   There are several important pests and diseases which are dealt with by silvicultural and phytosanitary measures. In order to prevent the rapid spread of the pathogens, an organization is being set up by the Direction of Forests, the public forestry establishments and the plant protection services: the new organization will watch out for outbreaks of damage and follow up with the necessary control measures, research and interregional cooperation. These actions are coordinated and financed at national level.

(vi)   Frost and wind damage occur periodically. Correct choice of species and silvicultural measures are considered the only practicable defence.

The conservation of nature has received increasing attention in recent years with the result that 31% of the land area enjoys some degree of special protection. The protected areas within forests include among others the following:

- in the forests of the State and collectivities, there are 60 reserves of special biological interest (rare species, etc.) with a total area of 4,300 ha. (1985)

- nature reserves

- forests acquired by the conservancy of the seashore and lakesides and managed by the Office National des Forêts

- National Parks

- areas where no clear fellings are permitted.

The State has decided to open its forests to the public and many collectivities have done likewise and have instructed the ONF to take the necessary measures. Tourist areas and urban areas are mainly affected. Information is made available to school children and the public at large.

In 1984, 46.4 M FFr. were spent on forest recreational measures by the State and the collectivities, of which about one-half was spent in the Ile-de-France. In 1985, a law was passed which sets out rules concerning forest recreation. Among other things, it provides for contracts with private owners under which they can receive financial contributions towards the management of woodlands that are open to the public.

There are now 23 regional nature parks covering over 3 M.ha.; the main purpose of these is to provide opportunities for the quiet enjoyment of nature by the public.

The responsibility for the protection of fauna rests with the Minister of the Environment. Legislation provides for three levels of protection for endangered species, depending on rarity and degree of danger of extinction.

There are also special measures for the reintroduction of species such as
bear (in the Pyrenees) and lynx (in the Vosges). There are 11,000 hunting
reserves with a combined area of 2 M.ha. and 645 km of water courses which
are designated as fishing reserves. Obligatory hunting plans are designed
to maintain a proper balance between fauna and their habitats and to
improve hunting facilities. Since 1972, there has been a National Council
of Hunting and Wildlife and since 1985, a Superior Council of Fisheries.
The Direction of Forestry and the ONF have first to manage the fauna in the
State forests and secondly to deal with relations between game and forests
everywhere.

The existence of separate agro-industrial chains and the forestry
chain is reinforced by the relative mutual ignorance of each other's
problems. Nevertheless, there are some contacts provided in part by various
agricultural organizations and a large number of forestry organizations,
some of which are very active.

The problem of converting agricultural land to forestry is nothing new
in France. Some 2 M.ha. have been afforested in the past one hundred years,
and 77,000 ha. since 1946, often in small plots. The tendency is likely to
be reinforced by the attempts to control agricultural surpluses in the
European Community. The views of the forestry services in the Ministry of
Agriculture may be summarized as follows:

- afforestation is no panacea; the technical difficulties are great;

- to start with, the emphasis must be placed on arousing the interest
  of farmers in their forests and in forest work as a means to
  complement their earnings;

- given the limited financial resources at the disposal of forestry,
  priority must be accorded to the improved management and
  productivity of the existing forest;

- a separate policy of afforesting agricultural land could be
  introduced, if necessary, provided that:

  * the farmers want to afforest and receive the necessary financial
    assistance;

  * the action is properly phased, is in accordance with sound land
    use, and results in forestry units large enough to be managed
    economically;

  * the afforestation is planned separately for each region and placed
    within the framework of the regional forestry guidelines;

  * the afforestation is accompanied by the necessary investment in
    wood processing industries.

The principles and objectives for the development and protection of the mountainous regions are contained in a law of January 1985. The main lines of action include the following:

- assembly of facts as a basis for planning at regional level; consultative committees have been established for the different mountainous regions;

- high priority is accorded to tourist facilities (rights of way for ski pistes, cableways, etc.);

- promotion of local arts and crafts;

- much greater involvement than in the past of the local authorities themselves in protective measures (avalanche and torrent control, afforestation, etc.); but the State continues to provide most of the finance;

- careful zoning according to level of danger, so that new installations can be located where they are safe and will do least harm to the environment.

5. UTILIZATION

Utilization policy is based on the link between forests and forest industries. The supply side is characterized by being relatively inelastic, composed of a very large number of partners, many of whom do not act commercially, and by the very long time required for investments to yield a return. The wood processing industries, on the other hand, must operate commercially and subject to the cyclical changes in the demand for their products.

The two main preoccupations are:

- balancing supply and demand by searching for new markets as the supply potential increases;

- improving the links between the segments of the forest-wood chain.

Harvesting is done either by salaried wood cutters or by felling contractors, most of whom are also involved with sawmilling. Transport is nearly all by road. Logs are usually sold standing, but some timber is also sold at the roadside, especially in the north-eastern part of France. The sales practices vary; they are mainly based on tradition and will be difficult to change.

Attempts are being made to standardize and codify the classification of roundwood (standing or felled) so as to facilitate supply contracts. For coniferous sawn wood, the Centre technique du bois et de l'ameublement (CTBA) has recently developed a classification system in collaboration with the timber trade. Some progress has been made with the classification of broadleaved sawnwood but many difficulties remain. There are many norms, technical rules, etc., for various forest products.

There is incentive for investment by groups of forest owners or users of sawn timber in sawmilling, while the sawmills themselves tend towards an integration downstream.

The forest industries are short of capital. A great effort is needed to improve structures and to modernize. Government financial support is given within the framework of a policy of industrial development which calls for a rapid change of mentality. The Government does not wish to replace free enterprise in the creation of new enterprises, but it encourages industries to go to areas with a rapidly developing forestry potential.

There are no specific ecological restrictions on forest industries, but they must conform to general rules and regulations (weight restrictions on road transport, planning permits for new installations, etc.).

The use of wood for energy is promoted by l'Agence Française pour la Maîtrise de l'Energie (AFME) in collaboration with the Ministry of Agriculture.

Attention has been directed in the first place to the use of forest residues, but research on the establishment of short rotation forest biomass plantations is also in progress. The main markets for the forest biomass from both sources are:

- the industries themselves for industrial use (pulp) or energy;

- domestic heating in rural areas near source of supply;

- heating of factories or district heating.

The industrial equipment for generating energy from wood is also being developed. It is estimated that forest biomass could provide the energy equivalent of about 10 M tonnes of oil, i.e. about 5% of France's energy consumption.

6. TRADE

There are no special rules concerning the timber trade, which is based on the concept of a free market.

Standing sales account for 82% of the sales in State forests and 70% in private forests. Methods of sale include public auctions, sale by sealed tender and sales at a fixed price based on the prices achieved in competitive sales.

Felled and prepared timber is sold either in lots already determined at the date of sale or in lots to be delivered later, in which case the quantities and qualities are specified by the purchaser.

The policy objective is to develop markets in step with rising production. The means of achieving this are:

- search for new markets;

- promotion of the use of timber;

- promotion of exports, especially of products with a high added value.

These actions are encouraged by persuasion and not by regulations. They have already caused a drop in the negative trade balance in the wood sector from 34% of consumption in 1980 to only 14.3% in 1985.

7. EMPLOYMENT

There are no special laws concerning employment in forestry and forest industry except for a statute of 1985 which distinguishes between individual forest working contractors and employees, mainly with regard to questions of social security.

Improved productivity has resulted in a sharp drop in employment in the forest and a smaller drop in the forest industries where the development has been as follows:

	1981	1985
Primary processing	10,400	10,700
Secondary processing	77,900	65,700
Furniture making	116,300	89,400

There are no special measures relating to the recruitment of personnel. There is an Interfederal Council of Wood of the various federations (woodland owners' associations, forestry communes, timber trade, furniture industries, etc.).

Salaries and wages are fixed by collective agreements in the same way as for other economic and social activities. Social security arrangements depend in part on the system for agriculture and in part on the general system for industry and commerce. Accident insurance for harvesting operations is extremely high; this results in "moonlighting" ("travail au noir"). The wearing of safety helmets and special equipment is now prescribed for these operations. The safety regulations for the wood processing industries are those for industry in general.

The forestry sector has regularly been asked to play its part in combating unemployment, delinquency, etc. The sector has accordingly recruited French people of Islamic stock who have been repatriated from North Africa. More recently, the forestry sector has been asked to offer work experience (stage) to young workers in jobs of public interest. 3,500 young people have thus been employed in the forests belonging to the State and collectivities and another 1,000 in private forests. The scheme is financed in part by the Ministry of Agriculture and organized by the ONF.

The scheme has encountered difficulties for various reasons: the work is difficult and without good career prospects, it is usually far from locations with other employment opportunities, the types of work for which the young people can be used are limited because of objections by the regular workforce.

8.   EDUCATION AND TRAINING

Education and training are given high priority and the resources made available for the purpose are increasing steadily. A closer link between forestry and agriculture will benefit the reforms which concern the sector, namely decentralization, modernization and the changing relationships between the State and the private sector.

Forestry education at university level is at a stage of rapid development, the present output of about 40 forestry engineers per year being quite inadequate. The main centre in France will continue to be at Nancy; but a parallel development of the centres at Montpellier (France), Pondichery (Rep. of India) and Kourou (Dept. of Guyana) will contribute to this development by enabling forestry to play a greater part in the global development of tropical regions.

The education of the public in forestry serves many objectives, and the public itself embraces very diverse interests. The main objectives are to:

- impart technical, economic, administrative or legislative information;

- reinforce forest policy by justifying and explaining it;

- influence the attitudes of the consumers of forest products and services (everybody from the rambler in the forest to the purchaser of forest products);

- initiate or improve an understanding of ecology.

The means of achieving these objectives are:

- a permanent service to respond to correspondence and telephone enquiries (the service "Allo-forêt" is jointly organized by the Directorate of Forests and the ONF);

- use of the media: radio, television, etc.;

- a network of nature centres, museums, etc., with forestry personnel specially trained in public relations;

- support of relevant associations and organizations.

The forest, with all its complexity, provides much scope for applying the modern interdisciplinary approach to education at schools. Some teaching of forestry is included as an option in the courses leading to some agricultural diplomas and also in some general courses in the biological sciences.

Further education and refresher courses in forestry are organized by the Ministry of Agriculture, by regional services, and by various professional and other organizations.

Looking to the <u>future</u>, the proportion of professional forest engineers who will become officials is likely to decrease and the proportion in other employment will increase. This trend calls for a reorientation of forestry education along the lines indicated below:

- increasing emphasis on a general scientific and technological education before any specialization in forestry or wood technology;

- "producing" cadres suitable for the new openings in the private sector;

- training specialists in international cooperation so that France can continue to play its part in developing tropical forestry;

- ensuring that graduates will also be qualified to manage non-forested natural areas and wildlife.

Education and training facilities at all levels - university, technical and vocational - will have to be increased in order to meet the rising demand.

9. RESEARCH

The basic objective is to promote, at minimum cost, the production of wood (in quality and quantity) while assuring the permanence of the ecosystems and without prejudice to the other forest functions (especially recreation and protection).

In the transfer of research results to forestry practice, it is important to take account of the fact that many forest managers outside the public sector are not professional foresters.

The main research organizations are:

- l'Institut national de la recherche agronomique (INRA - département forêts)

- le Centre d'études du machinisme agricole, du génie rural, des eaux et des forêts (CEMAGREF - département forêts)

- l'Institut pour le développement forestier (IDF, institut technique)

- l'Association forêt cellulose (AFOCEL)

- l'Association pour la rationalisation et la mécanisation de l'exploitation forestière (ARMEF)

- le Centre technique du bois et de l'ameublement (CTBA - centre technique industriel)

- le Centre technique forestier tropical (CTFT - département forestier
  du centre de coopération internationale en recherche agronomique
  pour le développement: CIRAD)

- le Centre technique des industries des papiers, cartons et
  celluloses (CTP).

In addition, there are other institutes with projects proposed by the
committee "Filière Bois" of the Ministry for Scientific and Technical
Research.

Research results are published at various scientific levels to suit
different needs. In technology transfer, the economics of the actions
proposed are emphasized. A large number of organizations are involved in
technology transfer including the organization of the chambers of
agriculture, the regional offices of forestry property, etc.

10. INTERNATIONAL COOPERATION

Bilateral relations with other countries and the participation of
France in international working groups of the United Nations, European
Community, etc., are dealt with by the Ministry of Agriculture while the
Ministry of Cooperation deals with tropical forestry. The Centre technique
forestier tropical (Technical Centre for Tropical Forestry) is the
institute primarily concerned.

France is particularly interested in cooperation with Mediterranean
countries on questions such as forest fires and it actively supports the
work of FAO's Silva Mediterranea. France is also greatly interested in the
studies on forest decline caused by atmospheric pollution. It must,
however, be pointed out that, with certain exceptions (e.g. protection of
forests against forest fires and atmospheric pollution), discussions on
forestry in the European Community are often incidental to discussions on
agricultural problems; the hope of achieving positive results depends
therefore largely on the direct relation between forests and agricultural
structures.

Although cooperation on tropical forestry is the responsibility of the
Ministry of Cooperation, the Ministry of Agriculture is also involved in
matters such as courses on tropical forestry and the financing of research
and investments with the help of the Fonds forestier national. The basic
aim in this development cooperation is to enable the tropical countries to
make better use of their forest resources.

Regular forestry contacts in temperate regions are maintained with
Canada (Quebec), USSR, Finland and Sweden, but scientific missions are
undertaken to most countries in the world. Cooperation in tropical forestry
is particularly strong with the tropical departments of France, especially
Guyana, and with Brazil, Indonesia and the francophone countries of Africa.

GERMAN DEMOCRATIC REPUBLIC

1. FOREST RESOURCE BASE

Forests cover an area of 2,977,563 ha. (1986), representing 27.5 % of the area of the country. This corresponds to 0.18 ha. of forest per head of population of 16.7 million. In spite of industrialization, the area of forest land has not diminished. The protection of natural resources and the conservation of land used for agricultural and forestry purposes are embodied in Article 15 of the Constitution of the GDR.

Forest ownership in the GDR is as follows:

State forest	68%
Cooperative forest	27%
Private forest	4 %
Church forest	1 %

The average timber growing stock per ha. in 1986 amounted to 188 m3 and the yearly increment to 6 m3 per ha.

The total economic area of the GDR is used as follows (1985):

	surface in percent
GDR, total	100 %
of which:	
1. Forests and small forests	27 %
2. Farmland	55 %
3. Lakes and rivers	2 %
4. Wasteland, uncultivated land and mining land	3 %
5. Roads, buildings, etc.	13 %

The consumption of water increases each year. The growing demand for water is met by 190 barrages, 164 of which have been built since the creation of the GDR.

The forest has a particular importance for water resources. It is distributed irregularly over the territory of the GDR. The size of the closed forest areas can be seen in the following table:

	Number	area in %	area in ha.
Forests over 1,000 ha.	500	58	1,700,000
Forests from 100 ha. to 1,000 ha.	2,300	27	800,000
Forests from 10 ha. to 100 ha.	9,000	10	300,000
Scattered tree groups under 10 ha.	93,300	5	130,000

The timber growing stock increased constantly between 1950 and 1986. It rose from 113 m3/ha. in 1950 to 188 m3/ha. in 1986.

The distribution of the tree species in percent is as follows:

77% softwood, of which 54% pine and 21% spruce;

23% hardwood, of which 8% beech and 5% oak.

Nature and landscape are protected by the law.

2.   FOREST ADMINISTRATION

The administrative structure of forestry in the GDR is as follows:

1	Ministry of Agriculture, Forestry and Food Industry with the Main Division for Forestry
14	Regional Councils with a Forestry Division each
77	State forest enterprises with an average size of 31,200 ha.
407	Forest districts with an average size of 6,800 ha.
2,197	Forest ranges with an average size of 1,200 ha.

After the land reform carried out in 1945, 36% of the forest area of the GDR was redistributed up to 1950 to farm workers, peasants with little land and to communal administrations such as counties, districts and communities, and to nationally-owned farms.

In the period that followed, these new forest owners joined forest communities and, later on, special inter-cooperative institutions for forest management belonging to Agricultural Production Cooperatives (LPG).

From 1959 onwards, the State forest enterprises started to take over the management of forests on a contractual basis, without changing the private or cooperative property status.

The Church forests are managed on 35,096 ha. by its own forest personnel.

It is the duty of the forestry sector to supply the national economy constantly with timber from domestic forests, to guarantee the yield of the forest stands and to increase their ecological functions.

Up to 1990, intensification measures in forestry are designed to bring about a higher effectiveness which will lead to an increased output of rough timber and improvements in the field of ecology.

Forest State enterprises are financed by the self-generation of resources from the sale of timber. Investments can be financed by bank credits. The rate of interest for investment credits amounts in general to 5%.

Some of the private forests are managed with the support of the personnel from State forest enterprises. A logging fee which amounts to 6% of the proceeds of sale is charged by the forest enterprise.

The State forest has to pay 4 DDR marks real-estate tax per ha. per year.

3. <u>FOREST RECREATION AND HUNTING</u>

Seven hundred and seventy-one nature reserves with a total area of 106,100 ha., or 0.9% of the surface of the country, reflect the diversity of ecology.

Four hundred and two landscape preserves cover more than 18% of the territory and have a total area of 1,957,400 ha. These are sites which are especially appropriate for recreational activities of the population or which have such natural characteristics as are worth maintaining.

They include excursion, holiday and health resorts. There are, moreover, 10,000 natural monuments in the GDR which consist of springs, geological formations, trees and avenues, etc. and are protected.

The Institute for Landscape Research and Nature Conservation is responsible for research in the field of landscape and nature conservation.

In addition to nature conservation in general, game management and hunting are legally regulated. Nine hundred and twenty hunting collectives with over 40,000 members manage and hunt the game in State-assigned hunting-grounds which can be used free of charge. The size of the hunting-ground for any one collective varies from 1,000 to 4,000 ha. The State forest enterprises are responsible for game management. The centre of game and hunting research is the Institute of Forest Sciences. A study group coordinates the research work of scientists and practicians.

4. <u>FOREST PROTECTION</u>

From the viewpoint of forestry, the wooded areas are divided into protection forests, special forests and commercial forests, which are also subdivided into very different groups.

A special task is the mobilization of a wide public for the protection of nature. This is performed by the Society for Nature and Environment which belongs to the Cultural Association of the GDR and has 50,000 members.

About 37% of the total forest area of the GDR is damaged by environmental impacts. The species which are especially affected are:

Pine	40.4%
Spruce	42.5%
Beech	12.2%
Oak	14.3%

Various measures are taken by the Government of the GDR to reduce the forest damage in a complex way.

Using 2,500 measuring points (indicator plots), the state of the forest is continuously controlled. A complex survey network of 500 plots is being established. Large-scale fertilization (in 1986 planned on 85,000 ha.) is designed to make damaged stands more resistant to pollutants affecting the environment. Despite increased industrial production, it was possible to reduce the dust load by 30% and the pollutant load on the groundwater by 12% during the last 15 years.

A special place in the GDR economy is occupied by brown-coal open-cast mining. At present the GDR produces 40% of the total brown-coal output of the world. Great expenditures are made to return the 4,000 ha. which are devastated annually to use in agriculture, forestry or water supply and distribution. After 5 to 6 years a new, efficient forest, water or field biocoenosis is developing.

In the pine stands of the lowlands endangered by fire, prevention and control of forest fires are of great importance. About 1.3 million ha. of forest are endangered. In recent years it has been possible to reduce the number of forest fires, and by using suitable measures of prevention and modern fire-fighting methods, the size of the area damaged by fire has significantly decreased.

5. FOREST UTILIZATION

In the field of forest utilization and wood processing, efforts are made to meet the growing demand for wood with complex measures.

At present, 70% of the wood grown is used.

Timber production was as follows in 1985:

Sawlogs and veneer logs	38.0%
Pitprops	1.9%
Pulpwood	27.4%
Other timber	32.7%
	100.0%

Timber makes up 93.4% of the total harvested raw wood. About 30% of the current wood demand has to be met by imports.

The State holds the monopoly for domestic and foreign trade in wood. Special foreign trade enterprises conduct foreign trade activities.

Increased wood production in forestry, a higher degree of finishing and better wood utilization in wood industry have to meet the rising wood demand and limit exports.

6. EMPLOYMENT

The employment of people in forestry and wood industry is regulated by the labour code of the GDR. The labour code defines the basic rights of the working people as guaranteed by the Constitution, e.g. the right to work, the right of co-determination, of pay in accordance to quality and quantity of the work done, the right of education, of recreation and leisure, of protection of health and working power, of participation in the cultural life, of pension in old age and in case of disablement, and of material security in case of illness or accident.

Detailed conditions are laid down in the outline collective agreement between the Board of the Trade Union branch for agriculture, food and forest and the Ministry of Agriculture, Forestry and Food Industry. The leading principle is the right to work and the orientation towards full-time employment.

The provisions of the outline collective agreement apply to State forest enterprises as well as to inter-cooperative forest enterprises.

7. EDUCATION AND RESEARCH

The level of education of people permanently employed in forestry is as follows (on the basis of 1987 data):

    1,510 university graduates
    4,700 technical college graduates
    1,072 foremen
  40,774 skilled workers
    4,664 with uncompleted qualification,

i.e. 90.6% of the permanently employed have completed vocational or professional training.

Presently, 67% of the people working in forestry are provided with a hot meal at their workplace and 76% of the workers are taken to the place of work in vehicles provided by their enterprises.

About 800 apprentices start their training in State forest enterprises every year. The objective of their two-year apprenticeship is to train and educate them to be versatile forest workers. Foremen for special fields of forestry obtain their qualification in an additional two-year training. Foresters are educated in three-year direct studies at three forestry technical colleges. This qualification can also be obtained through external studies.

Graduate foresters are educated at the Faculty of Forestry, Tharandt, of the Dresden Technical University in studies lasting 4.5 years. Further education, e.g. in order to obtain the licence to operate special machines or to train people from other vocations in basic forestry operations, is carried out by the forest enterprises or by the VEB Kombinat Forsttechnik Waren. Social organizations such as the engineers' organization "Kammer der Technik" and the agronomists' association "Agrarwissenschaftliche Gesellschaft" provide information on latest developments by means of short courses. Further education for university and technical college graduates is organized through special courses every five years.

The central research institution of forestry is the Institute of Forest Sciences, Eberswalde, with 700 employees. Affiliated to the Institute is a State forest enterprise with 45,000 ha. of forest area and 800 workers and employees.

8. INTERNATIONAL COOPERATION

International scientific and technical cooperation has existed for years between the member countries of the CMEA.

Bilateral relations are maintained with Austria, the Federal Republic of Germany and Finland, in addition to those with Socialist countries.

In the field of mechanization of forestry operations, joint research is conducted with the Soviet Union, Czechoslovakia, Hungary and Poland. Cooperation dedicated to the protection of forests and the environment is carried out with Poland, Czechoslovakia and the Federal Republic of Germany.

Apart from these direct relations with other countries, GDR forest scientists participate in the activities of international UN organizations and the ECE, including the Joint FAO/ECE/ILO Committee on forest working techniques and the training of forest workers. They work on research topics within the framework of the UN Environment Programme - Man and Biosphere (MAB), the International Biological Programme, the International Union of Forestry Research Organizations (IUFRO), the International Seed Testing Association (ISTA), and more recently the International Institue of Applied Systems Analysis (IIASA) in Laxenburg, Austria.

GERMANY (FED. REP)

1. INTRODUCTION

The success of German forestry in the 19th century laid the foundations of its good reputation. The principle of "sustained management" as a basic idea of a long-term oriented management method spread in Central Europe and was also introduced later on in overseas countries.

According to the 1985 survey, the forest area in the Federal Republic of Germany covered an area of about 7.3 million ha. or 29% of the total land area. Compared to previous years, the forest area had slightly increased despite losses occurring regionally.

The forest had already achieved its present-day extent and distribution by the 15th century. About 70% of the productive forests are coniferous (mainly spruce, pine, silver fir, Douglas fir, larch) and 30% are broadleaved (mainly beech and oak).

The forests of the Federal Republic of Germany are almost entirely managed as high forest with rotations ranging between 80 and 250 years, depending on the tree species. Generally speaking, the silvicultural treatment is primarily oriented towards the production of high-quality, heavy logs; wood of smaller dimensions results from necessary tending measures.

The greatly differentiated area and ownership structures are evident from the following table:

Structure of enterprises (1) with forests, 1983

Forest Area

	Enterprises	Total 1,000 ha.	%	Per Enterprise ha.
Enterprises with forest:				
State forest (2)	1,002	2,222.4	30.2	2,217.9
Corporate forest (3)	11,857	1,760.4	23.0	148.5
Total private forest (4) of which:	460,872	2,902.5	39.4	6.3
under 50 ha. forest area	455,530	1,687.7	22.9	3.7
50 ha.forest area and above	5,342	1,214.8	16.5	227.4
Total enterprises with forest	473,731	6,885.3	93.6	14.5
Very small forest areas (5)	–	474.7	6.5	–
TOTAL		7,360.0 (6)	100	

(1) The survey covers enterprises with a utilized agricultural or forestry area of at least 1 ha. and farms with an area of less than 1 ha. UAA whose natural production units correspond at least to the average value of an annual agricultural market production of 1 ha. UAA.

(2) Federal and Länder (there are 11 Länder in the Federal Republic of Germany).

(3) Districts, communes and their associations as well as churches and church institutions.

(4) Natural persons and legal persons under private law.

(5) Areas outside the enterprises covered, largely private forest.

(6) Result of 1985 Survey.

More than half of the private forest area is accounted for by enterprises with 1-50 ha. of forest. The average forest area of these enterprises amounts to 3.5 ha., the average size of parcels to 1.3 ha. only. The small size of parcels and the often inadequate infrastructural development make it very difficult to manage these small private forest areas which account for about 28% of the forest area.

The general aim of forest policy is to preserve the forest, to expand it where required, and to ensure its proper management (Federal Forest Act, Art. 1.1).

To achieve these objectives, forestry is entitled to Government support (Federal Forest Act, Art. 41.1). Government support is, in particular, to be directed towards safeguarding the general economic conditions required to preserve and maintain forests in a sustained way. For this purpose, forestry is to be put in a position - especially by means of economic, transport, agricultural, social and fiscal policies - to utilize and preserve forests under reasonable terms and conditions, while due regard is to be given to the distinctive natural characteristics of forestry and to its special economic character (Federal Forest Act, Art. 41.2). Financial support is given by the Federal Government under the Act on the Joint Task of Improving Agricultural Structures and Coastal Protection (Art. 41.1).

2. ADMINISTRATION

The distribution of ownership has remained comparatively stable in recent years. The Federal forests, which only account for 1.7% of the forest area, are mainly in military establishments. They are managed by the Federal Forest Service, depending from the Federal Ministry of Finances. Forests belonging to the Länder (28.5% of the forest area) are managed by their respective Forest Services.

The organization of the <u>Land Forest Services</u> varies from Land to Land, mainly for historical reasons. Apart from the management of the Land forests and the supervision of all other forests, they have other tasks, including: participation in master planning, regional and Land planning as well as in special planning activities of other authorities.

In the <u>corporate forests</u>, management is carried out by corporate forest personnel or by personnel from the Land forest administrative services.

<u>Private forest enterprises</u> manage their own forests, but are subject to the supervision of the Land forest administrative services.

To overcome unfavourable structures in private and corporate forests, <u>forestry groupings</u> were established with public support. Forestry groupings, in accordance with the Federal Forest Act, are:

- Recognized private silvicultural business affiliations - "Forstbetriebsgemeinschaften" (groupings of landowners under private law);

- public law silvicultural business organizations - "Forstbetriebs verbände" (groupings of owners of real estate having the status of public law corporations);

- forestry associations - "forstwirtschaftliche Vereinigungen" (groupings of recognized private silvicultural business affiliations, public law silvicultural business organizations or silvicultural cooperatives or similar groupings established under Land law).

The Federal Forest Act of 1975 established the framework for detailed legislation by the Länder.

The objectives of the Federal Forest Act are, in particular:

- to secure the forest in a sustained way because of its economic benefit, its significance for the environment, agriculture and infrastructure and recreation for the general public;

- to promote forestry;

- to reconcile the interests of the general public and forest owners.

The Federal Forest Act provides for the Federal Government to take a share in the financial support of forestry under the Act on the Joint Task of Improving Agricultural Structures and Coastal Protection of 1969. The procedure is mainly as follows: the farm ministers of the Länder deliberate each year, under the chairmanship of the Federal Minister of Food,

Agriculture and Forestry, on the concepts of the Federal Government and the
Länder with regard to the measures to be promoted in the agricultural
sector, including forestry. The result of the subsequent decisions is part
and parcel of the so-called "skeleton plan" which constitutes a binding
framework for the implementation of the agrarian structural (including
forest structural) promotional measures for the Länder. The Länder can,
however, supplement this promotion by their own forestry programmes at Land
level. Limitation of funds is the main constraint on the implementation of
forest policy.

The contribution which the forest makes through wood production
(economic function) in the primary sector can be outlined, in terms of
figures, as follows:

-   annual wood production: about 28-30 million m3 or about 4 m3 per
    ha. of wooded area;

-   contribution to the gross national product: about DM 3 billion;

-   value added: about DM 2 billion.

The forest produces less than 0.5% of the gross domestic product. It
thus shares, although in a particularly conspicuous way, the lot of the
other primary production sectors of our highly industrialized national
economy. Thus agriculture contributes about 3% and mining about 1% to the
national product. An increase in the relative share of forestry in the
gross domestic product is not to be expected. On the contrary, it will
continue to decrease, like the primary sector as a whole.

The importance of the economic function of the forest cannot, however,
be measured in terms of production figures alone. The forest meets about
half of the annual wood requirements. It thus provides the raw material
base of the German forest industries (share in the gross domestic product,
2.3%) and takes pressure off the balance of payments. The sustained forest
management ensures that the raw material base will not be exhausted and can
even be increased in the long term.

Moreover, the forest provides full-time employment for 50,000 people
(0.2% of the working population) and part-time employment for 700,000
people (3.4% of the working population). About 600,000 persons are employed
in forest industries.

The economic function is only a partial aspect of the services
rendered by forests and forestry. The financial importance of the
protection and recreational functions for the national economy cannot yet
be ascertained exactly. According to estimates, however, it is not lagging
behind the value of annual wood production.

3. FOREST CONSERVATION POLICY

Air pollution control to reduce forest damage continues to be one of the greatest environmental policy challenges. For this control, the Government of the Federal Republic of Germany has developed a comprehensive strategy which comprises the following points in particular:

- Drastic reduction of air pollution by reducing the emission of pollutants at source;

- complementary forestry measures to slacken and to mitigate the course of damage as far as possible;

- promotion of large-scale forest damage research;

- regular survey of the conditions of forests as an important source of information for policy and management decisions.

The main measures to reduce the emission of air pollutants are:

- Ordinance on Large Fuel Firing Plants (1983);

- Amendment to the Technical Guidelines for Air Pollution Control (1983 and 1986);

- Amendment to the Federal Emission Protection Act (1985); and

- the decision to introduce low-pollution cars in the EEC (1985).

Compared to 1982, these specific measures will reduce SO_2 emissions by two-thirds by 1993 and NO_x emissions by almost half by the mid-90s.

Forestry measures to reduce the new types of forest damage have been promoted since 1984 within the framework of the Joint Task of Improving Agricultural Structures and Coastal Protection. These measures include: fertilization, tending of young stands, underplanting and reforestation.

Coordination at international and Community level of the methods to assess and monitor forest damage made an important step forward in 1986. The ECE Task Force which was set up in 1985 on the decision of the Executive Secretary of the Geneva Convention on Long-Range Transboundary Air Pollution, and in which the Federal Republic of Germany is a leading country, could work out a Manual on the Assessment of the Effects of Air Pollution on Forests on the basis of the German forest damage survey.

Expenditure under the <u>forestry programme to improve structures</u> in non-State forests was as follows in 1985:

Measures	Federal Funds million DM
Primary afforestation (1,300 ha.)	4.3
Conversion into high forest	6.4
Silvicultural measures to improve the structure of young stands	3.5
Improvement of wood quality by pruning, separation of forest and pasture, setting up protective plantations	1.6
Forest road construction (1,500 km)	16.6
Forest owner associations (607 associations)	1.6
Measures due to new types of forest damage	15.7
TOTAL	49.2

The Länder contributed an additional DM 35 million to the above measures.

By ordinance of 10 March 1986 having the force of law, the Federal Minister of Food, Agriculture and Forestry ordered a <u>Federal forest inventory</u> to be carried out for the period from 1986 to 1989.

To secure the supply of proper <u>forest reproductive material</u>, a General Administrative regulation is being prepared to implement the Act on Forest Seed and Planting Stock. It will mainly regulate questions relating to the licensing of tested reproductive material, the implementation of comparative tests, and the keeping of Crop Authorization and Arboricultural Registers, as well as the issue of official certificates.

As the new types of forest damage are not only a threat to the present forest resources, but are also an acute danger to the genetic potential of the forest, the Federal Government considers the conservation of natural genetic resources a priority area among forestry measures and has taken steps to set up a <u>forestry gene bank.</u>

Forestry Taxation System

Forestry is incorporated into the generally applicable tax system. The most important taxes are those based on the possession of property, including transfer taxes, and on income, particularly turnover tax. The capitalized value of the forest is the standard for property tax, inheritance tax and land tax. The income from forestry is subject to income tax, and payments for deliveries and other services provided by forest enterprises are subject to turnover tax (which in forestry is, however, negligible).

The aforementioned taxes affect the various forest ownership categories as follows:

Property tax: private forest only

Inheritance tax: private forest only

Land tax: State forest, corporate forest, private forest

Income tax: private forest only

Turnover tax: State forest, corporate forest, private forest

Specific tax concessions for forestry are covered, in relation to income tax, by the Income Tax Act (Art. 34b – taxation of extraordinary income) and the Act on Compensation for Damage to the Forest (taxation in emergency cases), in relation to turnover tax by the Turnover Tax Act and in relation to property tax, inheritance tax and land tax by the Valuation Act, which ascertains the basis for assessment (capitalized value for these three tax areas). The capitalized value ascertained under the Valuation Act (assessed value) is minimal for forestry.

With a few exceptions, the Federal Government has legislative competence in the fiscal field. In the field of forestry, the Länder largely have their own legislative competence, but they cannot make any fiscal arrangements in their forestry laws. For this reason, the Federal Government sees to it that tax laws take forestry concerns into account to the greatest possible extent.

4. FORESTRY AND FOREST PROTECTION

The modern forestry enterprise is both a wood-producing and a service-rendering enterprise. Forestry enterprises, however, still have mainly economic, business and entrepreneurial functions.

Three other main forest policy objectives are:

1. To ensure the protection of water resources, soil, climate and wildlife by simple and natural means through forest conservation and improvement;

2. To preserve multiple and stable ecosystems;

3. To offer people relaxation and recreation in the forest.

Forest Protection

Activities towards protection against forest fires include prevention through communication of fire danger and reporting methods and through silviculture. Extension is also directed towards fire fighting. During the last 10 years, the average area burned has been approximately 800 ha.

The emphasis in forest protection against other dangers is on forest planning and silvicultural measures such as:

-   setting up stable mixed stands adapted to site conditions;

-   management based on forest hygiene standards (sound silviculture);

-   maximum use of biological or integrated control measures;

-   regulation of hoofed game populations (deer, etc.).

Primary afforestation has been supported at Federal level since 1969 within the framework of the Joint Task of Improving Agricultural Structures and Coastal Protection. The Federal Government has recently come to the following conclusions:

Under the aspect of raw material supplies, there is no immediate need, in particular for the EEC member states with large forest resources, like the Federal Republic of Germany, to substantially expand the forest area. But to secure raw material supplies in the long term, the expansion of the forest area is to be assessed positively and should be aimed at both in the EEC as a whole and in the Federal Republic of Germany.

If one includes, however, the agricultural policy aspects, it seems extremely useful to make a contribution towards taking pressure off the agricultural markets by mean of afforestation in line with environmental requirements of part of those areas which have so far been used intensively for agricultural purposes. Forestry is one of the possible alternatives and at the same time an economically useful alternative for the farmer who wants to give up production voluntarily. Forests that are in harmony with nature ("naturnah") fulfil in addition ecological functions in a far better way than intensive agriculture. Therefore, environmental aspects as well as the suitability of the forest as a recreation area speak in favour of afforestation of part of the land that may be abandoned by agriculture.

If agricultural production is to decline to the extent desired, it must be abandoned on part of those areas with high yields. It goes without saying that, in the beginning, good soils will be abandoned only reluctantly. If, however, a 55-year-old farm owner - this could be the target group of the EEC - without a successor wants to give up his farm in an area with intensive agricultural production and use it for afforestation, this should be welcomed also by the agricultural advisory services.

5. and 6. TIMBER TRANSPORT, TIMBER MARKETING, FOREST PRODUCTS POLICY

Except for the skidding of wood from stump to roadside, timber transport in the Federal Republic of Germany is subject to strictly controlled statutory provisions of transport. The Federal Government, with the aim of providing the best transport facilities, has to see to it that the conditions of competition between the carriers are fair and in line with market requirements and that they permit a division of functions which is useful for the national economy.

Raw wood marketing in the Federal Republic of Germany takes place within the framework of the principles of the market economy.

According to the EC directive to harmonize the legal provisions of member states concerning the grading of raw wood, the raw wood cut in the Federal Republic of Germany is classified by assortments of comparable quality and dimensions and is thus a standardized merchandise.

The Act on Compensation for the Effects of Special Damage to Forestry was established in 1969 and amended in 1985. It authorizes the Federal Minister of Food, Agriculture and Forestry to restrict fellings of individual species under certain conditions, for example after natural disasters.

Changes in forest industries in the last few years have sprung from the increasing need to rationalize. For example, in the furniture industry, new styles require machinery of highest precision which, with the aid of microprocessors, can also be used for the manufacture of small unit numbers at optimum cost. The same applies in principle to the sawmilling industry where a structural change is taking place in favour of modern processing technologies for small-dimensioned wood.

Standardization of wood products is the task of industry. The central body is the "Deutsches Institut für Normung (DIN)" (German Institute for Standardization).

The DIN is the German member of ISO and CEN, the international and European standardization organizations. The international standards of ISO are, like the German standards, recommendations which are not binding. They can, however, be made binding by inclusion in national regulations.

Standardization gained special importance in building and safety regulations. Freedom of furniture design is safeguarded by the fact that the only decisive criteria are safety and suitability for use.

Substitution by competing materials and the declining volume of new building associated with the population trend in the Federal Republic of Germany do not allow us to expect much growth in the traditional sales markets for wood products. In view of these perspectives, the efforts of forest industries have recently been concentrated to a greater extent on the possibilities of securing and/or increasing sales by:

- identifying existing market gaps;

- intensified efforts to educate and inform potential decision-making bodies (architects, engineers, builders);

- translating innovative ideas into practice by specific wood product research.

The relationship between forestry and forest industries is characterized by relative inflexibility of supplies on the one hand and considerable short-term fluctuations in demand on the other.

Residues have been used by forest industries for a very long time. Apart from energy production from wood residues and bark, mention should be made in particular of the use of sawmill residues and waste paper in the derived timber products industry, as well as in the pulp and paper industry. Recycled wood products are used in particular as a decorative and at the same time functional element for gardens, playgrounds and similar facilities. The development of various methods of processing bark into high-quality humus products or bark mulch has brought about new uses in gardening and landscaping.

The aim of structural policy is to help also smaller enterprises to become more efficient and competitive. An important contribution in this respect is the granting of funds for research and development projects by the Federal Government. The public funds serve to promote industrial joint research as well as external contract research.

Environmental policy constraints are topical and, in some instances, very controversial developments which directly affect forest industries. Apart from restricting the maximum formaldehyde concentration in rooms, the constraints include stricter maximum emission values for dusts from wood-firing installations and the classification of oak and beech wood dusts as carcinogenic by the Senate Commission of the German Research Society.

7. WORKFORCE AND LABOUR ASSOCIATIONS

The table below shows a breakdown by type and area of employment (enterprises with a forest area under 50 ha. are excluded).

Persons employed in forestry in 1982/83
(in 1,000s)

	Officials & employees	Enterprise workforce,incl. family labour	Non-enterprise labour
State forest	9.9	19.6	–
Corporate forest	1.7	21.2	–
Private forest	1.6	18.2	–
TOTAL	13.2	59.0	18.1

Standard wages in forestry in 1985/86 averaged about DM 11.43 per hour.

8.   FORESTRY EDUCATION

University Education

- The Graduate Forester (Diplomforstwirt)

There are faculties of forestry at the Universities of Freiburg, Göttingen and Munich. The regular courses comprise eight semesters. After graduation, the preparatory service (Referendarzeit) is obligatory for those who seek employment in the civil service. This preparatory service is generally concluded after 2 years by the "major forestry state examination".

- The Graduate Wood Technologist (Diplomholzwirt)

This type of study is only possible at the University of Hamburg in cooperation with the Federal Research Centre for Forestry and Forest Products. The course normally covers 8 semesters.

College for Higher Professional Training

- Forest Engineer (Forstingenieur)

Until very recently, the technical training of foresters at upper and medium level took place at the forestry schools run by the forest services of the Länder.

There is now a tendency for this training to be moved from the forest service to colleges for higher professional training ("Fachhochschulen"). Three institutions of that type already exist.

To be enrolled at these colleges, the applicant must have the university entrance qualification restricted to a specified field of study or equivalent.

Because of the special characteristics of the forestry field service, the applicant has to submit a medical health certificate before starting his practical training, certifying that his eyesight and hearing are good and that he is able to distinguish colours.

- The Wood Technology Engineer (Ing.-grad.)(Ingenieur für Holztechnik)

Wood technology training facilities at this level are only offered at the colleges for higher professional training at Rosenheim and Mosbach. The aim of this type of training is to provide the wood industry with technically qualified managerial staff.

Technical Training

- The Trained Forest Worker ("Forstwirt") and the Master Forester ("Forstwirtschaftsmeister")

Since March 1974, the Ordinance on Vocational Training to the professional status of trained forest worker has been in force; the Ordinance was issued under the Vocational Training Law and applies throughout the Federation. Training normally takes 3 years. The training centre must be a forestry enterprise of at least 500 ha.

Under the Vocational Training Law, and based on the regulations on the requirements for the master craftsman's qualifying examination in forestry, the trained forest worker may move up to the status of master forester.

9.   RESEARCH

The Federal Government and some of the Länder have forestry and forest products research institutes. Research in these fields is also undertaken at universities and other institutions. A description of the great number of activities would go beyond the scope of this publication. Further information may be obtained from the Federal Ministry of Food, Agriculture and Forestry and the appropriate ministries of the Länder.

10.   INTERNATIONAL COOPERATION

The Federal Republic of Germany takes part in the relevant international activities relating to forestry and forest industries, in particular within the framework of EEC, FAO and OECD.

Moreover, contacts exist with many countries, e.g. Austria, Switzerland, the Scandinavian countries, Spain, Portugal, Hungary and China; these contacts are mainly based on government agreements on mutual agricultural trade.

Mention should also be made of the great number of international
contacts of the Länder and of the exchange of scientific findings between
the research institutions and international research organizations, for
example within the framework of IUFRO.

The Federal Government, through its participation in many
supra-national bodies, organizations and conferences (e.g. at EC level,
within the framework of FAO, Lome III, World Bank, International Tropical
Wood Agreement, etc.) supports the conservation of tropical forests and the
establishment of planned forestry in the developing countries; it believes
that the industrialized countries should commit themselves to a greater
extent in that field.

GREECE

1. INTRODUCTION

The total land area of Greece is 13.2 million ha., broken down as follows:

Category of Use	Million Hectares	%
Cultivated area	3.96	30.0
Forests	2.51	19.0
Partly forested area	3.24	24.5
Forest grassland	2.49	18.9
Lakes, rivers, marshes	0.31	2.3
Area covered by buildings	0.47	3.6
Waste land (rocky)	0.22	1.7
Total	13.20	100.0%

Sources: CEPE and Ministry of Agriculture (General Directorate of Forests) Programme of Forestry, 1976-1980.

2. OWNERSHIP

The ownership distribution of the 2.5 million ha. of forests is as follows:

	%
State	66
Community	12
Monasteries	4
Private	8
Other	10
	100

The category "other" includes charitable organizations, cooperatives and joint ownerships involving more than three persons. The ownership distribution of the partially forested areas is similar.

3. PRINCIPLES AND OBJECTIVES OF FOREST POLICY

    The most important are:

    -   to recognize the social value of forests and prevent speculation
        in forest land;

    -   to develop a forestry conscience and a better understanding of the
        benefits of forests;

    -   to protect forests against fires and others risks including
        illegal fellings;

    -   to protect soils and combat erosion, especially in mountainous
        regions;

    -   to protect, conserve and encourage forest flora and fauna
        including fish, especially in mountain streams;

    -   to safeguard the environmental and landscape functions of the
        national forests;

    -   to manage the State forests and to care for the forests in other
        ownerships.

4. ADMINISTRATION

    The Minister of Agriculture is responsible for forestry. On the basis
of the Presidential Decree issued in October 1981, the Forest Service was
decentralized and is organized as follows.

    The Central Forest Service consists of the following ten divisions,
each of which has 3 to 4 sections:

    -   Planning and Studies

    -   Research, Training and Information

    -   Forest Cadastral Survey

    -   Mapping, Forest Survey and Land Classification

    -   Forest Ownership

    -   State Forest Management

    -   Reforestation and Management of Watersheds in the Mountains

    -   Wildlife, Fishery and Range Management

    -   Forest Protection and Forest Environment

    -   Non-State Forestry.

In addition, there is an independent Section of Financial and Accounting Services.

The Central Service is also responsible for:

- 3 forest research institutes (only 2 are in operation)

- the central forest seed store

- the central store and workshop for the control and maintenance of mechanical equipment.

The Regional Forest Services consist of:

- Inspectorates of Forest at interprefecture level	7
- Divisions with forest districts	31
- Divisions without forest districts	24
- Forest districts	80
- Forest offices	290
- Forest guard stations	1,115
- Divisions of reforestation	3

The seven inspectorates at interprefecture level are the responsible regional instrument of the Ministry of Agriculture for forest development and the application of forest policy within its jurisdiction.

The divisions with forest districts are responsible for coordinating the work of the districts under their jurisdiction and for approving the decentralized activities realized by the districts.

The forest districts are exclusive agencies for the execution of projects and they also are empowered to take decisions up to a certain level on many decentralized activities.

The divisions without forest districts have all the competences of the forest districts.

The forest offices and the forest guard stations are mainly concerned with forest protection. They also have a limited but important decision-making role in serving the country people.

The reforestation divisions are agencies for the planning and execution of reforestation projects. They have considerable powers and are located in Attica, Thessaloniki and Rodopi.

The Presidential Decree 332/1983 completed the process of
decentralization of all operational activities. The Central Service
remains, however, as the administrative agency responsible for: planning
forest policy, drafting legislation, giving guidelines to the Regional
Services, drawing up long-term programmes, financial matters relating to
both State and non-State forests, recruitment and distribution of
personnel, international aspects of forestry, the preparation of training
and information programmes and, finally, the collection of relevant
statistics and other information.

5.   FACTORS AFFECTING FOREST POLICY

The main factors are:

-   Site and climate: 70% of the country is mountainous and most of
    the forests are in the mountains. The climate ranges from
    continental in northern and central Greece to mediterranean in the
    south and on the islands.

-   The vegetation zones, of which five are distinguished, namely:

    * Eu-Mediterranean vegetation zone (Quercetalia ilicis);

    * Sub-Mediterranean vegetation zone (Quercetalia pubescentis);

    * Zone of beech-fir forests and mountainous sub-mediterranean
    conifers (Fagetalia);

    * Formation of humid western mountain stage (Vaccinio-Picetalia);

    * Dry sub-alpine zone (Astragalo-Acantho Limonetalia).

-   Social, economic and demographic conditions:

    * between 1920 and 1980, the population increased by an average
    of 1.1% annually and there was a marked shift of population from
    the mountainous regions, some of which have become virtually
    abandoned, to the plains and towns;

    * the proportion of people engaged in agriculture fell from 44%
    in 1961 to 30% in 1981;

    * between 1965 and 1983, GDP rose by 4.5% per year and per capita
    income by 3.7%;

    * during the past 15 years, there has been a great development in
    the plains of food and of other agricultural and horticultural
    crops such as cotton, flowers and fruit; these developments have
    been aided by land consolidation measures and major irrigation
    projects;

* pig and cattle breeding has also moved to the plains and near towns, but the development has been slower than for crops;

* goat and sheep breeding remain in small units; the protection of vegetation against damage by grazing and fire is therefore almost impossible;

* tourism has developed greatly along the coast and in the more populated regions, but not in the mountains;

* the modest industrial developments that have taken place have also been confined to the agricultural regions.

The above factors, combined with existing property problems, have created unfavourable conditions for the development of forestry.

6. PUBLIC AGENCIES FOR FOREST POLICY

In Greece, the only service responsible for the application of the forestry policy and all other activities mentioned above is the Forest Service of the Ministry of Agriculture.

7. LEGISLATION

No forest policy is applied without legislation, but the problem is that there are many laws and there is a need for codification and modernization. An effort to do this has been made in recent years, but it is not yet known by when the task can be completed.

8. NATIONAL FORESTRY POLICY AND DEVELOPMENT

Forestry in Greece aims to meet the needs of society for products and services in a variety of ways, namely:

- protection of forests and the natural environment in general against fire, pests and damage by man;

- increase of forest production, especially of industrial wood;

- increase of other products and services, particularly:

* acceleration of torrent control, land reclamation and other infrastructural works;

* creation of the necessary infrastructure so as to enable the public to reach and enjoy the natural environment;

* increase of the grazing potential of the forests;

* protection and development of the wildlife and fishery of the mountain rivers and streams in order to obtain revenue from hunting and fishing;

* improvement of the economic and social situation of the population in the mountains by creating new jobs and better working conditions.

Important programmes to implement these objectives have been undertaken. They have been financed from various national sources as well as from loans by the European Investment Bank, World Bank and the Rehabilitation Fund of the European Council.

Forestry accounts for about 1% of the total State budget and for 3% of public investments. The rules governing forestry investments are the same as for the rest of the public sector and nearly all are undertaken by the Forest Service.

9.   MONETARY AND TAX POLICY

Taxes

Primary forest produce from non-State forests is subject to direct taxation. The tax is named State Forest Tax and is paid by the forest owners when they receive the logging permit from the local regional forest services. The tax is based on the official price list for forest produce.

The official prices and the State Forest Tax are fixed each year by Presidential Decree on the proposal of the Minister of Agriculture and after obtaining the view of the Technical Council of Forests. The price list records the kind of primary forest products, together with the measurement unit, the unit price, the purchase price (official) and the State Forest Tax, which is determined as a percentage of the purchase price as follows:

14% for technical wood (timber), bark and forest plants

10% for charcoal, fuelwood and shrubs

11% for all other products (leaves, flowers, seed, etc.)

In addition, there is a land tax levied on all non-State forests. The object is to cover part of the cost of supervision. At present, the tax is 1 dr/ha./year on the total area of forest owned, but with the proviso that the tax must not exceed 1/12 of the potential annual yield as estimated from the price list.

Development of Non-State Forestry

Until 1974, very little development took place in the non-State forests. In order to promote such development, incentives were introduced in 1974 for "economic support of agriculture, livestock and forest and fishery production". As a result, subsidies of 40-60% of the total cost of the following works and materials are available from the State:

  * reforestation and nurseries

  * forest roads

  * fire prevention

  * measures in hunting areas

  * range works

  * preparation of management plans

  * supply of machinery and tools.

As a follow-up, Law 998 of 1979 requires owners to undertake measures for forest protection, such as erosion control, flood control, fire breaks, etc. These works may be undertaken:

-   by the forest owners, in which case the whole cost is reimbursed by the State;

-   by the State; in this case, the owner bears half the cost unless the forest where the works are to be realized does not produce sufficient income, in which case the total cost is borne by the State.

Under the same law, 998/79, forest owners are obliged to spend up to 30% of their forest income on forestry development. In spite of the above incentives and obligations, forest development in the non-State forests leaves much to be desired.

10. MANAGEMENT AND FOREST PROTECTION

Torrents

Over 4 million ha. have been either completely or partially eroded. It is estimated that 1000 m3 of material per km2 is eroded by torrents each year. Erosion has been so serious that major rehabilitation measures must have a very high priority.

Torrent control by the Forest Service began in 1932 in Macedonia. These measures complemented the big productive plain development of the region. The Forest Service spent 2.5 bn drs between 1931 and 1985 (at 1970 prices) on torrent control, and about 80,000 ha., i.e. about 20% of the worst affected areas, are now under control.

There is now a special project in the Programme of Public Investments for financing the engineering and reforestation works for the purpose of torrent control and watershed management.

Forest Management

About 38% of the forests are coniferous and 62% broadleaved. The total annual increment is 4 million m3. The average stocking of conifers is 112 m3/ha. and the average increment 2.8 m3/ha./year. The corresponding figures for broadleaved species are 69 m3/ha. and 2.1 m3/ha./year. The partially forested areas and the evergreen broadleaved forests produce an additional 0.45 million m3/year.

Between 1850 and 1950, the forests suffered severely from unreasonable exploitation and forest destruction. The reconstruction started 35 years ago and includes the various measures that have been mentioned.

Forest Production

The sustainable yield is estimated at 3.6 million m3/year. The annual cut is about 2.9 million m3/year, of which 15% are sawlogs, poles, pitprops and plywood logs, while the other 85% are fuelwood and pulpwood (for the manufacture of pulp and chips for particle board). Annual cut is less than the sustainable yield, partially because of lack of demand for fuelwood, partially because of insufficient forest roads, partially because of high cost of harvesting and mainly because there is not any industry for utilizing the smaller dimension wood.

Forest Exploitation

Under existing legislation, the management of all forests is conservative. This is because of the overriding importance of the environmental and protective functions of the forests in Greece. The more important State forests are all managed according to management plans drawn up every 10 years, while 5-year plans are drawn up and approved for the non-State forests. Harvesting in the State forests is carried out by forest cooperatives, groups of workers or by individuals. The wood is delivered to the purchaser after bidding procedures at the roadside. This system has proved to be excellent.

Forest Protection

The main dangers are fire, disease, illegal felling and conversion to other use, the latter mainly in coastal regions and near towns. About 65,000 ha. of forest are destroyed by fire each year. Fire prevention and fire fighting involves the forest services, the local population, the army and the civil airforce.

11. NATIONAL POLICY FOR PROTECTED AND OPEN RECREATION AREAS

The first protected area was declared in 1938. The policy for the reservation and management of protected areas is governed by law 996/79 which forms part of the forest legislation. In 1966, a section for "National Parks and Groves" was created in the Directorate General of Forests. By 1970, 45 million drachma had been spent on land acquisition and works such as fencing, roads, etc.

On the basis of law 997/71, there are now ten national parks, nineteen amenity forests (for landscape and recreation purposes) and 37 preserved monuments of nature which include areas of paleolithic, geomorphic and historical importance or trees or woods of particular botanical, phytogeographic, aesthetic or historic interest. Recently, a new law was passed by parliament for the protection of the environment, but the decrees for its implementation have not yet been issued. Provisions for the recreational use of forests have only been made recently, but within the last five years, 500 recreation areas have been created throughout the country, but more especially in Attica where one-third of the total population lives. The facilities offered include picnic sites, nature walks, etc., in order to provide opportunities for simple open air activities and the observation of wildlife. It is intended to increase the number and scope of recreational areas.

Hunting and Fishing

In 1985, there were over 340,000 hunters. While the numbers of hunters has been increasing, game populations have been reduced by the destruction of biotopes, unreasonable use of pesticides, illegal hunting, etc. To counteract this disturbing situation, 558 refuges for game have been established on an area of about 850,000 ha. In addition, there are twenty public breeding areas in which game birds (pheasants, partridges, quails) and deer, rabbits, wild goats and wild sheep are bred. There are also 8 controlled hunting areas, totalling about 130,000 ha. The main objectives are: the protection and maximum development of the game populations, their reasonable exploitation, the reconstruction of the biological balance between fauna and flora, the promotion of winter tourism, and the securing of additional income for the population of the region.

In the freshwater fishing sector, four trout breeding stations have been established with an annual production of 500,000 trout, which are released in the mountain streams of central and northern Greece. There are 152 trout streams in Greece with a total length of 1,860 km.

12. AFFORESTATION

Four categories of afforestation may be distinguished:

a) for the economic production of timber

b) for protective purposes: erosion control, etc.

c) for recreational and aesthetic purposes

d) for the growing of special short-rotation crops such as poplars.

A total of about 2 million ha. has been afforested, and afforestation continues at about 4,000 ha. each year, which is very little in relation to the 5.5 million ha. of partly forested areas and pastures which would be suitable for the purpose. The intention is to increase the rate of afforestation to 25,000 or 30,000 ha. per year. A necessary precondition will be the classification of the soils in the mountains.

13. RANGELANDS

A substantial attempt to improve and manage rangelands began in 1949. Particular importance was attached to works such as the construction of access roads and the provision of drinking water for the animals, as well as to the management of pastures and the protection of the soil.

The areas used as rangelands are classed as:

Alpine	400,000 ha.
Partly forested	3,240,000 ha.
Grasslands	1,520,000 ha.
Areas covered by shrubs	270,000 ha.

In addition, there are over 1 million ha. of forest where uncontrolled grazing takes place. Overgrazing of the rangelands has resulted in an impoverishment of the vegetation, a reduction in livestock production and a deterioration of the soils in many parts of the country. Suitable improvement measures and proper management could reverse the process.

The State, which owns 75% of the rangelands, has granted its right of income to the communities where people graze their animals free of charge. Everybody thus has the right to use the land but nobody is responsible for maintaining these areas.

14. THE USE OF FOREST PRODUCTS

Forest Roads

The existing density of forest roads in Greece averages only 5-6 m/ha. It is intended to increase this density in a first phase to 12-15 m/ha., and in a second phase to 20-25 m/ha. About 60% of the skidding of roundwood from stump to roadside is done by animals and the other 40% by mechanical means. Fuelwood of small dimensions is nearly all brought from stump to forest road by animals.

Policy concerning the Development of the National Wood Industries

Sawmills and particle board factories suffer from overcapacity and out-of-date equipment which results in very low productivity. The creation of the so-called cooperative units for wood production was a first step to confront this situation. Little progress, however, has been made in the standardization of forest products because of lack of interest.

Suitable industries have been developed to utilize the best qualities of wood, but not wood of second quality or of small dimensions. Only about one-half of the 40% of wood residues from sawmilling are at present utilized for the manufacture of pulp and particle boards, etc. The present possibilities for new forest industrial developments appear to be limited, but 3 large industrial wood processing units are being established by rural cooperative organizations within the framework of the agricultural policy. Whenever new wood processing industries are established, all necessary measures for the protection of the environment are taken.

15. MARKETING

State Forests

In the major State forests, the Forest Service harvests and transports the produce to the forest road, where most is sold by auction. A small percentage is processed by the State at its own industries and another small amount is sold at cost price to forest cooperatives.

In the less important State forests, harvesting and sales are agreed with the forest cooperatives on the basis of the fixed price lists. The forest cooperatives either process the produce in their own industries or sell it on the open market by auction or direct negotiation.

Non-State Forests

Private forest owners may dispose of forest produce as they wish. The Communities and Municipalities are obliged by law to offer the produce standing or delivered at forest road or to sell it to the forest cooperatives on the basis of the fixed price list. The produce from the forests belonging to the cooperatives and monasteries is sold on the open market either competitively or by direct negotiation.

Supplies to Primary Consumers

The big industries generally purchase the raw material direct from the growers. Small industries, on the other hand, usually buy from merchants although they could easily participate at auctions because the produce offered at these is split into small lots. Fuelwood is generally bought from merchants. Long-term contracts between growers and industries are rare.

16. EMPLOYMENT

Forestry labour, which accounts for 2.3% of the country's labour
force, enjoys the same social security benefits as workers in other sectors
of the economy. The Ministry of Labour operates training schools for all
sectors of industry including forestry. The privately-owned forest
industries recruit their own labour. Recruitment in the two State-owned
forest industries follows the procedures applicable to the whole of the
public sector.

The Regional Forest Services hire labour for work in the forest, where
most operations are seasonal, after obtaining the approval of the head of
the Prefecture concerned.

The Forest Service undertook special programmes for the unemployed in
1983, 1984 and 1985, but most of the unemployment programmes are
implemented by the Ministry of Labour.

17. EDUCATION

Compulsory education in Greece consists of six years of elementary
school followed by three years of Gymnasium. Then follow three years at
High School and finally University.

The School of Forestry and Natural Environment at the University of
Thessaloniki offers a five-year degree course in forestry.

Three Technical Training Foundations provide three-year courses in
forestry. Admittance to both the University and these Foundations follows
after successful graduation from High School. Forest guards are trained at
special schools giving courses lasting 2-3 months. The Forest Service
determines the required entrance qualifications, which include graduation
from Elementary School or Junior High School. Forest workers learn mainly
by experience, but there are also short courses of 2-3 days or 1-2 weeks
for specific jobs. The main requirement is therefore for the better
vocational training of forest workers, and the establishment of four forest
Vocational Training Centres is under study. All forestry training is
undertaken by the public sector.

The Ministry of Labour, which is responsible for the training of
personnel in the wood processing industries, has organized some vocational
schools offering various types of training.

18. FOREST RESEARCH

Forest research comes under the Ministry of Agriculture and is carried out by the Institutions of Forest Research in Athens and Thessaloniki. The subjects for investigation are agreed between the research institutions and the relevant Divisions and Sections of the Central Service, one of which is also responsible for coordination and financing. The aim of forest research is to assist in the accomplishment of forestry policy goals.

Some forestry research is also carried out by the School of Forestry and National Resources of the University of Thessaloniki. All research results are published in the magazine "Forest Research", of which there are 2-6 issues every year, depending on the research results achieved. The magazine is distributed free of charge to all forest services and the most important libraries of the country. Numerous copies are also distributed to foreign libraries and universities.

19. INTERNATIONAL COOPERATION

The main aim of national policy for international cooperation in the forestry sector is the formulation and application of a common EEC policy for the effective protection and development of the Community's forests. The main purpose of contacts with countries outside the EEC are exchanges of knowledge, technology and experience.

Relations on subjects of technical assistance have developed with FAO, OECD and ECE (the Economic Commission for Europe). The Ministry of Foreign Affairs and the Ministry of National Economy are together responsible for all the above external relations in forestry.

HUNGARY

1. INTRODUCTION

1.1 Major characteristics of the country's forests

The area registered as forest in 1985 was 1.6 million ha., i.e. 17.7% of the total land area of 9.3 million ha.

The proportion of forest managing organizations has changed during the past 15 years as follows:

Forest Managing Organizations	Percentage of Total Forest Area	
	1970	1985
State forest enterprises	70.9	64.2
State farms	3.2	4.8
Other state organizations and communities	2.3	0.2
Cooperative farms	22.8	30.4
Others	3.1	0.4
Total	100.0	100.0

Eighty percent of the country's forest area has wood production, 16% environmental protection and nature conservation, and 4% recreation and research as its recognized primary function.

About 85% of the forests are broadleaved, with oaks, beech, hornbeam and poplars as the main species, and 15% are coniferous.

1.2 Main principles and objectives of the national forestry policy

The main objectives of forestry policy are:

(1) Expansion of forest resources by afforestation and the conversion of existing forests to increase their yield and improve their quality.

(2) Increasing the felling and the industrial utilization of wood, and improving the country's supply of wood. Between 1950 and 1985, removals increased from 2.7 million m3 to 6.8 million m3.

(3) Expansion of non-wood services of forests: nature conservation, recreation, etc.

(4) Improving the working conditions of forest workers by social
measures and increased mechanization.

1.3 Legal measures and decisions bearing on forestry policy

Bases of the Hungarian forestry policy are laid down in the Forest Law
enacted in 1961 and modified in 1981. In 1985, the National Planning
Committee decided upon the tasks of the timber economy for the next 5
years.

Forestry policy is reflected also in national development plans, since
within the framework of national economic planning, the laws enacted by
Parliament on the development plans of the national economy determine also
the major tasks of forestry for each year and for the medium-term planning
periods too.

2. ADMINISTRATION

2.1 Organizational pattern of forestry administration

The organization of forestry administration has changed several times
during the past 40 years. The present organization was formed in 1979, when
the Office of Forestry and Forest Industries was established within the
Ministry of Agriculture and Food. This Office is responsible for
administration in the field of forestry, primary wood processing and timber
trade, as well as game management. It also coordinates the sector's
activities with other sectors of the economy in the field of environmental
protection and nature conservation.

The second part of the sector's administration is the Forest
Management Planning Service, having a national sphere of competence, and
the State forest inspectorates, organized territorially. Its function is to
provide 10-year management plans for forest owners and submit them for
approval to the Office of Forestry and Forest Industries.

Planned forest management, i.e. the implementation of management
plans, is obligatory under the Forest Law for every forest owner.

Supervised directly by the Office of Forestry and Forest Industries,
the State forest inspectorates supervise the forest owners' annual and
medium-term management plans, as well as the fellings and reforestation
carried out by the forest owners.

The organization and activity of State forest enterprises is built up
according to the principle of vertical integration since they are dealing
with wood growing, logging, wood processing and sometimes also with
furniture production and construction joinery as well as with marketing.
With effect from 1 January 1985, directors of enterprises are elected for 5
years by the board of the enterprise through secret ballot.

The National Forestry Association, being a voluntary association of professional foresters, also plays an important role in developing forestry policy, in continuing education and in the protection of the sector's interests. Its periodical, "Az Erdo" publishes scientific studies and informs its members about events in the Association's life.

Recently, the Timber Section of the Hungarian Chamber of Commerce has also played an increasingly significant role. It functions as a business federation of the enterprises towards the Government and government bodies.

2.2 Relationship of national forestry legislation with forestry policy

In accordance with the general rules of the Hungarian legislation, the following types of legal measures form the legal framework for forestry:

- Law, enacted by Parliament

- Law Decree, approved by the Presidential Council

- Government Decree, or decision endorsed by the Cabinet

- Ministerial Order, signed by a member of the Cabinet.

It is the task of the Office of Forestry and Timber Industry to take the preliminary steps in forestry legislation, i.e. drafting, consultation with relevant organizations, etc.

Implementation of the legal measures for forestry is supervised by the forestry authorities, but the different social organizations and associations also play an important part. Youth organizations, the Patriotic People's Front and the National Federation of Nature Lovers play an important role in questions related to forest protection, afforestation and plantation projects.

2.3 The national forestry policy and national development

As a consequence of the world economic recession, restrictions were placed on domestic consumption in the early 'eighties. In the forestry sector, this led to greater priority being given to the utilization of logging and industrial residues; replacement of imported wood products and the use of chips as a source of energy. Another consequence of the recession was a reduction in State subsidies to forestry.

However, the budget continues to cover all expenditures on afforestation and reforestation of uneconomic forests. Forest owners are partly compensated by the State budget also for their expenses on environmental protection and on the maintenance and establishment of recreational facilities. All other forestry investments, with the exception of forest road construction which is subsidised by the budget by 40-50%, are financed out of the forest owners' own resources and by bank loans. State forest enterprises may use on average 30% of their profit and 100% of their depreciation on fixed assets as their own resources for investment.

3. FINANCING AND TAXATION SYSTEM

   Taxes are imposed on forest managing organizations in two ways:

   a) All forest managing organizations are obliged to pay a certain
   amount as reforestation charge to the Reforestation Fund to cover
   the expense of silvicultural operations. This charge is imposed by
   the Ministry of Agriculture and Food.

   b) Income taxation for forestry, as for agriculture, is now based on
   gross income. The rate of tax increases progressively as gross
   income per capita rises.

   c) A so-called "accumulation tax" is levied on the enterprises'
   expenses on investment.

   d) In addition to the above, State forest enterprises are obliged to
   pay 3% of their gross income as a community development tax for the
   budget.

   The unfavourable impacts of the above taxation system, which is aimed
at centralizing a considerable part of the enterprises' income and at
restricting investments, were recently counterbalanced by a rise in the
fuelwood producers' prices proportionate to the prices of other fuels.

4. FOREST MANAGEMENT AND PROTECTION

4.1 Land-use policy

   One of the fundamental principles of the Hungarian land-use policy is
the utilization for food production of all lands that can be cultivated
economically. According to recent scientific investigations, there are
about 300,000 ha. in which agricultural production is not profitable.
Inundated flood plains along rivers, steep sides of hills and mountains,
and grasslands of low yield belong to this category. The afforestation of
170,000 ha. of this area is planned by the year 2000.

   A programme of planting trees outside the forests is also planned.
This is a social programme, the seedlings being provided free of charge by
the State.

4.2 Protection of forest resources

   The conversion of forest to other land use is only permitted in
exceptional cases. The preservation of the quality of forests is supported
by the regulations which provide for penalties if the regeneration of
forests has not been carried out in due time or inadequately, or if
thinnings have been neglected. In order to monitor biotic and abiotic
damage, a network covering the whole country is being developed in
conformity with the recommendations of the FAO European Forestry
Commission.

Recently, oak decline has been observed in about 120,000 ha. According to investigations carried out so far, this damage is probably due to the joint effect of several factors, among which acid rain, pollutant depositions, unfavourable concentration of heavy metals in soil-solution and drought play the determinant roles.

4.3 Nature conservation

The aim of Hungarian nature conservation is to explore and preserve the country's natural values of greatest importance from scientific or cultural viewpoints and to make them public property through demonstration.

At present, nature conservation areas of national importance occupy 480,000 hectares, the distribution of which is as follows:

- 4 national parks: 141,000 ha.

- 34 landscape protection regions: 311,000 ha.

- 102 nature conservation areas: 28,000 ha.

In addition, 35,000 ha. have been declared nature conservation area by local authorities. Ten percent of the conservation area is managed by the Nature Conservation Authority and the remaining 90% by the owners in accordance with nature conservation prescriptions. The extra costs generated by management restrictions are reimbursed by the Nature Conservation Authority.

About 50% of the conservation area is covered by forest, where the reservation of natural stands and the protection of native species are the primary goals.

4.4 Recreational forest management

In Hungary, there has been a high demand for recreation in forests since the second half of the 'fifties. From the mid-1950's to 1970, the basic principles for the recreational function of forests were laid down.

The second period of the development of recreational forests started in the early 1970's, when some finance approved in the national economic plans was made available for investment in and maintenance of recreational facilities. It was at this time that the elaboration of a long-term programme for the development of recreation forests up to 1990 was begun on the basis of a wide-ranging survey of demands. In this programme, the proportions of the three functions were scheduled as follows:

Recognized Primary Function	1985	1990
	percentage of total	
Timber production	80	73
Environmental protection	16	15
Recreation	4	12

The annual maintenance costs of the facilities established in recreational forests financed by the budget amount to 60-65 million HFt.

4.5 Game management

The right to hunt is exercised by the State all over the country.

According to the game management policy, hunting and game management should serve three objectives:

- meeting demand for sport-hunting;

- conservation and development of natural values;

- yielding profit through commodity production and lease hunting.

On the hunting grounds managed by hunting societies, meeting the demand for sport-hunting is the main objective, while on the State hunting grounds, profitability takes priority.

The ten-year game management development programme compiled in 1980 schedules a decrease in big game stock because of the considerable damage it causes to forestry and agriculture.

A new Hunting Law is being prepared, one of the most important purposes of which is to create legal conditions for harmony between game management, agriculture and forestry.

5. FOREST UTILIZATION

The basic objectives of the policy are complete utilization of domestic raw material and the development of a wood industry capable of processing this material into further-processed products of high value.

At present, 40% of wood products consumed are imported. At the same time, felling and removal potentials exceed the domestic processing capacity. Therefore 1.2-1.5 million cu.m., mainly of poor quality hardwood, are exported.

In contrast to the general situation, the biggest particle board manufacturing enterprise in the country, the Western Hungarian Wood-working Complex, has developed rapidly. By manufacturing new products (laminated and cement-bonded particle board), this enterprise has adjusted to the changed conditions and produces from its own products modern office furniture, wooden dwelling house components and complete dwelling houses.

The use of wood for energy has increased. In order to utilize logging waste and industrial residues, the production of wood briquet has been started and is increasing.

Programmes for the development of the wood industry are aimed at establishing new capacities suitable for processing domestic raw materials and at improving the timber trade balance. The programme includes, for example, the building of 2,000 energy-saving houses with prefabricated components and the manufacture of OSB and MDF.

6. TIMBER TRADE AND MARKETING

6.1 National timber trade policy

The organizational pattern of the Hungarian timber trade still bears the marks of a centrally planned and directed system of the economy. Thus there is only one wholesale timber trade enterprise, the ERDERT Company, whose main task is to receive, store and convert imported softwood logs, sawn softwood and panel products which are needed for domestic consumption and then to sell these products to retailers or consumers. During the last few years, more and more undertakings have started to deal in timber along with ERDERT Co. These firms, however, have very little trading capital and thus are not able for the time being to store goods and they act mainly as brokers.

Foreign timber trade is a State monopoly in Hungary. As regards its organizational pattern, however, it has been considerably decentralized since 1980.

The current State Administration's reform will result in a gradual liquidation of monopolies and the establishment of a more flexible trade organization.

The most important item of the Hungarian timber imports are the softwood products, which Hungarian forests cannot provide. At the same time, about half of the volume of exports is composed of non-coniferous pulpwood, because of the shortage in domestic processing capacities.

6.2 Timber marketing policy

State forest enterprises and timber industries distribute the timber products they produce direct to consumer enterprises and to the population. Direct marketing is also encouraged by the State in order to speed up the exchange of goods and reduce stocks.

7. EMPLOYMENT

At present, the sector employs about 50,000 persons, of which 40,000 are manual workers. Between 1970 and 1980, the labour force decreased by 5,000. Labour shortage is significant in silviculture and logging, where working conditions are unfavourable; the work is heavy and earnings are lower than in some other sectors.

Forest management organizations try to compensate for the disadvantageous working conditions by mechanizing the operations of especially heavy work and by improving social benefits. State forest enterprises also play a significant part in establishing small settlements of forest workers' homes.

The expanding offer of services by private contractors, mainly for logging and transport, may help management organizations to eliminate their problems of labour shortages.

8.   FORESTRY EDUCATION AND CONTINUING TRAINING

Forestry education and training has three grades in Hungary. Professional foresters of the first grade are educated in the two faculties (Faculty of Forestry and Faculty of Timber Industry) of the University of Forestry and Timber Industry at Sopron. This University has a third faculty, the Faculty of Land Surveying and Mapping, which educates engineers for this special career but without granting them a university degree. Fifty forest engineers, 30 engineers in wood technology and 50 engineers in land surveying and mapping graduate every year. The period of studies for a university degree is five years, and for engineers who do not take the university degree it is three years.

Professional foresters of the middle grade, the so-called forestry technicians, are educated in two institutes. Each year about 120-130 forestry technicians and 40-50 technicians of wood technology complete their studies.

The third grade of forestry education is the training of forest workers, which is carried out at four schools for skilled forest workers. There are about 18,000 skilled workers employed in forestry and in primary wood processing, of which 3,500 have special qualifications in forestry and 2,000 in wood technology.

No significant change in the system of basic education is envisaged for forestry, but greater stress will be laid on systematic continuing education and self-education.

9.   FORESTRY RESEARCH, EXTENSION AND INFORMATION

9.1 Research

Forestry research is coordinated by the Forestry Committee of the Hungarian Academy of Sciences. This Committee determines the main directions and priorities of research in conformity with forestry policy. Research work is carried out at two institutes (the Forest Research Institute and the Research Institute for the Wood Industry) and at two universities (the University for Forestry and Timber Industry, and the University for Agricultural Sciences). Seven hundred workers are employed at these institutions, the number of researchers totalling 180 persons. Forty researchers have obtained scientific qualifications.

On average, 50 million forints are allocated by the budget each year for research purposes, and research commissioned by enterprises totals about the same amount.

Experimental areas of several thousand hectares covering the most important forest regions of the country are at the institutions' disposal. Field foresters also take part in the research in these areas.

The University for Forestry and Timber Industry is the main institute for basic research, while applied research is mainly carried out by the Forest Research Institute.

At the Research Institute for the Wood Industry, significant results have been achieved in the development of particle board and fibre board manufacturing technology and in the consumption of domestic hardwood by the building sector.

9.2 Prospective development of the forestry sector

There are about 300,000 ha. suitable for expanding the country's forest area, but because of financial constraints, afforestation of only about 170,000 ha. is expected by the turn of the century.

The allowable cut is expected to be nearly 8.5 million cu.m. in the year 2000.

Demand for industrial wood products will continue to increase, but at a slower rate than before. Demand for oak sawnwood and other sawn hardwoods of excellent quality will increase in conformity with the rising standards of housing.

A notable rise in the consumption of wood-based panels by the furniture industry is not expected, while the market for these products in the building sector may increase if the product structure is properly developed.

The demand for fuelwood and the use of wood for energy purposes will also increase in the future, because of the high import share of the country's energy consumption.

It is necessary to unite society's forces for the preservation of the health of forests, since the major factors causing the devastation of forests (air pollution, acid rain, etc.) are beyond the control of forestry. The professional tasks of forestry are as follows: raising of stands which are ecologically stable, development of institutional systems of forest protection, and development of forestry machines which do not damage stands.

10. INTERNATIONAL COOPERATION

The international relations of Hungarian forestry are extensive, in conformity with the country's open-door policy. In addition to the professional-economic objectives, establishment of direct connections between people is also a matter of great importance. Through these contacts, people can become acquainted with each other's culture and traditions.

Nowadays, Hungary maintains bilateral cooperation with fourteen countries on the basis of approved agreements.

Hungarian foresters take part in the following organizations:

- FAO Committee on Forestry

- FAO European Forestry Commission

- Economic Commission for Europe, Timber Committee

- International Union of Forestry Research Organizations (IUFRO)

- International Hunters' Council (CI)

Cooperation within the scope of the activities of the Council for Mutual Economic Aid (CHEA) plays an important part in the international relations of the country. The CHEA's Permanent Agricultural Committee, Forestry Section, and the Permanent Light-industrial Committee, Working Group on the Wood Industry, deal with the questions in the sector.

IRELAND

1. INTRODUCTION

There are some 400,000 ha. of afforested land in Ireland comprised of 340,000 ha. in State ownership and 60,000 ha. in private ownership. Coniferous forests make up over 90% of State forests and 20% of private forests. Development of the current estate dates from the increased planting of the mid-1950s in response to a Government policy decision of 1948 to plant 400,000 ha. by annual increments of 10,000 ha. Thus, 55% of State forests are under 25 years of age. The 1948 Government planting policy decision was reaffirmed on a number of occasions and most recently in 1982.

The aim of this policy is to lead to the creation of a normal forest estate with a spread of even-aged plantations. It will also provide a sustained and uniform supply of raw material for the domestic sawmilling and pulpwood industries. It is the aim of the Government to develop policies which will allow for the economic development and management of State forests and which conform to national environmental, recreation and conservation considerations.

The aims of the Forest and Wildlife Services are:

To promote:

(a) sound national forest and wildlife policies;

(b) a pattern of land use so adjusted that forestry and wildlife will yield the greatest benefits, taking into account national economic and social policies, including environmental, industrial and employment considerations; and

(c) the development of a comprehensive programme for wildlife conservation.

Specifically in regard to forestry, the main activities of the Forest Service are conceptually grouped into two distinct programmes, viz. Forest Development which relates to the extension of the forest area by State and private planting, and State Forest Management which deals with the management of the existing State forest.

The objectives of the Forest Development programme are:

(a) To increase the State forest area at a rate which will

- be consistent so as to secure that the rate of increase will produce a balanced yield;

- enable national wood production to be expanded systematically so as to avail to the greatest extent foreseeable of home and export markets at competitive prices with an acceptable return on investment;

- have due regard to the conservation, amenity and recreational values of forestry.

(b) To foster private forestry in harmony with State forestry on suitable lands and to encourage good forest management thereon.

Note: The objectives of the State forestry programme are deemed to be met by planting 10,000 ha. per annum on land on which the average yield class is not less than 14 m3 per annum.

The objectives of the State Forest Management programme are:

To produce wood in State forests in the most economic manner and to manage land in the possession of the Forest and Wildlife Service to best overall advantage - with full consideration for amenity, recreational and conservation values.

More specifically, the management objective is to maximize the expected net income from wood production in the State forest.

2. ADMINISTRATION

While forest development in Ireland has been largely dominated by State investment, there is now a trend towards greater involvement by the private sector.

Administration of forest policy in Ireland lies principally with the State. Its functions under the Forestry Act 1946 in regard to land acquisition, planting management and forest products disposal are carried out by the Forest Service of the Department of Energy. The Forest Service has a central administration (in Dublin) and seven regional management divisions.

Promotion of private sector forest expansion is undertaken by the State, which administers national and EEC grant schemes for this purpose.

Other public bodies which contribute to the implementation of forestry policy are the universities and national research organizations such as The Agricultural Institute and EOLAS (the Irish science and technology agency).

The principal constraints on the implementation and expansion of national forestry policy are:

(a) the difficulty of obtaining increased public funding for forest development and management;

(b) suspicion in some rural areas as to the impact of forest development on other traditional agricultural land uses.

Ireland is primarily an agricultural country, and along with other agricultural economies in the EEC, forestry is seen as an ideal alternative land use which additionally can play an important role in diverting land from the production of agricultural commodities which are in over-supply.

The Industrial Development Authority - the national agency charged with promoting industrial development - realizing the potential which forestry offered for downstream timber industry development, embarked with the State forest authority in 1980 on a programme of development and improvement of the sawmilling and pulpwood industries.

The percentage of the total public budget allocated to forestry activities is 0.8%.

There are no restrictions on investment in forestry.

3.   MONETARY AND FISCAL POLICIES

Private Forests

General

Private planting averaged only 200 ha. per annum up to the early 1980s. In 1986, private planting exceeded 2,500 ha. while over 3,200 ha. were planted by the private sector in 1987, making a substantial contribution to the national planting programme.

Overall monetary and fiscal policy is directed to ensure that private forestry is treated no less favourably than agriculture and that there are appropriate incentives both by way of taxation reliefs and establishment grants to encourage greater involvement and investment by the private sector. Details of these incentives are given below.

Monetary Incentives

The State Private Planting Grant Scheme, in operation since 1931, provides grants for the planting and replanting of land in all parts of the country. The grants available are as follows: £500 per ha. for conifers; £800 per ha. for broadleaves.

The Western Package Planting Grant Scheme was launched in October 1981 and provides grants for the afforestation of land in the disadvantaged areas. The level of grant payable is related to the cost of each forestry development project. In the case of farmers, the maximum grant payable is 85% of approved costs, and for non-farmers 70% of approved costs subject to a maximum of £800 per ha.

The Western Package Forestry Road Grant Scheme was launched in 1984 for the construction and reconstruction of forest roads serving privately-owned forestry plantations in western counties. The maximum grant is 80% of costs subject to a limit of £12 per metre.

<u>Farm Forestry Scheme</u>. A new scheme of forestry grants for full-time farmers in all parts of the country was introduced with effect from March 1987. The following grants apply:

    Up to £550 per ha. for planting conifers;
    Up to £850 per ha. for planting broadleaves;
    Up to £8 per metre for forest roads;
    Up to £35 per ha. for the provision of firebreaks
    and waterpoints in forests.

<u>Compensatory Allowances (Headage Payments) for Forestry</u>. This scheme, which was introduced with effect from October 1986, allows farmers who are in receipt of headage payments in respect of livestock to continue to receive these if they afforest their land. The allowance is £74.13 per ha. per annum for 15 years after afforestation.

<u>The Technical Advisory Service</u> provides technical advice free of charge under the planting and road grant schemes.

<u>Fiscal Incentives</u>

The profits accruing to an individual or a company from the occupation of woodlands managed on a commercial basis and with a view to profit-making are exempt from both income tax and corporation tax.

Capital gains tax is chargeable only on the lands; the trees growing on the land are not chargeable. Gains arising on the disposal of felled timber are not liable to capital gains tax.

For value added tax (VAT), forestry is regarded as an agricultural activity and benefits from the relevant tax concessions.

Private forestry is liable to <u>gift and inheritance tax</u> when it is taken as a benefit under a gift or inheritance. However, where the beneficiary is an "Irish" farmer as defined, the taxable value of woodland is the open market value less 50% or £200,000, whichever is the lesser. In the case of other beneficiaries, the 50% relief applies to the market value of growing Irish timber, but not to the lands on which it is growing.

A maximum of 10% <u>Corporation Tax</u> is payable on profits earned on the sale of manufactured goods. This will continue until the year 2000.

Companies which qualified for <u>Export Sales Relief</u> (i.e. tax exemption on profits earned from exports) before the end of 1980 may continue with this concession until 1990. They will then be eligible for the 10% Corporation Tax incentive.

Seventy-five percent depreciation allowance against taxable income is available to the manufacturing industry for new buildings, plant and machinery. (This allowance will reduce to 50% with effect from 6 April 1989).

Personal income tax relief, for funds of up to £25,000 per annum invested in manufacturing firms, is available under certain conditions.

Dividends paid to overseas shareholders, corporate and individual, are fully exempt from Irish income tax. There are no withholding taxes on dividends.

Ireland does not offer financial incentives to owners' associations or cooperative groups but gives free technical advice on matters relating to the better management and expansion of private forestry. The Irish Timber Growers' Association represents private growers and maintains regular contact with the State forest service. A cooperative grouping aimed at encouraging farmers to pool their land into blocks for afforestation is receiving EEC aid. This grouping was encouraged and assisted with its application by the State forest service.

4. FOREST MANAGEMENT AND PROTECTION

The national forest policy on land use is to promote and increase the production of wood on the land categories where forest crops can be formed, and that are marginal or sub-marginal for intensive livestock or farm crop production.

The main principles for management of existing plantations are:

(a) orderly production of wood as forecast in order to supply sawmills and pulpwood industries;

(b) protection of plantations against fire from planting to first thinning stage (crown fires are a rarity).

The relatively low level of industrial development in Ireland does not constitute an air pollution threat to forests.

The use of timber extraction machines which can cause damage to the forest is not allowed.

Appropriate insecticides and fungicides are used where necessary to combat the threat of insect and fungal infestations.

National legislation provides for the establishment of three categories of protected areas:

- national nature reserves
- refuges for fauna
- national parks.

Nature reserves and refuges are the responsibility of the State forest service. National parks are the responsibility of the Office of Public Works.

In addition, legislation also provides for negotiation of agreements with landowners ensuring that the management of the land shall be conducted in a specified manner which will not impair wildlife or its conservation.

The objectives are to:

- create a network of nature reserves which is representative of all national habitat types;

- protect native species of wild fauna;

- acquire and preserve large wilderness areas which are relatively untouched by man.

In the case of national parks, the criteria for establishment are those laid down by the International Union for the Conservation of Nature. Nature reserves and refuges for fauna are selected on the basis of either their unique scientific value or their representativeness of habitats of their type.

Use of State forest areas for recreation is encouraged, provided that the primary objective of commercial timber production is not unduly compromised. The "open forest" policy dating from 1970 began as part of European Conservation Year and has resulted in the creation of twelve forest parks and four hundred minor amenity facilities for public use (picnic sites, nature trails, forest walks, scenic view points, etc.).

Some forest parks incorporate caravan and camping facilities. Boy Scouts, Girl Guides and other youth organizations are provided with camping sites and other facilities. In addition to the foregoing, the State forest authority has established a unique development of 20 timber holiday chalets in a forest/lakeside environment which will complement existing forest recreational facilities.

The Minister for Energy is responsible for management of State forest leisure amenities.

The emphasis in Ireland on afforestation has necessitated the initial enclosure of the land and exclusion of domestic grazing animals. This (coupled with fertilization and ground preparation), while effecting a change in ground vegetation, has resulted in an increase of invertebrates, small mammals, birds of prey and in some cases deer. The underlying principle in wildlife management in forest areas is to sustain this diversity of species, thereby adding to the national spectrum of wildlife conservation.

The statutory base for this activity is the Wildlife Act, 1976. The Act is now administered by the Office of Public Works on behalf of the Minister for Finance.

Participation of Rural Organizations

The State forest authority - the Forest Service - cooperates with rural organizations such as the Irish Cooperative Organization Society (ICOS) and the national agricultural research institute (ACOT) in promoting the development of forestry.

Use of Abandoned Agricultural Lands for Forestry

Abandoned agricultural land as understood in the EEC context does not exist in Ireland.

5. FOREST UTILIZATION

Logs are cut at the forest into lengths appropriate to the requirements of the end uses for which they are to be converted. The main objective is to maximize the degree of economic conversion from the forest produce. Logging is generally carried out by contract labour on behalf of the purchaser of the logs.

The main institutions involved in logging and transport are:

- The Forest Service;

- Contractors to the Forest Service (approximately 10 mechanized main contractors and numerous smaller contractors);

- Sawmills and pulpwood plants;

- Various contractors;

- The Industrial Development Authority, which assists in harvesting development by grants aiding the purchase of harvesting machinery;

- Local Authorities who maintain county roads which adjoin forest properties.

Policies on the Development of the National Wood Industry

In view of the forecast increase in the volume of timber becoming available in the 1980s from Ireland's developing forests, the Industrial Development Authority carried out a sectoral study of the Irish timber industry with the objective of:

(i) drawing up a medium-term development plan for the national softwood timber industry which would ensure that the increasing timber resources would be utilized to the best national advantage;

(ii) devising an implementation programme for the development plan.

The Irish Timber Industry is composed of three sectors, which are interdependent. These are the forests, the sawmills and the pulpwood industry.

The Sawmill Industry

The Industrial Development Authority has embarked on a restructuring and development programme for the sawmilling sector which embraces such areas as new mill development, mill organization and layout, machinery improvement and replacement, and kiln drying. The objective of the plan was to improve the quality of production by sawmills to a standard acceptable to the needs of the market place. This policy resulted in the establishment of two new automated sawmills and in technological improvements being implemented in 27 other mills which were regarded as having the capacity to upgrade and add value to their production. This has resulted in improved harvesting, conversion (grading, sawing, drying) and presentation of Irish timber to the market.

The Pulpwood Sector

Ireland had four pulpwood plants in the 1970s - two producing particleboard, one fibreboard (wallboard) and one woodpulp mill for export. The industry was severely affected by the rise in energy costs caused by the oil crisis of 1974 which, together with competition from abroad, resulted in the closure of three of the plants, the fourth, which was put into receivership, requiring Government support to remain in business.

Pending the establishment of alternative pulpwood-using facilities, some temporary exports of pulpwood were arranged.

Agreement was reached with an American firm to establish a medium-density fibreboard plant. At a later stage, the remaining particleboard plant was purchased by a Spanish company and has continued production on an increasing scale. It is now likely that within five years a further pulpwood-using facility will be required to utilize supplies surplus to existing needs.

Other Matters

Good relations exist between the Forest Authority and the wood industry in matters of industrial development and timber promotion, but difficulties understandably do arise at times in matters of supply and price.

The two pulpwood plants have guarantees of supply and this is a source of complaint from the sawmill sector which has to compete on the open market for its supplies. These guarantees were essential elements at the time to attract the appropriate investment in the pulpwood sector. The acquisition, since the setting up of the two pulpwood plants, by some sawmills of modern sawing technology capable of sawing down around 10 cm. diameter (as compared to previously accepted sawable limits of 14 cm) has exacerbated the situation.

Grants are available to encourage the industry to improve the quality of its technical production. Assistance is also available to encourage the industry to engage in and develop export markets for its surplus production.

The legal basis for the development of the forest and wood industries is the Forestry Act of 1946.

Promotion of new industries is undertaken by the Industrial Development Authority. Because of the limitation on supplies - less than a half of the national forest estate is at productive stage - development of the wood industries is carefully monitored.

The wood industry, like other industries, is subject to environmental controls in matters of fellings, transport and pollution.

6.   TIMBER TRADE AND MARKETING

The bulk of timber from State forests in Ireland has traditionally been sold by a sealed tender system. Some departures from this method of sale have taken place in recent years. As previously indicated, certain guarantees of supply have been given to the two pulpwood plants.

The Forest Service, with the agreement of the industry, introduced a Quota Scheme for the sawmilling industry whereby those mills with the requisite technical and marketing capacity qualified for direct purchase at market price outside of the Tender System of up to 45% of their annual purchases of large sawlogs. This scheme has proved very successful. Some sales by public auction have also been used in recent years. The pulpwood and sawmill sectors have arrangements for exchanges of small and large diameter logs.

In addition to the foregoing, the Institute for Industrial Research and Standards introduced an Irish standard recommendation for structural timber for domestic construction.

The principal results of these policies are that:

(i)   a new industrial outlet for pulpwood and residues has been established which is supplying domestic and export needs;

(ii)   penetration of the domestic market in constructional timber has increased from 15% in 1980 to around 50% in 1988.

7.   EMPLOYMENT

While there is no specific industrial legislation relating to employment in forestry and forest industries, industrial employees in this area are embraced in general legislation relating to conditions of employment, industrial relations, etc.

Industrial disputes in the forest and timber industries are rare; this satisfactory state of affairs may be attributable to use by management and employees of Conciliation and Arbitration machinery and local labour councils.

While it is an objective to maximize the economic level of employment in forestry, it is not feasible to increase employment at present due to funding constraints.

8.   FORESTRY EDUCATION AND TRAINING

The orientation of professional education in forestry is to produce graduates qualified in subjects relating to all aspects of forest establishment, management and timber harvesting.

Technical and vocational education and training is undertaken by the national forest authority relative to resources and needs.

There is no formal education of the general public in forestry matters, and forestry has not yet been introduced into the general education system.

The objective of continuing education is to keep technical and professional staff abreast of developments in forestry. Extension courses are held in two centres.

The orientation of these courses is towards staff employed in the State forest sector. However, private forestry personnel are tending to be included in these courses as participants in specialized aspects of forest operations.

The private sector per se has no formal education or training role.

9.   FORESTRY RESEARCH, EXTENSION AND INFORMATION

State forest research covers five areas:

- Inventory

- Crop structure and wood technology

- Soils and site productivity

- Genetics

- Forest protection.

State forestry research staff resources comprise 17 Research Officers (forestry graduates), 20 Research Foresters and 2 Laboratory Technicians. Physical resources include a research nursery and laboratory.

EOLAS carries out research under contract on the properties, characteristics and usages of Irish timber.

State forest research disseminates results by:

(a) Research communications and research notes (for internal distribution);

(b) International scientific journals;

(c) Research courses, field days and lectures.

Results involving major changes in operational policy are applied by means of directives to forest management.

EOLAS, as part of a timber promotion activity, disseminates results by:

(a) information sheets which are widely distributed to the industry, architects and engineers;

(b) seminars and lectures.

The extension of forest research results outside the State service is carried out at various levels:

(a) Advisory service to farmers and landowners who already own forests or who wish to plant trees. This advisory service is available free throughout the country and is normally carried out as part of the grant aid and regulatory function of the forest managers.

(b) Specialist private woodland officers who liaise with agricultural extension officers and promote private forestry generally;

(c) EOLAS provides an advisory service to the timber industry;

(d) International scientific journals;

(e) Courses, field days and lectures open to non-government organizations;

(f) Personal contact with individuals such as university personnel, private forest owners, etc.

As the forest estate has now begun to mature, the general public is very much aware of the level of forest expansion in Ireland. This developing physical presence of forests, coupled with the public's active use of forest amenities, contributes to a growing interest in forestry generally.

10. ENVIRONMENTAL ISSUES

Traditionally, public awareness of environmental issues in Ireland has been poor. However, there has been a noticeable increase in public interest in the past few years. It is the policy of the Wildlife Service to promote awareness of our wildlife resources and the need for their conservation.

Publicity and educational material on wildlife is regularly disseminated by the Wildlife Service to educational institutions and the general public.

The Department's interests are also represented by the Environmental Awareness Bureau which was established by the Minister for the Environment to increase public environmental consciousness.

11. INTERNATIONAL COOPERATION

The State forest authority's involvement is principally with international fora and countries with an interest in similar silviculture and wildlife in Europe, North America and New Zealand. Ireland participates in the activities of FAO, FAO/ECE Timber Committee, IUFRO, IUCN, etc., and the various forestry activities of the EEC.

The principal field for international cooperation is research. This has involved cooperative research ventures with forestry personnel from other countries, particularly under the European Economic Commission's funded research programmes. The principal Irish institutions involved at international level are:

The Forest and Wildlife Service

EOLAS

The Universities.

ISRAEL

1. INTRODUCTION

The area under forest cover is 112,000 ha. (5.5% of land area) -
72,000 ha. man-made and 40,000 ha. natural forest stands (end of 1986). 98%
of the forests are in public and 2% in private ownership.

Since the establishment of the State of Israel, the guiding principle
of forestry policy has been to restore ancient forests and to create new
forests, resulting in intensive afforestation activities mainly during the
first two decades of the existence of the State of Israel.

The trends in forest policy since 1970 have reflected the growing
concern with environmental problems and the ever-increasing demand for
social services provided by the forest. The Forest Department has therefore
devoted increased attention to conservation, recreation and landscape, but
the afforestation activities have continued.

Special attention has been paid to forest survey, and management
directives have been prepared for all man-made forests. With the maturing
of many young stands, silvicultural treatments and management questions
have also gained in importance.

During the 'seventies', two proposals for forestry policy were
published: in 1971, by the Society of Forestry Engineers, and in 1973 by
the Land Development Authority.

A special committee, appointed in 1977 by the Land Development
Authority and the Agricultural Research Organization, also prepared a
forestry policy statement. This represents the permanent framework for all
forestry activities and a guarantee for the professional and efficient
realization of the goals. The forestry policy statement is to be revised
every 10 years, the latest revision being due in 1987.

After defining the area considered as forest, the policy statement
deals with the following issues: the social role of the forest; provision
of social services by the forest; the forest and improvement of the
landscape; the forest as a basis for an economic infrastructure; forest
management; timber production; recreation; grazing; increasing the forest
area; forest protection; forest research; and education and extension.

2. ADMINISTRATION

The Forest Department, which is headed by a Director, is part of the
autonomous Land Development Authority. It is the sole forest administration
and as such is responsible for the management of all State and public
forests.

The structure of the Forest Department is decentralized. Four
territorial divisions (Regions) are responsible for all forestry activities
and forest administration at regional level. They are fully staffed and
subdivided into 3-4 districts, which are again subdivided into several
ranges.

Unfortunately, there is no faculty of forestry in Israel, so the persons employed are from other disciplines such as agriculture, planning, natural sciences or geography.

The forestry policy is influenced by the national general development policy. The institutions influencing the formulation are primarily the Land Development Authority, the Ministry of Agriculture with its affiliated bodies (Land Administration, Water Authority, Agricultural Research Organization, Nature Protection Authority, Soil Conservation Department), the Settlement Department of the Jewish Agency, and the Ministry of the Interior (Planning). The implementation of the forestry policy is the responsibility of the Land Development Authority through the Forest Department.

Forest legislation is still based on the ordinance for the Protection of Forests and Management of Forest Reserves from 1926, with some later amendments (1945 and 1956). Additional amendments are being prepared relating to forest protection, forest fires, pollution and illegal fellings and should be dealt with during the present term (to 1988) of the Knesset (parliament) by the legal committee.

Since the establishment of the State of Israel in 1948, forestry policy has been dictated by national development interests, and forestry projects have constituted an important factor in the dispersion of the population, particularly in development areas.

Master Plan

Since 1971, several surveys have been carried out, aiming at the integration of forestry into regional and national planning. As a result of these surveys, a "Master Plan" for the forest was prepared and implemented in 1982. According to the plan, 50,000 ha. of new forests are to be established by the year 2000.

The National Planning and Construction Council is the public body responsible for physical planning and for the implementation of the Planning and Construction Law (1965). In the Council, which is appointed by the Minister for the Interior, are represented: the Government, experts (engineers, architects, nature conservators, sociologists, etc.), mayors of the main cities, representatives of the Jewish Agency and others.

The Council is preparing a country-wide master plan for the classification of agricultural land.

The budget for forestry reflects the fluctuations in the general economic situation of the country. Although the financing of forestry activities is met mainly by grants and donations from abroad and from Israel as well as by income from property in Israel, timber sales, etc., and some allocation from the Government - the activity is coordinated with general trends of development and overall planning. The yearly budget of the Forest Department for 1986/87 was the local currency equivalent of US$ 14,500,000.

3.   MONETARY AND FISCAL POLICIES

Since no special tax categorization exists for the forestry sector,
the level of taxation depends on the category into which forests are
placed. If considered an agricultural crop, forests would not be taxed by
the State. Otherwise, a State tax of as much as 2 1/2 % of the land value
could be levied. For timber sales, a tax is levied for each cubic metre of
wood removed from the forest. Grazing licences in forest areas are issued
in return for a fee.

As mentioned before, only about 2% of the forests are privately owned;
they are widely scattered all over the country and are highly productive,
being located mostly on good agricultural soil. Small woodlots and
windbreaks in citrus groves contribute about 40% of the yearly removals.

The Ministry of Agriculture is encouraging farmers to plant trees by
offering grants and loans. The Forest Department provides nursery stock and
technical advice free of charge.

There is no organized form of cooperation among the private forest
owners.

4.   FOREST MANAGEMENT AND PROTECTION

In principle, the "multiple use" approach is accepted as a guideline.
To improve the basis for management, a new general survey of the forest
area has been prepared. This includes mapping on a new 1:5,000 scale, using
aerial photography as well as field measurements. At the same time a
re-division of the forests into management units has been carried out.

The forest inventory is centralized and is conducted by the
Headquarter Division for Survey and Forest Management. The survey is based
on periodic measurements of permanent sample plots on the basis of a
seven-year cycle. All man-made forests are included in the survey.

Tending

The rotations for conifers are planned for 60-70 years, with 4-5
thinnings. Eucalypt coppices are managed on a 7-12 year rotation, according
to site and production aims, up to 10 rotations being possible. Also
rotations of 20 years are in use. The mean annual increment is 2-8 m3/ha.
for conifers and 5-35 m3/ha. for eucalypts.

Existing forests are to be managed with the aim of providing benefits
on a multi-purpose basis. The protection role of the forest is still of
great importance, especially in the southern part of the country. Landscape
and recreation are receiving more attention than in the past. In certain
areas, grazing space has to be provided in some parts of the forest. The
natural Mediterranean oak forest is especially suitable for silvo-pastoral
use.

The problem of forest fires represents an important part of the Forest Department's activity, 10-15% of the yearly budget being allocated for this purpose. The semi-arid climatic conditions in Israel and the composition of the forest area - Mediterranean oak-shrub and coniferous plantations - create a situation favouring the outbreak and spread of forest fires. All forest fires in Israel are caused by human factors as none result from natural phenomena. The fire suppression activity may be defined as good. Eighty percent of the forest fires are detected by Forest Department personnel and most of them (75%) are extinguished with damage contained under one acre.

Protection of the forests from insects and diseases is of growing concern. Bark beetles and processionary caterpillars are causes of damage, but the main concern is the continuing decline of the Aleppo-pine stands, due to the pine bast scale affecting about 15% of all stands. Some cypress stands are also attacked by Seiridium cardinale and Diploida.

For the present, there is no significant damage to forests by air pollution.

In 1963, the "Law of National Parks and Nature Reserves" was promulgated. Since that time, 97 National Parks and 150 Nature Reserves have been gazetted and managed by the National Parks Authority and the Nature Reserves Authority.

The management of wildlife resources comes under the Nature Reserves Authority. The wildlife situation could be characterized as unstable. Rural development and the increase in agricultural area has restricted wildlife habitats, but the severe reduction and extermination of beasts of prey has led to an increase in some animal populations.

The aim is to protect and re-introduce some species. Selective hunting is controlled. Some 4,000 hunters are registered in Israel.

Grazing

The ever-growing demand for more grazing land could not be neglected by the forestry sector. In cooperation with the Ministry of Agriculture, a special organization was set up, including regional authorities and cattle-breeders, as well as the Forest Department. Projects are under way to combine grazing with proper forest use. In some instances, controlled grazing is allowed in order to destroy weeds and reduce fire hazards. This operation requires strict regulation and control on behalf of the Forest Department.

Soil Conservation

Soil conservation and watershed management are included in the activities of the Forest Department. In cooperation with the Land Reclamation Department of the Land Development Authority and the Department of Soil Conservation of the Ministry of Agriculture, various plantations have been set up all over the country aimed at soil conservation and water-flow regulation, including collection and storage of run-off water.

The various forms of swamp drainage and reclamation, taken together, have increased Israel's agricultural potential by almost 30%.

Watersheds

The planning of watersheds must seek to reconcile the needs of various uses (agriculture, residential areas, industry, forestry, recreation, tourism, etc.) with the distribution of the main roads, water courses, drainage and water supply.

The management includes nine large catchments totalling about 50,000 km2 and an additional number of smaller catchment areas.

One of the main activities of the Land Reclamation Department is devoted to the problems of drainage in its various forms. After several years of drought, the water supply system in Israel is in a state of acute crisis, even the ground water resources being endangered.

Combined soil conservation works are carried out with the Forest Department by planting of trees and shrubs along the water courses in the wadis in the Negev.

In the area with an annual rainfall of 50-150 mm, the "liman" plantation has been introduced.

After examination of the topography from aerial photographs and field surveys, suitable locations are selected to collect the run-off from small catchments. The ratio of liman to watershed is usually 1:50 and more.

Preparation of the liman consists of levelling to ensure an equal distribution of the floodwater and the erection of a low earth dam to arrest the water flow. Once the soil has been made wet by the first rains or flood of the season, trees such as eucalypts, tamarisks, acacias, etc., are planted at a spacing of 4x5 m.

Soil cultivation is by ploughing prior to the rainy season to facilitate infiltration, and harrowing and disking in the spring to reduce soil moisture loss by evaporation; after heavy floods, some additional levelling and repairs to the earth dam may be necessary.

Some 300 "limans" covering about 50 ha. have been established, creating "green spots" in a treeless desert.

They can serve for recreation as well as for fuel production in developing countries.

5-6. FOREST UTILIZATION - TIMBER TRADE

The wood removed from the forest in Israel originates from three main sources:

1. Planned clear felling of eucalypts;

2. Thinning operations in coniferous stands as well as tending operations in natural oak stands;

3. Unforeseen removals due to fire, insects or development activities.

Logging and transport is carried out mainly by contractors, and only to a lesser extent by Forest Department workers.

The average annual production has reached 110,000 m3, broken down as follows:

Wood for chipping	50%
Sawlogs	15%
Agricultural posts	10%
Fuelwood	25%

Israel's annual consumption of timber is about 650,000 m3, about 85% of which is imported. The total value of these imports is approximately US$ 120,000,000. Utilization of locally produced timber currently saves about US$ 7,000,000 yearly.

Production of local timber provides permanent employment opportunities for about 300 workers in logging and transportation operations, as well as for some 400 more in forest-based industries. In Israel there is a highly developed wood-using industrial sector. Five mills produce both plywood (using imported logs) and chipboard, the latter composed of a mixture of the residue from plywood production and locally grown raw materials. A sixth mill produces chipboard utilizing local wood exclusively.

Many small sawmills operate using locally grown timber for the production of agricultural posts, poles and freight pallets. A paper mill is also in operation, using imported pulp exclusively.

There are practically no limitations on timber imports, except that they may be made subject to barter agreements based on reciprocity. The customs duty on imports of sawn coniferous and beech wood was reduced on 1.1.1987 from 32% to 18%. To overcome the shortage of raw material for the particle board industry, the customs duty on waste and low-grade wood has been abolished.

7. EMPLOYMENT

Legislation relevant to employment, social conditions, salaries, etc., in the forestry sector is the same as for agriculture. In the past, employment in forestry played an important role in the absorption and training of new immigrants. Most of them were employed in forestry until absorbed into other branches of the economy.

As many stages of forestry operations, especially felling and transport, are carried out by contractors on a piecework basis, there is an increased interest in this kind of employment and the number of such workers has increased.

The general regulations for industrial workers apply also to the
timber industry. Health and safety regulations are very strict and are
controlled by the Ministry of Labour. In general, the employer is
responsible for social and health security and is obliged to insure workers
against all risks.

8.   EDUCATION AND TRAINING

There is no faculty of forestry in Israel, but some forestry subjects
are taught in other faculties. Periodic courses are organized and conducted
by the Forest Department for all levels of staff members. Lectures are
given by university professors, research specialists and senior officers of
the Forest Department. Secondary agricultural schools also have some
courses on forestry in their teaching programme.

9.   FORESTRY RESEARCH

Organized forestry research was established in 1949. Since 1961, the
research has been carried out by the Forestry Division of the Agricultural
Research Organization of the Ministry of Agriculture.

At present the whole of the forestry research is in the process of
reorganization. Most facilities are to be moved to the Centre of
Agricultural Research Organization at Beit-Dagan. A Department of Natural
Resources has been established and the Division of Forestry will be
included in this new department.

Every research project is scrutinized by a Referees Committee of
university professors and research specialists.

10.   INTERNATIONAL COOPERATION

The Forest Department has established close contacts with other forest
services in many countries, as well as with FAO and IUFRO. Israel is a
member of the Committee on Forestry (COFO), the European Forestry
Commission (EFC), the Committee on Mediterranean Forestry Questions (Silva
Mediterranea) and also participates occasionally in meetings of other
forestry organizations such as the World Forestry Congresses. Several
international forestry meetings have taken place in Israel.

ITALY

1. INTRODUCTION

The forests of Italy occupy 6.4 M. ha. which is equivalent to 21% of the total land surface of 30.1 M. ha. The distribution of forest types by categories of ownership is as follows:

1000 ha.

Type of forests	Category of Ownership				
	State and Regions	Communes	Other Public	Private	Total
High Forest	198	1,019	193	1,379	2,789
Coppice	148	600	167	1,932	2,847
Coppice with Standards	30	157	32	548	767
Total	376	1,776	392	3,859	6,403

About 60% of the forests are situated in the mountains, 35% in the hills and only 5% in the plains.

The average size of State and regional forests is about 850 ha., of Communal forests 150 ha., and of private forests only 3 ha. About 80% of all forests are broadleaved and 20% are coniferous. Most of the productive high forest is in the north, but there are also considerable areas in the south. Coppice predominates in the centre of the country.

The average annual trade balance during the period 1980-85 was as follows:

$M.m^3$

1.	Internal production	8.9
2.	Imports	26.1
3.	Exports	2.6
4.	Apparent consumption (1+2-3)	32.4
5.	Deficit (4-1)	23.5

Forestry policy has mainly been concerned with the mountainous regions, where soil and water conservation and the improvement of the living standards of the local rural populations have been the prime objectives. The measures adopted to achieve these objectives include, among others: maintenance of the existing forest, afforestation, improvement of pastures and hydrological projects.

The legal basis for this policy is provided by the Royal Decree of 30 December 1923, No. 3267 on "Zones of Hydrogeological Importance" and on subsequent legislation concerning Mountain Communities. Some 16 M. ha., including the 6.4 M. ha. of forests are covered by this legislation.

Recent trends in forestry policy have been to progress from the protection of the "forestry system" to a more dynamic policy to:

- increase wood production for industry and energy;
- to promote actively the environmental role of forestry.

2.   ADMINISTRATION

The forestry sector contributes only 0.12% to the gross domestic product. In the private sector, forestry is oriented mainly towards production while in the publicly owned forests ecological considerations take precedence.

The efficient management of private forests is hindered by the fragmentation of ownership (size of average holding is only 3 ha.), the long time scale of forestry investments, lack of forestry knowledge, and inadequate market structures.

These factors have led to a neglect of many private woodlands, but Project No. 24 of the Cassa per il Mezzogiorno (Fund for Southern Italy) which is designed to promote private forestry has demonstrated that the position can be much improved.

Publicly owned forests are required, under Forest Law No. 3267 of 1923, to be managed according to a management plan, but only about half of these forests have such a plan. The decentralization of forest administration to the Regions in the late 1970s has caused some at least temporary difficulties in forest management.

Up to 1971, the central State Forest Service in the Ministry of Agriculture and Forestry had provided the necessary technical and supervisory services, both centrally and throughout the country.

During the 1970s, the responsibility for forestry was devolved by a series of administrative decrees to a variety of organs such as the Regions, Mountain Commmunities, Communes, and associations of individuals. All these organs have a public responsibility in law to submit projects of public interest which, after approval by the administration, may be financed wholly or in part by the State or Region.

Before 1970, approximately 400,000 ha. of State forests, including denuded areas, were managed by the Azienda di Stato per le Foreste Demaniali (ASFD) (State Forest Enterprise). With the transfer of the forestry responsibilities to the Region, the ASFD have remained with approximately 20% (80,000 ha.) of these areas which includes protected areas, reserves and seed stands.

The Regions now have their own forest services and they also make use of the personnel of the "Corpo Forestale dello Stato" (State Forestry Corps) which is put at their disposal by the Central Administration under bilateral agreements.

In addition to the laws already mentioned, there are various others dealing with matters such as protection of the beauty of the landscape, the establishment of a National Forestry Plan, plant health and prevention of forest fires.

Public finance for forestry comes from various sources including the already-mentioned Cassa per il Mezzogiorno and the EC under Regulation 269/1979. A framework for these individual measures has been provided by the Piano Agricolo Nazionale (National Plan for Agriculture) of 1979.

These programmes have given a new impulse to forestry. The EEC programme, for example, has achieved the following:

- reforestation: 38,000 ha.
- improvement of degraded forests: 88,000 ha.
- fire protection: 165,000 ha.
- forest roads: 2,000 km.

The whole question of forestry programmes and finance is at present at a delicate stage. The first National Plan for Agriculture of 1979 and the programme EEC 269/1979 have both expired and the new measures to replace them have not been finally settled. Some indication, however, can be given of what is planned. The main point is that there will be a separate National Plan for Forestry (Piano Forestale Nazionale). There were two reasons for no longer including forestry in the National Plan for Agriculture. First, forestry differs markedly from agriculture, in its characteristics and functions; and secondly, forestry tends to be treated as a residual appendage when combined with agriculture.

The new National Plan for Forestry came into force on 9 February 1987. The broad intentions are:

-   to combine the interventions by the State and the Regions with those of the EC and other sources;

-   to ensure continuity with what has been done to date;

-   to do justice to both the protective and productive functions of forestry;

-   to integrate forestry plans into general land use planning especially in the mountainous regions;

-   to promote both public and private forestry;

-   to promote efficiency by:

    .   structural measures (land consolidation, management associations etc.)

    .   improved technology, (including training of personnel)

    .   combination of forestry with other activities (agrisilvipasture, tourism, rural crafts etc.).

-   to improve the sytem of monitoring projects, which is, at present, purely financial and without any reference to the achievement of technical objectives.

Among the problems to be resolved are:

- the existing lack of coordination between the various agencies
  concerned: national, regional, EC, etc.

- the adaptation of existing programmes to changed conditions.

Within the context of the Plan, the setting up of a permanent
monitoring body is being considered for the whole "Forest-Wood-Environment"
complex. This monitoring body would keep the system as a whole under
review. In particular, it would seek to ensure the balance between
production, trade and wood processing industries by suggesting measures as
the implementation of the National Plan for forestry progresses.

3.   MONETARY AND FISCAL POLICIES

About 90% of all private forests form part of agricultural holdings.
Forest owners face a number of difficulties which render forestry
unprofitable. These difficulties include:

- heavy taxation on private property and forest management;

- inadequate markets for wood;

- weak bargaining position vis-à-vis the intermediary who is
  virtually a monopoly buyer;

- absence of legislation that would specifically favour the
  formation of producers' associations;

- lack of trained forest labour;

- absence of technical extension services.

Forestry taxation is analogous to taxation on other land uses, except that
there are certain deductions and exemptions.

Taxation is generally based on the land registry. For each parcel of
land a distinction is made between:

- income from the land;

- income from the capital and labour input.

Individual owners pay both these income taxes at rates which progress
with the level of income. Juridical persons such as companies pay a fixed
rate of 25%. In addition, all owners pay a local tax of 15% which is
levied by the local authorities concerned.

Taxes on succession and gifts are based on market values, they are
progressive and they vary according to the degree of relationship between
donor and recipient.

Value added tax ranges from 2% on sales by producers, and 9% on sales by
non-producing merchants, to 18% on final forest products.

Capital gains tax is levied at rates ranging from 2% to 30%.

Registration tax is levied on transfers of property, but is considerably reduced for farmers and cooperative societies.

Levy in favour of the Ente Nazionale per la Cellulosa e Carta (ENCC) (National Organization for Pulp and Paper). This is a levy ranging between 0.6% and 3% of the invoiced price of several pulp and paper products. The proceeds are used by the ENCC for promotion, distribution of nursery plants, technical assistance and research on pulpwood plantations.

Tax concessions include

- a 50% reduction of income taxes for Communes, Provinces and State forests;

- temporary exemptions (15-40 years) from the local authority tax are planned after certain improvement measures have been undertaken;

- reduction of income taxes for properties above an elevation of 700 m.;

- exemption from succession tax of properties which have been established or improved as a result of legislation concerning mountainous regions;

- exemption from succession tax of properties transferred to public ownership or organizations such as cooperatives in mountain communes.

4.   MANAGEMENT AND PROTECTION

4.1 General principles

The main objective is a fundamental attack on soil degradation and atmospheric and water pollution. The damage inherited from the past is compounded by present events and by the inadequacy of the technical and legal measures which have been taken up to now.

Specific problems include among others: water erosion, industrial discharges, acid rain, intensive use of fertilizers and pesticides, conversion of fertile land to urban use, and abandonment of rural areas. It is for example estimated that about 1,000 tons of soil per km2 is carried down to the sea each year, and that about 30,000 ha. to 40,000 ha. of land become sterile each year as a result of erosion. To these dangers must be added others such as earthquakes and forest fires.

Clearly, forests must play a key role in halting this disastrous environmental degradation. While it is true that Italian forestry has always worked towards these ends, it has not always received the necessary political support.

What is now needed is a major long-term policy of reforestation and anti-erosion measures on mountain slopes, supported by the necessary legislation and organizational measures. The State, Regions, Mountain Communities, Provinces, Communes, etc. must all cooperate. Environmental impact assessments and the definition of a minimum index of forest cover are being considered in this context. The key role to be played by the "local autonomies" and the need for the constant monitoring of progress must be underlined.

Some not-too-rigid classification of forests according to their main
purpose seems indicated: production forests, forests for solving
environmental problems, protection forests, recreation forests, etc.

4.2 Financial resources should be allocated for:

- all improvements to the national forest heritage;

- meeting part of the cost of management of forest cooperatives and
  other relevant groupings;

- the preparation of working plans;

- surveys to identify areas suitable for afforestation;

- an inventory of poplar resources;

- planting trees outside the forest;

- fundamental improvements to water catchment areas;

- improvements of mountain pastures;

- improvement of forest fire prevention structures;

- support measures after calamities;

- phytosanitary measures;

- strengthening scientific research on all aspects of forestry.

Other types of incentives are needed to enable Regions and the various
local authorities to acquire abandoned land for the establishment of parks,
pastures and nature reserves.

Finally, funds are needed to enable forestry enterprises to
participate in EC programmes and some additional tax concessions appear
desirable. The main lines of necessary action have been established as a
basis for inclusion in the National Plan for Forestry.

4.3 Combating losses

Fires constitute the most serious threat to the forests in Italy.
There are an average of 11,800 fires per year damaging some 163,000 ha. of
which 62,000 ha. are forested. The number of fires and the damage done
varies considerably from year to year. Nearly all fires are caused by man,
either accidentally or on purpose. The fire danger has been increased by
the accumulation of combustible material on land abandoned by agriculture
and by the influx of tourists. Practices such as the burning of stubble
and setting fire to grasslands in order to improve the grazing also
persist.

Fire prevention measures include:

- publicity;

- a law that prohibits any construction or change of land use on
    areas that have been burnt;

- switch to less fire-sensitive species.

The responsibility for fire fighting rests with the State Forestry
Corps of the Ministry of Agriculture and Forestry, as well as with various
regional and provincial authorities and voluntary organizations. Aircraft
of the Air Force are available when required.

In 1982, the Ministry for the Coordination of Civil Protection set up
a Unified Operations Centre for fire fighting with personnel from the
Armed Forces and the State Forestry Corps.

In the fight against pests and disease some notable successes have
been achieved in recent years with biological control, e.g. of chestnut
cancer. The damage from air pollution is being monitored in the context of
the relevant EC programme.

4.4 Protected Areas

Up to 1968, Italy had only 5 national parks with a total area of
270,744 ha. By 1984 the position had developed as follows:

252	Nature Reserves	144,391 ha.
5	National Parks	270,744 ha.
40	Humid Zones	49,000 ha.
42	Regional Parks	501,940 ha.

Of the nature reserves 147 are under the Ministry of Agriculture and
Forestry and the other 105 come under the tutelage of the Regions. These
nature reserves may either serve nature protection in general or have a
more specific purpose (e.g. biogenetical). Numerous further proposals for
nature reserves are being considered. Most of the humid zones have been
established in the context of the Ramsar convention. Measures are taken to
reconcile the recreational use of the various protected areas (and
especially of the National and Regional Parks) with their conservation
function.

A point that needs emphasizing is that much valuable work in the field
of conservation in Italy is done by non-governmental organizations (Italia
Nostra, WWF, Federnatura etc.). Also the national Research Council and
various other scientific and academic institutions play an important and
constructive role.

4.5   Recreation

The original more or less "spontaneous zoning" of recreation areas in response to demand as it arose has been replaced by a policy of programmed development. The following three main categories of recreation areas may be distinguished:

(a)   Town Parks, more or less specially equipped;
(b)   Nature Parks near towns, more or less specially equipped;
(c)   Nature Parks and/or Reserves (communal, provincial, regional) or areas equipped for recreation or mixed use.

The institutions responsible for managing these facilities may either be public (communes, etc.) or private (foundations, clubs, etc.).

4.6   Management of fauna

Up to the early 1970s, fauna was considered a res nullius in legal terms. Since then things have changed.

Law No. 968/1977 established that all animals are an inalienable heritage of the State. The more important provisions include:

-   the introduction of a list of species that may be hunted (thus virtually overturning previous legislation);

-   prohibition of bird catching;

-   prohibition of hunting in Nature Reserves and National Parks;

-   elimination of the concept of the harmful animal;

-   elimination of non-selective trapping (poison traps, etc.);

-   introduction of penalties, beyond the administrative ones.

The whole question of fauna is being debated very intensively and there is even a proposal that there should be a referendum on whether hunting should be abolished completely throughout the country.

There is also a proposal for legislation before Parliament to adapt Italian rules more closely to international directives and conventions, some of which are at present only partially applied, although Italy is a signatory (Ramsar, Paris, Bern, Bonn, Washington).

4.7   Involvement of rural organizations

Given the high degree of decentralization of Italian forestry, a large number of organizations can participate actively in the development of forest policies. A stimulus is provided by gatherings such as Euroforesta in the context of the Fair of Verona, broadcasts, etc. There is, however, a continued need to try to integrate the forestry sector more closely with other sectors of the economy and national life (industry, environmental issues).

4.8 <u>Afforestation of abandoned agricultural land</u> is one of the few possible uses of such land and EC Regulation 797/1985 provides a basis for EC financial support for afforestation by farmers.

4.9 <u>The Development of mountain economy</u> requires an intersectoral approach in which forestry is an important component. Over 50% of the country is mountainous and most of the country's forests are in the mountains where they not only produce timber but are vital for soil and water conservation.

5. <u>UTILIZATION</u>

Harvesting has generally been undertaken by private enterprises which are independent of the growers, public and private. The economic situation of these enterprises has deteriorated, because labour costs have increased much more rapidly than the price of wood; the number of these enterprises has therefore been in decline. In some areas, especially in the coppice forests in the Appennines, they have been partially replaced by cooperatives. The measures needed to render harvesting operations more economic include:

- development and introduction of modern harvesting technology;
- construction and improvement of access roads;
- training of personnel in modern harvesting technology.

Italian <u>forest industries</u> must be adapted to changing conditions on the world market.

The <u>construction industry</u> must seek to improve efficiency by rationalization, standardization of products, improved knowledge of external markets, etc. The Administration can help by: promoting the use of wood in public buildings; incentives to modernization and promotion of exports.

The <u>furniture industry</u> requires: some rationalization (but leaving scope for the small craft enterprises), downstream integration into installation, greater diversification of external markets and the support of research.

The basic problem of the paper industry is its dependence on imports for its raw material and pulp. Carefully phased measures are needed along the following lines:

- financial support (national and EEC);

- rules to oblige the Administration and other public bodies to use paper of the minimum quality standards needed for the intended use (this is to eliminate the norms which limit the content of recycled fibre and high-yield pulp);

- increased collection of waste paper for recycling;

- the extension of the facilities of the Fund for Technical Innovation to the paper industry;

- the greater involvement of the EC and National Administration to enforce GATT and EC rules against unfair trade practices (dumping, etc.);

- research.

The Interest in <u>wood for energy</u> varies cyclically with the price and supply problems associated with fossil fuels. The studies that have been made suggest that the development of wood energy could play a modest but useful role in the mountains for local use, where such a development would also create some jobs.

6. TRADE

Commercial policy in Italy is based on freedom of trade and economic initiative. This applies both internally as well as externally and is also in harmony with the general policies of the EC. A few restrictions on this freedom may result from the application of phytosanitary measures and measures against dumping.

There are some technical norms for wood and wood products which have been prepared by the Ente Italiano per l'Unificazione (UNI) (Italian Organization for Standardization). Classification by quality follows commercial practice; there are no general rules. Model forms of contract have, however, been drawn up for coniferous sawn wood imported from Sweden, Finland, Austria and Bavaria. The object is to reduce the possibility of misunderstandings between the trading partners. A similar procedure is being considered for the import of broadleaved timber from France and Yugoslavia.

7. EMPLOYMENT

According to unofficial statistics about 900,000 persons are employed in the forest industries. There are some 120,000 enterprises of which only about 10,000 employ more than 10 people.

There are 2,000 registered harvesting enterprises, but only about half of these are actually operating. Most of these are small family firms using only a modest degree of mechanization. There are few larger enterprises of an industrial character.

There are no reliable statistics on the total number of forest workers because much of the work is part-time by people whose main occupation is farming. According to unofficial statistics, public agencies (State, Regions, Mountain Communities) employ about 150,000 persons.

There are various rules and regulations concerning matters such as salaries, social security, safety, special programmes to combat unemployment, etc.

8. EDUCATION, TRAINING AND INFORMATION

The responsibility for forestry training was transferred to the Regional authorities in 1977. After an initial hiatus caused by the reorganization, the Regions have undertaken some promising initiatives, often promoted by the Mountain Communities or the Regional Administrations in collaboration with the education authorities.

The most active Regions have been the more heavily wooded ones in northern and central Italy but there is now a general call by the whole forestry sector for a greater degree of nationwide coordination between the central administration and local authorities. Everybody is now aware that forest workers need better training and that the training needs to be interdisciplinary. Instruction is at three levels:

- at primary level, basic information is given about the forest resource and the traditional occupations connected with forests and wood.

- at secondary level, the object is to enable students to become better qualified technicians at intermediate level than the traditional forester or forest guard.

- at tertiary level, the object is to improve the technical and professional training of future managers in the public and the private sectors of forestry and forest industry.

9.   RESEARCH

Research of national significance is promoted by the State, while research of more local interest is conducted at regional level.

Up to now research has been conducted at a large number of centres, by different institutions and with diverse objectives. Individual research projects are often excellent, but forestry research as a whole suffers from the dispersion of initiative, the heterogeneity of intentions, the fragmentation of effort (also in financial terms) and lack of technology transfer.

Forestry and forest products research must, above all, become more practice-oriented; it must also look ahead; identify emerging needs; seek to reduce costs; simplify cultural operations and improve our knowledge of forest genetics. In addition, research workers must keep abreast of developments abroad which might benefit Italy.

10.   INTERNATIONAL COOPERATION

International cooperation is the responsibility of the Ministry of Foreign Affairs and is conducted through the normal bilateral and multinational channels. Development aid is given mainly to Ethiopia, Somalia, Zimbabwe, Mali and Sudan.

Italy cooperates and undertakes some joint projects with countries in the EC and Mediterranean regions on matters of common interest such as the prevention of forest fires.

LUXEMBOURG

1. INTRODUCTION

The 88,350 ha. of forests constitute 34% of the country's total land area of 258,600 ha. The distribution of ownership is as follows:

Category	ha.	%	No. of properties
State	7,000	8	1
Communes	30,000	33.5	126
Other public establishments	1,250	1.5	about 120
Total Public forests	38,250	43	
Private forests	50,100	57	about 12,000
Total:	88,350	100	

The forests of the Communes range in area between 0.48 ha. and 1,137 ha. 95% of the private woodlands extend to less than 5 ha.

The types of forest are as follows:

Broadleaved high forest	40,800
" coppice (oak)	13,200
" Total	54,000
Conifers	31,150
Unstocked	3,200
Total	88,350

The main objective of forestry policy in Luxembourg is the conservation and protection of the forest so as to:

- prevent the degradation of the forest ecosystem and the consequences for the environment of such degradation;

- assure the maintenance of the ecological, economic and recreational functions of the forest.

In order to achieve this objective, the accent is placed on the following points:

- Conservation and enlargement of the forest area;

- Improvement of the regional distribution of the forests through reforestation in the south of the country;

- Improvement of the composition of the forests by favouring the indigenous broadleaved species;

- Improvement of the age class structures which are characterized by the fact that most old stands are broadleaved while an alarmingly large number of young stands are coniferous;

- Improvement of the structures of the private forests which are characterized by extreme fragmentation.

2. ADMINISTRATION

The Law of 4 July 1973 deals with the reorganization and definition of the duties of the Administration of Water Resources and Forests (which for the sake of brevity will henceforth be referrred to as the Forest Service). The Forest Service comes under the Ministry of the Environment and its responsibilities include the following:

- The conservation, supervision and administration of all public forests;

- Various duties relating to private forests including supply of silvicultural information and the supervision of work carried out with State aid;

- The conservation of game and fish resources in cooperation with the relevant consultative bodies;

- The maintenance of forest statistics and the preparation of economic studies;

- The supply of information and reports to national and international organizations.

The formulation, approval and implementation of national forest policy are influenced mainly by the following governmental organizations: The Superior Council for the Protection of Nature, the Superior Council for Hunting, the Superior Council for Fisheries, and the Professional Chamber.

The Ministry of the Environment accounts for 0.5% of the ordinary national budget which in 1986 amounted to some 66 bn LFrs, and the Forest Service for 0.37% (248 million LFrs). About one-half of the forestry budget is spent on salaries.

3. MONETARY AND FISCAL POLICIES

Subsidies are available for planting, conversion of coppice to high forest, first thinnings, pruning of Douglas fir, fencing against damage by game, and the construction of forest roads. These subsidies are available to private owners of agricultural or forest land, to public owners other than the State and to associations approved by the Minister of the Environment.

Income tax is based on the difference between receipts and outgoings without taking into account changes in the value of the growing stock except that a distinction is made between normal fellings and exceptional fellings (e.g. resulting from wind throw). In the case of exceptional fellings, the rate of tax on all fellings above the normal level is reduced, usually to one-half. The losses may be deducted from income from other sources and the excess profits may be carried forward for up to a maximum of five years. These rules apply to the large forest properties which are obliged to keep accounts. Small properties are taxed on the average income (normal or estimated).

Property tax is negligible.

Succession tax and gift tax are levied at the same rate and in the same way. The basis is the net market value, which is higher than a valuation based on income. The rate varies according to the degree of relationship between donor and beneficiary. The direct heir is exempted from these taxes.

The turnover tax at about 2% is relatively unimportant in forestry.

Observations. The taxation system is very unsuited to the conditions in Luxembourg where most private forests are very small. The income tax on fellings leads owners to delay the felling of mature trees as well as thinnings. The tax system also does not encourage regeneration or other forest investment, because the costs cannot be set against income.

Because of the fragmentation of forest ownership, investments such as forest roads are uneconomic except where forest owners collaborate.

As only costs directly connected with harvesting can be deducted from income, the owners tend to neglect other operations which could improve the quality of the growing stock. On most private forest holdings, which are very small, income from forestry constitutes only a very small part of total income.

The payment of succession and gift taxes often forces the new owners to carry out excessive fellings or to sell part of the forest. The State is keen to buy parcels over 10 ha. if they are near existing State forests.

4. MANAGEMENT AND PROTECTION

The Law of 20 March 1974 concerning general land use is based on the premise that the objective of land use is to ensure for the inhabitants of the country, in the long term, the best living conditions, both material and moral; this objective is to be achieved by promoting, for the common good, the harmonious valorization of the land through the utilization and optimum development of its resources.

- 167 -

In its framework programme on land use of 11 November 1977, the Council of Government decreed that all projects must be examined for their environmental impact.

The implications for forestry of this programme and subsequent legislation include the following:

- Any forest clearing must be compensated by the afforestation of an equivalent marginal agricultural area, preferably in the vicinity;

- Near towns forest land cannot be converted to other use except to serve an overriding public interest;

- Afforestation of agricultural or unused land requires the permission of the Minister;

- The Minister is empowered to prohibit leisure activities in forests, which could damage the environment or create undue noise. Motor vehicles are only permitted on public forest roads with a tarred surface;

- The Government may prohibit excessive fellings in private forests in the public interest (e.g. for reasons of soil conservation on slopes).

The main objects of management in public forests are to conserve the forest and to secure a rising sustainable yield. The Forest Service plans the management and utilization for a ten-year period and prescribes the measures needed for implementation.

With regard to the control and monitoring of atmospheric pollution, the following approaches have been adopted:

(i)   Measures to reduce industrial pollution at source;

(ii)   Monitoring of the situation by means of aerial photography and ground sampling (using the Gauss-Kruger system of plots in a systematic 2km x 2km grid);

(iii)   An observation station has been installed to measure atmospheric depositions.

For the protection of nature the following areas are defined in the relevant decisions of Government of 24 April 1981:

- The nature parks

- The valleys of the Eisch and Mamer

- The green belt of the town of Luxembourg

- The region of la Rochette

- The green zones between the conurbations north and south

- The landscapes to be protected along river banks

- Other forest areas of special interest

- Nature reserves:

  . dry grass land
  . wet zones
  . miscellaneous reserves
  . forest reserves

- natural sites and monuments.

- the remaining rural area, which is subject to general basic rules.

The protective measures which are prescribed in each case are designed as far as practicable so as not to interfere with other land use (agriculture, etc.) except for limited priority areas requiring special attention.

Some protected zones of recreational value are accorded special treatment so as to protect their beauty and character while at the same time making the necessary arrangements to welcome the public.

The objective in game management is to achieve the right balance between agriculture, forestry and wildlife and to ensure the maintenance of a healthy and varied game population. Every year, the Minister of the Environment, acting on a proposal from the Director of the Forest Service, fixes a hunting calendar and issues other relevant prescriptions.

It is also necessary to maintain or re-establish an adequate stock of fish in the great variety of water habitats in Luxembourg. The Forest Service has adopted measures to this end.

Luxembourg has also ratified various international conventions for the protection of fauna, flora and their biotopes.

The question of the afforestation of agricultural land is covered by the Law of 11 August 1982 on the protection of nature and natural resources which decrees that all afforestation of agricultural or unused land requires ministerial authorization.

5. UTILIZATION

In the public forests, harvesting is subject to various rules designed to prevent damage to the remaining crop and to regeneration. Normally all work is carried out by the Forest Service. Felling in broadleaved high forest must be completed by 15 April. Conifers are normally debarked immediately after felling.

There are few wood processing industries in Luxembourg and 65% of the wood produced is exported. A recent study found that the volume of conifer logs exported corresponds to the amount of processed timber that is imported. The study suggests, as a first step, the establishment of a sawmill with an annual capacity of 40,000 m3 and capable of sawing logs of small dimensions.

6. MARKETS AND TRADE

Wood from public forests is sold either standing or felled. The Forest Service is responsible for the measurement, classification and numbering of the logs. Sales are either local or regional, by tender, auction, or direct negotiation. Sale by public tender is the rule.

Wood in the rough may be classified according to:

- species and normal destination
- dimensions
- quality
- destination.

The classification according to quality uses the EEC standards: A/EEC, B/EEC, C/EEC, C1/EEC, C2/EEC.

7. EMPLOYMENT

In the public forests, workers are employed by the Forest Service in agreement with the forest owners. These workers are treated as workers of the State. Payment is either:

- by piece work, according to the rates fixed annually; or

- by the time or hours worked; the hourly rates are based either on the collective agreement in force for workers employed by the State, or on the collective agreement of the owner, whichever is more.

In private forests the work is often done by the owners themselves.

Some of the forest workers are small farmers who would have to give up farming without this ideal way of complementing their earnings.

In April 1985 the Government established a pilot scheme to provide work in the forest to unemployed persons. In this way 58 unemployed were found work in State forests in 1985 and 25 in 1986.

In the anticrises programme for extraordinary work 550 million LFrs were spent in the State forests between 1980 and 1984. The money was spent on normal forestry operations (e.g. planting, clearing, thinning, protection against game damage) which could not be carried out within the normal annual budget of the Forest Service.

8. EDUCATION AND TRAINING

In order to raise the standard of forest work, the Forest Service organizes logging courses every year. A team of young forest engineers is put at the disposal of private forest owners to teach them how to work more efficiently and thus improve the structure of their forest and increase the income from it.

9. RESEARCH AND INFORMATION

Being a very small country, Luxembourg has no forestry research institute, but it occasionally participates in the research programmes of foreign institutes.

In order to promote a better understanding of forest conservation among the public and especially among young people, the Forest Service collaborates closely with other services and organizations such as the National Youth Organization and the Natural History Museum. The Forest Service has also issued a number of brochures on silviculture which are available to forest owners on demand. The Ministry of the Environment has also had great success with its ecological exhibitions, and a permanent ecological centre is now planned in one of the State forests.

10. INTERNATIONAL COOPERATION

Luxembourg contributes financially to the following international organizations:

- The International Hunting Council

- The International Commission for the Protection of the Rhine and its Tributaries against Pollution

- The International Union for the Conservation of Nature

- The Research Institute for Forest Work and Methods

- The International Union of Forest Research Organizations.

Luxembourg is a member and regularly participates in the meetings of the following bodies: Benelux, Council of Europe, EEC, FAO.

Luxembourg has no universities or higher technical schools that offer forestry courses, but it collaborates with various foreign universities, technical colleges and specialized institutes in a number of research and development projects.

NETHERLANDS

1. INTRODUCTION

Of the total area of The Netherlands (33,930 km^2), 3,340 km^2 (9.8%) is forest, according to the fourth Dutch Forest Survey (Nederlandse Bosstatistiek). Of this, 94% is closed forest and 6% open forest.

The categories and trends of ownership of Dutch closed forest are as follows:

	1952-1963		1964-1968		1980-1983	
	in ha.	in %	in ha.	in %	in ha.	in %
State	55,300	21%	68,300	24%	97,800	31%
Provinces	1,700	1%	2,000	1%	2,400	1%
Municipalities	40,400	15%	43,700	16%	47,000	15%
Private Nature Conservation Organizations	10,200	4%	14,200	5%	34,600	11%
Private Owners	152,600	59%	150,900	54%	126,800	41%
Other	200	0%	500	0%	2,400	1%
Total:	260,400	100%	279,600	100%	311,000	100%

The most recent statement on forestry policy in the Netherlands is in the Regeringsbeslissing Meerjarenplan Bosbouw (governmental decision for a long-range forestry plan).

This main objective of the Government's forestry and silviculture policy is: the promotion of conditions and circumstances within the framework of total government policy such that the forested area in the Netherlands, in terms of size and quality, corresponds as nearly as possible to the wishes of society regarding the use of forests, now and in the future, at a cost level acceptable to society.

The main objective has been further broken down into the following subdivisons:

- the enduring conservation and development of existing forest in its current location;

- the promotion of a forest management such that the uses normally attributed to the forest are maintained and, in general, simultaneously implemented in its current location. For the period leading up to the year 2000 the most important uses are considered to be as follows:

  . the offer of possibilities for open-air recreation
  . the production and supply of timber
  . the maintenance and development of natural assets
  . contribution to the quality of the landscape;

-   ensuring that the conservation and functioning of the forest can
    be implemented at a cost level acceptable to society;

-   the expansion of forest area by or through the Government, the
    promotion of forest expansion by private persons and the promotion
    of the planting of fast-growing production forests.

These long term aims will be 'translated' into a policy for the
planning period leading up to the year 2000.

During the period up to the year 2000 a number of steps will be taken
aimed at the realization of the long-term policy. This will involve
further examination of the following elements:

- policy with regard to existing forest;
- policy with regard to (open) forest;
- policy with regard to expansion of forest area;
- policy with regard to special topics:

    . air pollution
    . management freedom and subsidizing
    . buying policy and privatization
    . regionalization of forestry policy
    . plant material provision
    . training, research and information;

- policy evaluation.

2. FOREST MANAGEMENT

The governmental influence on forests and silviculture is twofold. On
the one hand there is the public responsibility, and on the other hand
there is the management responsibility for the State forests.

In the Netherlands the public and private governmental
responsibilities for forestry and forest management are within the
jurisdiction of the Ministerie van Landbouw en Visserij (Ministry of
Agriculture and Fisheries) in which the Staatsbosbeheer (National Forest
Service) has the actual job of implementing policy.

The Staatsbosbeheer operates at a national, provincial and regional
level, the provincial and regional respresentatives see to the
implementation of the policy formulated and dictated at a national level.

The organizational structure of the Staatsbosbeheer is such that a
strict division is maintained between policy which applies to the entire
forestry sector, and the management of the State forests. This division
between policy and management also applies at the provincial and regional
levels.

The Ministerie van Economische Zaken (Ministry of Economic Affairs) is
politically responsible for matters which involve the handling and
processing of timber. In order to raise timber production to a permanently
higher level, the Minister for Economic Affairs publicized in 1983 a number
of policy resolutions for Dutch timber production. Insofar as they are
relevant, these policy resolutions have been incorporated into the
aforementioned long-range forestry plan.

The Minister for Agriculture and Fisheries, besides the political responsibility for forestry, has since 1982 also had the responsibility for policy regarding nature conservation and open-air recreation.

Government guidelines on priorities at national level do not in general lend themselves to a direct conversion to management plans for a specific forest area. For this it is necessary to have available a further elaboration of governmental policy at a more local level. It is moreover desirable that with such an elaboration, a relationship be established with other elements of government policy, such as physical planning policy at provincial and municipal levels. The Government, therefore, considers it advisable that the provincial authorities take a pioneering role in the drawing up of so-called regional forest plans.

3. FINANCIAL AND FISCAL POLICY

The Natuurschoonwet (NSW) (nature protection act) attempts to lighten the tax burden on private estates by way of a number of fiscal measures. Apart from this there are also specific tax laws which provide a number of fiscal allowances for forestry.

Classification of an estate under the NSW offers allowances regarding the following:

- wealth tax;
- income tax;
- corporate tax;
- death duties, capital transfer tax and transition tax;
- conveyance and capital levy.

These allowances are included in the separate tax laws. According to the Wet op Inkomstenbelasting (income tax law) everyone must pay income tax on income earned. Forestry as a whole, however, is excluded from the tax; in other words, benefits obtained from forestry are not considered to be profit.

According to the Wet op de Vennootschapsbelasting (corporate tax law), corporations, foundations, associations and others are obliged to pay corporate tax on profits made. Forestry is also exempted from this tax.

Estates not covered by the NSW are obliged to pay an annual assets tax, but the assets tax is levied on a much lower sum, provided that the estate is open to the public. According to the Gemeentwet (municipal law) municipalities can charge property tax. Forests are exempted from this.

According to the Successiewet (succession law) the new owner must pay death duty or capital transfer tax for the inheritance or receipt of gifts respectively. Forests are in principle valued according to their value on the open market, the same as for the wealth tax. The tax rate is partly dependent on the degree of kinship.

In the case of an NSW estate, application of the succession law is applied in a manner similar to that of the wealth tax. Unlike the wealth tax, however, there is a sanction if the estate is not maintained as such for a period of 25 years. The sanction consists of the advantage enjoyed by the receiver still being taxed with interest.

According to the Wet Belasting Rechtsverkeer (tax law in judicial matters) in acquisition other than by inheritance, a <u>conveyance tax</u> is levied. The rate is 6% of the value.

No conveyance tax is due if a person resident within the Kingdom, whose principal purpose is the maintenance of one or more NSW estates, has obtained an NSW estate.

There are a number of subsidy arrangements applicable in Dutch forestry.

The most important are as follows:

- A contribution for conservation can be awarded to the owners of forests for management and maintenance expenses.
  Included in the conditions are an approved management plan and opening of the property to the public. If a management plan provides for the implementation of certain kinds of work, 75% of the net costs can be reimbursed;

- Anyone satisfying the legal replanting obligation according to the Forestry Act can receive a contribution of 75% towards the costs;

- Anyone planting, other than to satisfy a legal replanting obligation, according to the Forestry Act can receive a contribution of 80% towards the costs;

- Subsidy given in connection with the opening up of forests (80% of the costs) and for the drawing up of a plan for this (100%);

- A contribution towards the costs of collaboration is 80% in the first year and drops to 20% in the fourth and last year;

- A once-only contribution of Dfl.3000-/ha. is given to promote the planting of new fast-growing forest. This contribution serves as compensation for the lack of income during the first years following planting. The timber should be felled between 15 and 25 years after planting.

4. FORESTRY AND FOREST CONSERVATION

4.1 The Legal Apparatus

The Forestry Act of 1962 forms the most important legal instrument for the conservation of forests; the Act also applies to timber grown outside the forest except in built-up areas.

The Forestry Act has three main provisions:

(a) Anyone intending to fell timber must give a minimum of one month's notice to the director of the Staatsbosbeheer.

(b) If timber is felled or in any other way destroyed, its owner is obliged to replant within three years on the same ground or on other ground if permission for this is granted by the director of the Staatsbosbeheer. Replanting must be carried out in a manner appropriate to responsible forestry.

(c) For the conservation of nature or the beauty of the landscape, a timber-felling ban of a maximum of five years can be imposed by the Minister for Agriculture and Fisheries.

Apart from the Forestry Act, which is above all aimed at the quantitative conservation of the forest, there are a nmber of other laws which play an important role in qualitative forest conservation.

The Nature Protection Act offers financial incentives to owners for the conservation of the natural beauty of their estates. The Ontgrondingswet (Erosion Act) regulates, among other things, the removal of humus in forests.

The Wet Bodembescherming (Soil Conservation Act) is important for the consideration of growth locations. The Meststoffenwet (Fertilizer Act) contains rules for the protection of the forest aginst the dumping of fertilizers.

The Natuurbeschermingswet (Nature Conservation Act) makes possible the designation of forests as protected natural monuments and in this way can limit the forest owner in his freedom of management.

Finally, zoning schemes based on the Wet op de Ruimtelijke Ordening (Physical Planning Act) are important for the preservation of scientific values.

4.2 Forest Conservation

The problems of vitality which have arisen in recent years in association with air pollution have given rise to the greatest concern. Since 1983 the Staatsbosbeheer has conducted annual surveys of forest health.

In 1985 about half of the forests showed signs of diminished vitality. Two percent of the forests showed such a pronounced reduction in vitality that recovery must virtually be ruled out, while another 13% could be called critical.

In the Indicatieve Meerjarenprogramma's (IMP's) Milieubeheer (indicative long-range programmes for environmental management) the Government explains its policy concerning reducing emissions in Holland.

The measures being supported, which include the reduction of emissions aimed at by the IMP, will produce results only in the long term.

Within the forestry sector, an effort is meanwhile being made to increase knowledge of the mechanism of air pollution and to carry out research into measures that can retard the process of forest deterioration. Here the aim is also to contribute to the determination of the level to which air pollution should be reduced.

The number of fires and the amount of surface burned annually is relatively small. This is partly the result of the limited forest area and its fragmentation, but by far the most important factor is the existence of a well-functioning warning system.

For the prevention of forest fires, the regional forest fire fighting organizations are of great importance. Local authorities, provinces, forest owners and managers work together in these organizations whose activities are coordinated by Bosschap (The Industry Board for Forestry and Tree-growing).

4.3 Nature Conservation

The national policy for nature conservation and the management of protected areas is explained in the Structuurschema Natuur-en Landschapbehoud (structural scheme for nature and environmental conservation), the definitive version of which was completed in 1986.

An indication of the importance to be placed on various aspects of conservation is given in the table below:

Characteristics relevant to the natural merit of the forest	Share of the future acreage in %
Indigenous tree species	69%
Mixed forest	60%
Small-scale management	24% for 0 - 0.25 ha.
	69% for 0.25 - 1 ha.
Forest with developed ground vegetation	65%
Forest with layer of bush	35%
Forest with large proportion of dead wood	18%
Forest with long period of rotation	40%
Forest with spontaneous regeneration	18%

The Government emphasizes that the distinction made among the various characteristics can never be as sharp in practice as the designation appears to imply. In forests with an accent on nature there will also be an average harvest of 1.4 m3 of timber per year.

4.4 Open-Air Recreation

The national policy concerned with open-air recreation is explained in the Structuurschema Openluchtrecreatie (structural scheme for open-air recreation), the definitive version of which was made in 1986.

The policy is aimed at reducing the tension between the demand for and the supply of opportunities for open-air recreation along the following lines:

- facilities for day recreation should preferably be located within the urban districts;

- the creation of facilities for overnight recreation will be spread throughout the country, but special attention will be given to areas within the sphere of influence of cities.

The Government itself will participate in the effort to alleviate the shortage of day recreational facilities by contributing to the realization of about 7,000 ha. of recreational area during the next 15 years. Of this, 4,000 ha. will be forested, mostly in the urban agglomeration of Western Holland. As a rule of thumb, in open landscape an area of about 100 ha of adjoining forest is necessary to make a specific forest recreational area possible.

One of the most important factors which determines the recreational value of forest is their visual diversity, but no attempt will be made to achieve as varied a vegetation as possible in every separate forest. Uniformity would be the final result of such an approach.

The long-range policy takes as its point of departure the need to keep the forests open to extensive recreational use. Only where conservation of nature is of prime importance can there be limitations to the recreational possibilities.

4.5 Wildlife management and hunting

Wildlife densities which hinder natural forest renewal over larger areas cannot be justified from the point of view of forestry and ecology.

When a forest owner maintains excessive wildlife populations he will not be eligible for the forest contribution subsidy because of the extra measures which will be necessary to maintain his forest. The micro-economic impact of hunting is manifold: hunting provides food and income for the land user, prevents damage to forests and/or claims for damages from nearby agricultural areas, contributes to the supervision of the forest, and provides work for game-wardens.

5. USE OF FORESTS

The primary wood processing industry in the Netherlands is largely based on native raw materials. This is also true for a significant proportion of the secondary processing companies.

A specific policy for the timber processing industry does not exist. The number of firms, turnover and numbers employed are as follows:

Sector	Number of Firms	Turnover x Dfl, 1 mil.	Number of Persons
Saw and planing mills	4	10	200
Plywood industry	22	180	800
Carpentry and parquet industry	266	1,501	9,900
Packaging and pallet industry	47	440	2,600
Other timber products industries	58	182	1,400
Brushes industry	14	54	500
Wooden furniture industry	402	1,463	11,400
Paper and board industry	35	2,322	7,400
Total	848	6,152	34,200

There is no national policy to stimulate the production of timber as a source of energy; research in this field does not support the conclusion that timber plantations for energy will be cultivated on a significant scale.

6.   THE MARKETING AND SALE OF TIMBER

In 1983, the Ministry of Economic Affairs issued a number of policy resolutions aimed at achieving the fastest possible acceleration in the production of domestic timber and timber products. The target is an increase from the current 8% self sufficiency to a minimum of 25% within a period of 50 years. This means that in 50 years the current production of about 1 million m3 of roundwood equivalent will have to be boosted to 3.9 million m3 r.e. per year.

Possibilities for this are as follows:

a) increase in the use of industrial wood residues and the recycling of timber;

b) increase in roadside and border planting by an extra 10,000 km;

c) increase of the timber production from existing forests from ca. 0.85 million m3 r.e./year to ca. 1.6 million m3 r.e./year by the year 2030;

d) improvement of timber harvesting methods; and finally,

e) an increase of forest area through afforestation.

7.   EMPLOYMENT

An estimated 3,650 people are currently employed in forests and nature areas. There is structured work for about 6,200 persons working full time.

In addition, there are another 7,500 working years of overdue forest maintenance. The incomplete use of this potential is the result of the current financial situation in forestry.

34,200 persons are employed in the wood processing industries (see table in Section 5: use of forests).

Concerning working conditions in forestry, the Industry Board for forestry and tree-growing plays a central role. There are no specific forestry unions.

8.   INSTRUCTION AND TRAINING

For many years now the three-part unity of education-research-information has constituted the solid basis for the development and realization of the agricultural policy. Until now this basis has not been equally well developed in the forestry sector. Special measures are planned to improve this situation. The links between training and practice will be strengthened through the financial participation of the commercial world in university education.

Through existing forestry training (Agricultural University, Higher and Intermediate Forestry and Agricultural Engineering Colleges, Lower Forestry College, College of Practical Forestry, Agricultural Engineering and Open Space Planning, and the Apprentice system), new insights in the area of forest development and use will continue to find their way into practice. In addition, the possibility exists to set up post-doctoral training, joined to the two-phase structure of the university and colleges, which is oriented towards the needs of the market, commerce and government. Feedback of practical experience to education takes place through consultation groups. The Minister for Agriculture and Fisheries is responsible for ensuring that the facilities for forestry education meet the demand.

9. RESEARCH AND INFORMATION

9.1 Research

The Government will place extra emphasis in the coming years on the following research topics:

- tree physiology and forest ecosystems
- forest reserves
- forest management
- management of forest enterprises
- timber market
- environment
- fulfilment of function
- expansion of forest
- relation between forest and surroundings.

There already exists a framework for the research programme to which all the institutions involved in forestry and commercial forestry can make a contribution. Through discussion structures the attunement of research and practice will be improved in the coming years.

It is the policy of the Ministry of Agriculture and Fisheries to promote the participation of commerce, both in the financial sense and as regards content. In addition, use will be made of knowledge and experience from foreign institutions. Companies and organizations from the private sector will be involved in the implementation of the research.

9.2 Information

The Staatsbosbeheer is responsible for the dissemination of forestry information to the general public, local authorities, etc. An improvement of the through-flow of research results is necessary in practice.

Special attention will be devoted to the economic aspects of forestry in dissemination of information and advice.

10. INTERNATIONAL COLLABORATION

The collaboration with developing countries is mainly with the poorest tropical countries and regions: Bangladesh, Egypt, India, Indonesia, Kenya, North Yemen, Pakistan, Sudan, Sri Lanka, Tanzania, the Sahel region, Southern Africa, and Central America.

The coordination of the policy regarding timber as a raw material for Dutch industry lies with the Ministry of Economic Affairs. Within the framework of the policy for raw materials as a whole, the assumption is that the Netherlands are to a great extent dependent on the import of raw materials for industrial processing and are significantly involved in the trade in raw materials. Thus Dutch interests are central to this policy.

Conversely, the development cooperation policy, coordinated by the Ministerie van Buitenlandse Zaken (Ministry of Foreign Affairs), is in the first place aimed at the interests of the people of developing countries.

The forestry activities which have been carried out in recent years with Dutch support in developing countries have as common objectives the contribution to the provision of fuelwood especially for the rural population and the combating of erosion and desert formation. Of equal importance to the achievement of specific physical objectives is often the institutional strengthening of national or regional forestry services and the counselling of the local population.

At present forty projects are being implemented in the programme, nearly all of which were started after 1980. The total investment in these projects to date is about 140 million guilders. The Government is resolved to raise the country's participation in development projects in this area to a level of 100 million guilders per year.

Research collaboration will, in the first place, be supportive of policy. In addition, a combined effort will be made by a number of ministries to develop permanent management systems for tropical rain forests.

The International Tropical Timber Agreement, worked out within the framework of UNCTAD, creates the possibility of conducting the trade in tropical timber in a responsible way.

NORWAY

1. **INTRODUCTION**

The total land area of Norway (Svalbard not included) is 306,885 km^2, of which 66,596 km^2 or about 22% is productive forest land.

Table 1.1   Productive Forest Area by Groups of Ownership

	Number of properties	Productive forest area		Pr. property
		total		ha.
		km2	%	
Individual owners	118,039	51,354	77.1	43.5
Various types of private common ownership	1,739	6,769	10.2	389.2
Public ownership	1,159	8,473	12.7	731.1
Total	120,937	66,596	100.0	55.1

A considerable part of the public forest is located in the northern part of the country or at high altitudes.

Combined ownership of forest and agricultural land is very common.

The yearly roundwood cut from the forest is currently around 10 million m^3, of which 8.8 million m3 is for industrial use.

The actual increment is about   16 million m^3

Strict sustainable yield, about   13 million m^3

and future realistic potential   17-20 million m^3

The basic objectives in the forest policy of the Government are given in laws and in reports to Parliament. Three laws are particularly important:

a)   The Concession Act: this Act regulates the ownership of agricultural and forest land;

b)   The Land Act: this Act regulates the use of agricultural and forest land;

c) Act on Forestry and Forest Protection: the objective of this Act is to increase the productivity of forest land and to promote afforestation and forest protection. The main principle is that, as long as a forest owner manages his forest in accordance with the intentions of the Act, he shall have the right to manage the forest himself without interference from the authorities.

Among other laws of importance for forestry, the following should be mentioned:

- The Act on Scaling of Industrial Roundwood

- The Nature Conservation Act, and

- The Open Air Recreation Act.

During recent years, two reports to Parliament have given general policy statements:

Report 110 (1974-75): Public attempts to increase the annual cut from the forest.

Report 18 (1984-85): Forestry policy in Norway.

The main policy objective as formulated in these two reports is:

The forest resources in Norway should be used in such a way that maximum benefit for the population is achieved, aiming simultaneously at conservation and further development of resources.

2. ADMINISTRATION

Forestry in Norway has a comprehensive organizational network both on the public and the private side. Relations between the two sides are more cooperative than competitive.

The Public Forest Administration (PFA) is organized under the Ministry of Agriculture, where there is a Department of Forestry. This department has a direct responsibility for matters concerning private forestry. Publicly owned forest is managed by a Directorate of State Forest and Land which is established with a certain autonomy outside - but linked to - the Ministry.

Private Forestry

The part of the PFA dealing with private forestry is called the Forest Authority. It consists of three levels of governing bodies. At each level there is a professional and/or technical staff (the Forest Service) serving the system.

(i) National Level

The governing body here is the Ministry of Agriculture, through its Department of Forestry.

Other Ministries have responsibilities in fields that are very closely linked to forestry. For example, the Ministry of the Environment administers the Nature Conservation Act and the Open Air Recreation Act.

Non-governmental organizations are also frequently brought into the decision-making process in an advisory capacity.

(ii) County Level

There are 19 counties in the country. In principle, each county has a County Land Board and a corresponding County Forest Service.

(iii) Local Level

There are 433 municipalities in the country. Each of these - except for a few towns - have a Municipal Land Board. These boards are served by 184 units of the District Forest Service.

Public Forests

The Directorate of State Forests and Land is linked to the Ministry of Agriculture which takes decisions in matters of a political nature. Day-to-day decisions are taken by the Director General and his staff.

The Directorate is the executing agency for areas belonging to various ministries. Apart from the Ministry of Agriculture, also the Ministry of Church and Education, the Ministry of the Environment and the Ministry of Defence have certain parts of the areas which are managed by the Directorate.

Non-governmental Organizations (NGOs)

Forest Owners' Organizations

(i)   The Norwegian Forest Owners' Federation has about 56,000 members and covers a significant part (3.7 million ha.) of the productive forest area of the country.

(ii) The Forestry Association of 1950 has only about 250 members. It represents, however, a productive forest area of about 500,000 ha. and a similar area of non-productive land.

Other Organizations:

The Forestry and Land Workers' Union is established as a part of the National Federation of Labour.

The Forestry Employment Association is the corresponding association for employers.

The Norwegian Forestry Society, which was established in 1898, has as its objective to promote forestry, in particular by indicating the multiplicity of benefits offered by the forest.

Related Organizations:

There are many other organizations which have some interest in forestry, e.g.:

Norwegian Farmers' Union
Norwegian Society for Conservation of Nature
Norwegian Sawmill Industries Association.

A series of matters is of concern to more than one of the organizations and institutions mentioned above. The necessary contact between them is mostly handled on an ad hoc basis. One more organized form of cooperation is an arrangement over a few days every year where problems in forestry and forest industry as discussed. Meetings are open to the public.

3. MONETARY AND FISCAL POLICY

In a country where the main part of the forests is privately owned and where "freedom under responsibility" is a leading principle, the monetary policy is most important. In an attempt to influence the behaviour of forest owners so that it comes reasonably close to national policy objectives, various arrangements have been established.

Since 1932, it has been compulsory (by law) to set aside a certain part of the income from the forest for investment purposes in the same forest. This levy is administered by the local PFA, and the forest owner gets no interest on his money as long as it is not used for this purpose. The interest in this period is used for various activities in general promotion of forestry. The owner, on the other hand, enjoys tax exemption by using this part of his income for investments. Because of this latter arrangement, the levy has gained considerable popularity, and has greatly influenced the level of investment in the period after World War II.

State subsidies to private forestry are mainly used for silvicultural improvements (especially planting) and for roads and transport. The total amount of these subsidies is equivalent to some 4.5$ per harvested m3 industrial wood, or 6.25$ per ha. productive forest land.

Credit - also for forestry - can generally be obtained from most banks. Some institutions have as a specific objective the offering of credit to forestry.

It is generally accepted in Norway that equity should be a basic principle for taxation. There is a tax on income and a tax on capital. For most forest owners, the income tax is the dominating part. The income is defined for this purpose as the net income from the wood harvested (not the increment). To permit a certain flexibility, income tax is calculated on the basis of average income during a five-year period.

To stimulate activity, there are possibilities for immediate deduction of expenditures - and investments - in the calculation of income. This is particularly profitable for the forest owner when the expenditures come from the forest levy.

4. FOREST MANAGEMENT AND PROTECTION

Change of use from agriculture to something else (including forestry) will require special permission. This has been a rather strict regulation. The Act on Forestry and Forest Protection states:

"This Act - shall not prevent forests from being cleared and the land cultivated for agricultural purposes, or used as a building site, road, gravel pit, industrial plan, storage, loading or landing site."

In the case of coniferous forest, however, permission of the Forest Authority is necessary in certain circumstances.

In view of the increased agricultural production of the country and the increased demand for forestry products, more restrictions on clearing forests for agriculture are being considered but no decision has yet been taken.

The Nature Conservation Act (which is administered by the Ministry of the Environment) opens the possibility to set aside National Parks, various types of Reserves and special areas where it is desirable to protect the landscape against human disturbances. In these areas, wood production is not regarded as an important objective.

Other forest areas of particular value to recreational interests and nature conservation, but where wood production is still important, can be regulated under the Act on Forestry and Forest Protection.

Also outside these particular areas, special restrictions can be imposed on roads and other construction work in connection with forestry.

Measures against attack by insects, fungi, etc., are dealt with in the Forestry Act, which states:

"If owing to fire, wind, landslide, avalanche or other causes, there is a danger that a forest may be exposed to extensive damage by attacks from insects or fungi, the Ministry may initiate the necessary public measures in order to counteract the attacks, no matter who is the owner of the forest.

The Ministry, under the same circumstances as mentioned in the first subsection, may decide that a forest owner shall undertake in his forest those felling operations and timber extractions which are considered necessary to combat the attack".

5. FOREST UTILIZATION

There is a general political objective to develop a network of forest roads, aiming at increasing accessibility and profitability. The official policy has been to keep the level of mechanization in reasonable balance with the general employment situation.

Short-distance transport out of the forest is increasingly carried out by machines specially designed for the purpose. Amongst these, the forwarder dominates over the skidder. The agricultural tractor still holds 40-50% of the volume, and the horse about 1%. There is no reason at present for the Government to influence the situation.

Of land-based industrial processing, the forest industry accounts for 14.5% of the value and 13% of employment (1984). The forest industry is largely in private ownership, and about half of it is owned by the forest owners' organizations.

The timber industry and the pulp and paper industry each use about 50% of the available industrial wood. Some 10% of the industrial wood is net import - mainly from Sweden.

A certain influence on the establishment or expansion of the forest industry is exercised by the Government by means of monetary incentives.

The yearly consumption of fuelwood in Norway is estimated at around 2 - 2.5 million m^3.

6. TIMBER TRADE AND MARKETING

Marketing of industrial wood is mainly carried out by the forest owners' organizations for their own members and for others who require their services. Some industries have recently also formed groups for the purpose of organizing the purchasing and transport of wood.

Wood prices are generally fixed through centralized negotiations between sellers' and buyers' organizations. In principle, the price for logs delivered at the roadside is the same all over the country. In cases where negotiations do not lead to agreement, there is provision for arbitration and, if necessary, intervention by Government and Parliament.

There is a special act on grading of wood for sale. According to this law, there shall be "grading associations" for regions or districts. All wood for use by domestic industries shall be graded by personnel from these associations.

The pulp and paper industry is clearly export-oriented. About 85% of the produced value is sold on the export market. The timber industry, however, produces mainly for the domestic market.

7. EMPLOYMENT

Employment in forestry, expressed as number of man-years work, has decreased drastically during the postwar period. This has been necessary because of the change in cost structure.

At present, employment is about 11,000 man-years, of which 5,400 man-years are provided by the owner and his family and 5,000 man-years by hired workers. About one half of the man-years from hired workers are provided by full-time forest workers, and the rest by part-time workers.

In forest industries, employment is of the magnitude of 60,000 man-years per year, depending on what type of industries are included. Research, education, administration and extension in forestry and the forest industry absorbs about 1,200 man-years.

A total of 6-700 professional foresters and 1,200-1,500 forest technicians are employed in forestry and forest industries, including education and research. There is a well-developed general system in Norway for social security, including health insurance and pension.

8. EDUCATION AND TRAINING

Professional education in forestry is given at the Agricultural University of Norway. Studies take 5 years, including a preparatory year which includes practical work.

Education at technical level normally takes 4 years including vocational training.

One-year courses in vocational training are given, mainly for the training of forest workers.

Postgraduate courses of various kinds can be taken at the Agricultural University.

The Forest Extension Service Institute serves the whole forestry sector. It arranges conferences and gives short courses on various topics. It has recently developed material for introducing some forestry aspects to classes in the primary school.

Engineers for the pulp and paper industry are educated at the University of Trondheim. Sawmilling engineers, however, will soon be able to obtain graduate education at the Agricultural University. There is also a school at technical level for sawmilling.

9. FORESTRY RESEARCH, EXTENSION AND INFORMATION

Research in forestry is the responsibility of the Norwegian Forest Research Institute (NISK) and the Faculty of Forestry under the Agricultural University of Norway. Most of the related research in industry and wildlife management is handled by other institutions.

The target group for <u>extension</u> mainly consists of forest owners and forest workers. The extension work is generally carried out by public and private organizations.

Two periodicals are published which reach a relatively broad group of readers. The Forest Owners' Federation has the publication "The Forest Owner" which is distributed to all members. The Norwegian Forestry Society has another called "Norwegian Forestry".

The Norwegian Forestry Museum gives information in very illustrative form about forestry, hunting and fishing.

10. INTERNATIONAL COOPERATION

Under the umbrella of general political cooperation within the "Nordic Council", there is a "Cooperative Committee for Research in Forestry" with several branches. A common Nordic course in tropical forestry is ambulatory between the countries. Norway also takes part in the various activities within the International Union of Forestry Research Organizations (IUFRO).

There is also a "Nordic Forestry Union" which in principle is private but in practice involves also the Public Forestry Administration.

Contact for Norwegian forestry outside the Nordic countries is mainly through membership of FAO and the Timber Committee of the ECE, including their subsidiary bodies.

<u>Development cooperation in forestry</u>: most goes bilaterally to a few selected countries. A smaller part is channelled through the FAO Trust Fund.

POLAND

1. INTRODUCTION

The forests of Poland cover 8.6 million ha., which is almost 28% of the total area of 31.2 million ha. There are 0.23 ha. of forest per person.

Forest ownership in Poland is as follows:

1) State forests: 7.1 million ha.

- controlled by the Ministry of Agriculture, Forestry and Food Economy: 6.8 million ha.;

- other ministries and central offices: 329,000 ha. (including 84,000 ha. of national parks).

2) Non-State forests: 1.5 million ha., belonging to:

- agricultural cooperatives and neighbouring groups of farmers;

- parishes, territorial communities, forest companies;

- individual owners.

The forest cover has increased from 24.6% in 1960 to the present 27.7% and a further increase in forest area of 225,000 ha. is expected to raise the forest cover to 28.4% by the year 2000.

Since 1970, there has been a gradual reduction in the area of non-State forests. Some of these have been taken over by the State in return for annuities or cash payments. This trend is likely to continue so that the share of non-State forests is expected to decrease from the present 18% to 15% by the year 2000.

The main principle of forestry policy in Poland is to ensure the ecological and economic conditions that enable forests to fulfil all their functions at an optimal level.

The policy relates to all forests in the country and it makes demands on all sectors of the economy and on all public institutions concerned. The State ensures by law the permanence of the forest area and the efficiency of the forest economy, irrespective of ownership.

Forestry is among the basic branches of the national economy. The implementation of forestry policy rests mainly with the Ministry of Agriculture, Forestry and Food Economy.

2. ADMINISTRATION

a) Organization

The Minister of Agriculture, Forestry and Food Economy has overall responsibility for forestry. His authority derives from:

-   Article 6 of the Act of 20 December 1949 on State forests;

-   Article 3 of the Act of 22 November 1973 on the management of non-State forests;

-   decision of the Council of Ministers No. 217/85 of 27 December 1985 on the status of the Ministry of Agriculture, Forestry and Food Economy.

The Minister exercises his functions mainly through the Director-General of State Forests, directors and chiefs of forest districts of State forest enterprises, and directors of national parks.

The regional forestry administration is also concerned with the supervision of forests which are not owned by the State.

The Director-General is personally responsible for the State Forests. He is also the Chairman of the Forestry Board, which has both decision-making and advisory functions. In addition to the Director-General, the Board comprises the Deputy Director-General, the Controller of Finance, the Inspector-General of Forests and directors of the regional offices of the State forests.

The following subjects require Board decisions:

-   plans and programmes concerning activities of the State forests as a whole, and especially annual and longer term economic plans;

-   the common initiatives organized by State forests and financed by member enterprises;

-   construction and use of dwellings and buildings erected for social purposes;

-   preliminary plan of maintenance costs of the General Board of State Forests.

In an advisory capacity, the Board considers a variety of matters relating to administration, finance, personnel and research, but the decisions rest with the Director-General.

The regional offices of the State forests include:

- forest districts

- forest transport centres

- reconstruction and building centres

- log sorting and despatch depots

- other special units.

b) Relationship between National Forest Law and National Forest Policy

There are several legal instruments relating to forestry but, together, they deal with the matter coherently and comprehensively.

The Act of 20 December 1949 on the State forest economy regulates the principles of forest policy in State forests. The basic thesis is contained in Article 9, which states:

"The State forest economy should strive to execute the following tasks on the basis of the instructions contained in the national economic plan:

- maintain the permanence and continuity of the production of wood and forest by-products in order to satisfy the present and future needs of the national economy;

- increase the national productivity of the forest;

- ensure favourable impact of forests on the country's climate, water management and national culture".

Forest management plans are an important element of policy implementation. These plans are designed to ensure that:

- the harvest is less than the current increment;

- all forest land as well as other land intended for forestry is afforested or restocked;

- the productive potential of forests is increased.

The Act of 22 November 1973 on the management of the non-State forests states in Article 7:

"The forests should be managed so as to ensure their productivity and their ability to fulfil their conservational, sanitary and cultural functions".

At present, preparatory work is in progress on a consolidated forestry act embracing all aspects of forestry and all categories of ownership.

3.   FINANCIAL AND TAX POLICY

a)   Share of Forestry in National Budget

In 1984, forestry accounted for 1.3% of national income, 0.87% of national investment and 0.95% of the working population of 17 million people.

b)   Investment Regulations

Forestry investment is not met from funds allocated for new capital investment and is divided into four categories:

- buildings and constructions, including houses;

- machines and technical devices;

- transport;

- tools;

- other movable items.

The sources of finance for forestry investment are:

- development fund;

- forest fund.

The development fund is financed from mortgages and part of the income. It is a basic component of investment finance. The means of the forest fund are an additional source.

According to the Order of the Council of 28 June 1982, the expenses connected with the following developments and purchases can be paid from the forest fund:

- basic equipment for nurseries;

- fire detection equipment;

- roads, forest railways, log-handling depots;

- water management devices;

- equipment for forest management, pasture management and agriculture, fishery management;

- forest settlements and houses.

c)   Tax Principles

The Act of 15 November 1984 on taxation in agriculture provides the legal basis for forestry taxation. State forest land is generally free of the agriculture tax. Land in other ownership is free of agriculture tax as long as the tree stand on it is less than 50 years old. This is more favourable than the previous Act of 26 October 1971 which limited the tax-free period to 30 years.

Although the forests of State forest enterprises are free of agriculture tax, they are subject to the turnover and income taxes generally applied in the economy. Sale value is the basis for the turnover tax, and net income for the income tax.

4.   FOREST MANAGEMENT AND PROTECTION

a)   Outline of National Policy on Land Use

The principles for allocating land to agriculture, forestry and nature reserves were laid down in the Act on landscape management planning of 1946. The Act of 1949 on the protection of nature foresaw a possibility of increasing the area under forests in view of their multiple functions.

A significant increase in the areas under agriculture and forestry has been achieved by land improvement, afforestation of wasteland and of submarginal agricultural land, as well as by reclamation of mining and other land relinquished by industry. As a result, the area of forests rose from 6.5 million ha. in 1946 to 8.6 million ha. in 1981.

The principles of land use policy are set out in several Acts, including: the Landscape Planning Act of 1984, the Protection and Environment Shaping Act of 1980, the Agriculture and Forest Land Conservation Act of 1982. These Acts severely limit the use of land for purposes other than agriculture and forestry.

The main goals of water management in the country are:

-    step-by-step liquidation of existing and potential water deficits;

-    prevention of floods and water pollution;

-    increased utilization of river and other inland waters for navigation, generation of energy, tourism and fisheries.

b)   Main Principles and Directives Concerning Forest Management and Afforestation

The growing stock in the forests is 1,348 million m3 over bark. The annual harvest, which is defined by the allowable cut, was 18 million m3 in 1985.

The basic tasks of forest management fall into three groups:

- forest inventories at 10-yearly intervals;

- regulation of production;

- monitoring changes.

The following directions for the maintenance of existing forest resources in Poland have been adopted:

a) Harvest

- based on productive capacity and taking account of calamities, damage caused by industries, ecological and social considerations;

- prompt utilization of timber resulting from calamities and sanitary measures undertaken to prevent the spread of pests;

- maximization of wood processing near the main sources of supply, elimination of wood storage in forest and creation of storage facilities outside the forest.

b) Silviculture

- establishing quasi-natural multi-use forest associations and communities;

- plantations tending to form artificial forest communities to produce timber on degraded soils;

- change of species in areas subject to pollution from industry; the main objective here is to create tree vegetation to serve ecological and social needs.

c) Principles and Directions in Forest Protection

The threats to health and productive capacity of the forests in Poland are caused mainly by unfavourable site and adverse climatic conditions. In this situation, all external pathogens, and especially air pollution, endanger the ecological, productive and social values of forests.

It has been estimated that about 75% of the forests in Poland are threatened continually or periodically by various factors. Serious attacks by Geometridae and green tortrix moths occurred between 1981 and 1985 mainly in stands of oak; pine stands were attacked mainly by pine-shoot beetles, weevils and Cerambicidae, while spruce stands suffered from attacks by the eight-toothed bark beetle. In 1985, chemical control of insect pests was carried out on about 118,000 ha. In that year, parasitic fungi were controlled by chemical means on about 1,800 ha. and by mechanical means on 4,300 ha.

The removal of the dying trees is followed by measures to improve the resistance of forests to disease. These measures include fertilization, replacement and the matching of species with site, especially the replacement of sensitive conifers with less sensitive broadleaved species.

Fire prevention measures include forecasts of fire hazards, fire breaks and observation from fire towers and aircraft; television cameras are also used.

d)   Policy for the Conservation and Management of Protected Areas

Nature protection in Poland began towards the end of the 18th century and the first reservations were established in 1886. Between 1912 and 1917, an inventory of areas of outstanding natural interest was started. The Provisional State Commission of Nature Protection, appointed in 1919, was the forerunner of the State Council of Nature Conservation which was established in 1926. The decisive year for nature conservation in Poland, however, was 1949, when the Act on Nature Conservation was passed, which is still valid today. This Act regulates the conservation, rehabilitation and proper utilization of natural objects of special interest. They include single trees or groups of trees growing on an area of less than 0.2 ha., avenues, certain rocks and caves. The total number of such objects recognized in 1984 was 14,027, of which nearly 13,000 were trees, groups of trees and avenues, and about 1,000 were rocks, caves and caverns.

A protected area of between 0.2 and 500 ha. is called a reservation. A reservation can either have a single purpose, such as the protection of a single rare plant, or it may serve to protect a whole plant community which, however, must be strictly defined.

A protected area of 500 ha. or more with numerous and complex conservation objectives is called a national park. The establishment of a national park is by an order of the Council of Ministers on the recommendation of the Minister of the Environment and Natural Resources. There are at present 14 national parks covering a total area of 125,000 ha., of which 70% are forests.

Landscape parks and areas of protected landscape also receive legal protection. They are designated by resolutions of "vovoidship" administrative councils on the basis of the Act of 20 July 1983 and subsequent legislation concerning a system of administrative councils and local governments. There are now 24 landscape parks covering a total of 1 million ha. and the total area of protected landscape is 1.7 million ha.

e)   Policies Connected with Recognition of Protected Areas

The following kinds of recreational areas occur in Poland:

-    community forests;

-    forests around urban and industrial agglomerations;

-    forests destined for public mass recreation and tourism, on territories of forest districts (mainly for day visitors near cities, camping facilities farther afield);

- health-climatic forests (mainly around health resorts);

- forests of high "verdure zone" (mainly around industrial plants).

Community forests are a part of State forests, but are excluded from the State forest economy on the basis of Article 14 of the Act of 20 December 1949 on State forest economy; they are managed by the city administrations. The forests located within the administrative limits of cities form an integral component of urban green areas.

f) Principles for the Management of Nature Reserves

Nature reserves are created on the basis of the Act on Nature Protection of 7 April 1949 by orders of the Minister of the Environment and Nature Resources Conservation.

Reserves are divided into the following categories:

- strict reserves where no interference with the environment is allowed, and economic activities are prohibited;

- partial reserves where protection of some components of nature is the goal, and economic activities are limited accordingly.

Nine kinds of reserves are differentiated in Poland, namely:

	number	ha.
Faunistic	82	37,856
Landscape	83	28,382
Forest	430	23,929
Peat	70	4,876
Floristic	127	2,034
Water	10	1,816
Non-living nature	38	496
Steppe	28	364
Halophytes	4	25
TOTAL	872	99,778

Only 123 reserves are subject to strict protection; the mean area of strict reserve is 62 ha., and mean area of reserve in the country is 114 ha.

Management principles in nature reserves, where forests are included, comply with the "Instruction on forest management in national parks and nature reserves" which was accepted by the Ministry of Forestry and the Woodworking Industries in December 1961 and introduced for implementation in 1962.

Strict protection of a forest reserve tends to sustain the natural state of the forest. Partial protection tends to conserve some elements in a definite state through application of proper cultivation, silviculture and protection measures. Detailed management plans are prepared for all reserves.

5. FOREST UTILIZATION

The level of mechanization in felling, limbing and bucking amounts on average to 95%. The level of work mechanization in the whole process of wood harvest is about 55%.

Use of gas motor saws with 2 and 4 KM power will predominate in the wood harvest of the Polish forest economy. The use of agricultural tractors with accessory equipment, and of tractors of medium and high power is forecast for wood skidding; medium and high-tonnage trucks are foreseen for the transport of the wood.

A higher degree of mechanization which eliminates manual work is forecast for lowland forests.

Operations linked immediately with wood harvest are executed by forest districts, but skidding and wood transport is done mainly by special forest transport centres.

Polish forestry transport is organized at 24 centres of forest transport (OTL) with a two-level technical base:

- transport brigade bases and technical service stations (SOT)

- regional service stations (OSO).

6. EMPLOYMENT AND STAFF TRAINING FOR FORESTRY AND THE WOODWORKING INDUSTRY

Employment in forestry and the woodworking industry exists mainly in the State sector. The great fragmentation of non-State forests does not create either the need or the conditions for the employment of highly qualified personnel. State enterprises also play a dominating role in the woodworking industry while privately owned sawmills have a limited, local range of activity.

The basic problems of employment policy in the forestry and woodworking industry are regulated by legal acts concerning the whole of the national economy. Specific to the branch are the following subjects:

- norms and tariffs for work

- job specifications

- determination of unit rates resulting from work norms

- some aspects of training.

The above-mentioned subjects, while complying with the needs of forestry and the sawn timber industry in detail, are based on general national criteria.

In past years, the basic problem was the lack of qualification of workers employed in the forestry and woodworking industry. The question has been partially solved by the development of the educational system.

Two agricultural universities have separate faculties for forestry and wood technology. A third, in Cracow, has only a forestry faculty. The number of graduates finishing their studies meets the needs resulting from normal staff turnover.

Special forestry colleges and wood industry colleges deal with the education of the staff for supervisory posts at technical level. Forestry colleges come under the Ministry of Agriculture, Forestry and Food Economy, while wood industry colleges operate in a general system of professional education administered by the Ministry of Education.

Forestry workers receive their training at enterprise schools and on educational courses. Both institutions enable them to get the title of qualified worker on the same basis as workers in other sectors of the national economy.

This well-developed system of higher, medium and basic education satisfies almost all needs. The demand for qualified workers is not yet fully satisfied, but significant progress has been made. In 1966, the ratio of qualified to unqualified workers was 1:3; in 1988 it is 6:1.

7. FORESTRY RESEARCH, DEVELOPMENT AND INFORMATION

Scientific and research activities are mainly directed towards forest conservation, multi-use of forests and optimization of forest raw material utilization.

Forestry research is carried out at the Forest Research Institute in Warsaw, at the forestry faculties of the Agricultural Academies of Warsaw, Cracow and Poznan, at the Faculty of Agriculture and Forestry Technology of the Warsaw Agricultural Academy, at the Institute of Dendrology of PAS in Kornik, and at the Department of Agriculture and Forest Biology of PAS in Poznan.

Papers on forestry topics are published mainly in three forestry journals and in eight scientific periodicals. Scientific papers appear in "Acta Agraria et Silvestria", "Folia Forestalia Polonica", "Prace IBL", "Prace z Zakresu Nauk Lesnych Poznanskiego Towarzystwa Przyjaciol Nauk", "Roczniki Akademii Rolniczej w Poznaniu", "Sylwan", "Zeszyty Naukowe Akademii Rolniczej w Krakowie" and "Zeszyty Naukowe SGGW-Ar w Warszawie".

The following publishers take an active part in the extension of forest knowledge: "Panstwowe Wydawnictwo Rolnicze i Lesne", "Panstwowe Wydawnictwo Naukowe", "Polskie Towarzystwo Lesne" and "Stowarzyszenie Inzynierow i Technikow Lesnictwa i Drzewnictwa".

8. INTERNATIONAL COOPERATION

There is bilateral cooperation in forest science with Czechoslovakia, the GDR, USSR, Hungary, Romania, Austria, Finland and France.

Polish foresters also take an active part in the activities of the following international organizations:

- Permanent Agricultural Commission of Comecon, Forestry Section

- Commission for Scientific and Technical Cooperation of Comecon - Finland

- IUFRO, of which the Forest Research Institute of Warsaw is an active member

- FAO

- MAB (Man and Biosphere Programme of Unesco)

- IUCN (International Union for the Conservation of Nature and its Resources).

In addition, the State Forest Service has taken part for several years in the tri-lateral cooperation Poland-Czechoslovakia-GDR concerning the reduction of industrial damage to forests near common frontiers. Meetings of the Vice-Ministers of Forestry of those countries are held yearly in the context of this cooperation.

The international cooperation of Poland in the field of forestry involves:

- scientific and research activities shared between cooperating institutes;

- participation in meetings, symposia and seminars;

- exchange of machines and equipment for investigations and technical tests;

- participation in and organization of common exhibitions of machines and forestry equipment;

- common action for insect pest control near frontiers;

- exchange of information, documentation, planting stock, etc.

PORTUGAL

1. INTRODUCTION

Forests cover a little over 3 million ha. or about one-third of the total land area of Portugal. The ownership structure is as follows:

Ownership Category	Area (1,000 ha.)	%
State	105	3.5
Communities ("Baldios")	300	9.8
Workers' cooperatives	160	5.2
Private, non-industrial	2,378	77.6
Industrial enterprises	120	3.9
Total	3,063	100.0

The main species are maritime pine (over 1M ha.), cork oak (Quercus suber) and other oaks (mainly Q. rotundifolia) (also over 1M ha.) and eucalyptus (0.4 M ha.). There has been much planting of eucalyptus in recent years; most of the plantations owned by forest industries are of this genus.

In our view, the essentials for implementing forest policy are:

- a clear definition of objectives for the sector

- the identification of available means

- the efficient use of these means

- the placing of the sectoral objectives into broader national objectives

- due consideration of the numerous and complex inter-sectoral relations.

These conditions can only be met by achieving a broad national consensus of all concerned. At present, while measures have been taken on certain matters, there is no coherent view of the sector as a whole.

In recent years the Government, in its statements on annual programmes, has made brief references to forestry. The year 1987 marks a turning point in that the Government for the first time submitted to the Assembly of the Republic "major options" for the four-year period 1987-1990. The specific reference to forestry is confined to a statement on the need "to afforest land unsuited to agriculture and to protect nature", but there are general references to matters such as "the improvement of infrastructures", which also concern forestry.

A major part of the initiatives on these matters falls within the
scope of the Action Plan for Forestry which is co-financed by the EEC under
Article 22 of the specific development plan for agriculture in Portugal.
The plan provides not only for afforestation but also for the
rehabilitation of degraded woodlands, fire prevention, etc. The level of
aid is increased where work is undertaken by groups of owners because
collaboration leads to larger units of management.

Very recently the Government has approved a set of legislative
diplomes, some of them not yet in force, which introduce some rules,
considered to have priority, in the forest activity: the prohibition of
prematurely cutting town forests; the conditioning of afforestation with
fast-growth forest species; the obligation to declare the cutting down or
uprooting of trees; the submission to forest regulation of areas swept by
forest fires; the cork oak forest protection; the establishment of rules
for tapping operations on pine trees; and the possibilities of access to
land through forest renting. The Government also created two commissions,
one of them to accompany and analyze the afforestation carried out and the
other to propose a national policy for an integrated development of the
forest sector, to harmonize the forest legislation and to prepare a forest
code. Forestry receives little public attention except for forest fires
and for forestry impacts in the environment.

2.   ADMINISTRATION

The ownership structure of the forest situation is unlikely to change
much, except that more afforestation will be undertaken by the pulp
industry if the problems arising from the fragmentation of land ownership
can be overcome. Most forest holdings are owner-occupied.

The forestry sector consists of a number of interdependent elements
which should be treated as a coherent whole. Unfortunately, this is not the
case. The Directorate General of Forestry in the Ministry of Agriculture,
Fisheries and Food is responsible for forestry, while the Institute of
Forest Products in the Ministry Commerce intervenes - although for a short
time, for it is to be abolished - on matters of processing and quality
control and international trade. There are also other ministries which take
decisions on environmental and industrial matters. For research, there is a
national forestry research station which constitutes a department of the
National Institute for Agricultural Research.

A complete concentration of responsibilities would not be necessary in
order to overcome the present unsatisfactory lack of coordination. The
situation would be much improved by:

a) adoption of a unified, stable and sufficiently detailed forestry
   policy;

b) more formal and efficient procedures of coordination between all
   concerned.

These are the aims of one of the above-mentioned recent legislation.

The Directorate General of Forestry is in charge of:

- contributing to the formulation and implementation of forestry policy;

- managing the following activities on State lands: forestry, silvopasticulture, wildlife, freshwater fisheries and beekeeping;

- giving technical assistance to the management of these resources on other land.

The Directorate General is assisted by two bodies. The first, the Forestry Council, is consultative and consists of senior officials of the Forest Service and the regional directors of the Ministry of Agriculture as well as representatives of various activities connected with forestry, including: the regional coordination committees, the higher forestry education establishments and the National Agricultural Research Institute. The second body is the Administrative Council which deals with the finances of the Service.

Apart from the central services, the Directorate General disposes of six regional offices which normally operate on the basis of annual programmes prepared by the central office in consultation with the regional forest offices. The "Regional Coordinating Committees" and other relevant bodies also participate in the planning of regional forestry programmes.

The Institute of Forest Products, which is to be abolished, has the following tasks:

a) to coordinate and regulate the production, processing and commerce of wood, cork, resin and their derivatives;

b) to regulate conditions concerning supply, imports and exports, taking account of the interests of the producers as well as the national interest;

c) to undertake economic and technical studies.

The issue of licences for external trade ceased with Portugal's accession to the EEC.

Some forestry policy decisions are taken by the Assembly of the Republic, and others by the Government. Proposals are generally submitted by the Director-General of Forests to the Minister of Agriculture after consultations with the Forestry Council. It happens, of course, that decisions are contested or that no agreement is reached.

The main obstacles to the implementation of a forest policy are the divergent views of the sector taken by agricultural, industrial and environmental interests. Moreover, a long-term view of the subject has been rendered difficult by the economic difficulties of recent years.

Forestry contributes to the following national policies:

(i)   improved production and productivity in agriculture;

(ii)   better and more complete use of the land resource;

(iii) increase of positive trade balance;

(iv)   improved balance between regions and stabilization of
       populations in sparsely populated areas;

(v)   strengthening of intersectoral relations;

(iv)   soil conservation and restoration and the regulation of water
       regimes in certain regions;

(vii) improvement of the quality of life and of the environmental
       equilibrium.

At regional level, forestry development is to be included in the
"Integral Plans for Regional Development".

There are virtually no official credits available at present for
forestry development; the joint project between the Government of Portugal
and the World Bank ended in 1987, and no decision on future credits from
official sources has been taken. Credits obtainable from private sources
are not usually on sufficiently favourable terms for forestry.

Besides the grants given to the projects undertaken under the Action
Plan for Forestry, in which some favourable conditions are given to
associations of small owners and to the growing of slow-growth high-quality
timber there are some grants available in certain areas for multiple use
forestry (afforestation, pasture management, improvement of resources of
game, bees and fish).

Privately occupied woodlands are subject to the rural land tax from
which State and community woodlands are exempt.

3.   MANAGEMENT AND PROTECTION

In the beginning of the eighties three laws were passed on these
matters. The first two limit or impose conditions on the use of certain
areas, namely "the agricultural reserve" and the "ecological reserve". The
third law, which refers to "regional plans for land use", confers on the
Minister responsibility for the planning of the task of promoting and
coordinating land management.

On land classed as "agricultural reserve", all actions likely to
reduce the agricultural potential are prohibited. The "national ecological
reserve" seeks to preserve, on certain sites, a biophysical equilibrium
between production and the cultural and socio-economic values which
characterize these sites. The sites include beaches, dunes, estuaries,
small islands, river banks, etc.

There is legislation which dates from the beginning of the century, which has rarely been enforced and reflects the need to regulate water regimes, protect the cultivated land, render arid lands productive, improve the climate, conserve soil in the mountains, etc.

The regional land use plans cover a 12-year period, after which they are revised. They are of course subordinated to national plans and they are linked to other socio-economic plans which affect all private and public operators in a region.

At the level of communes, land planning is achieved by municipal indicative plans which are conceived as an instrument of an integrated development policy.

Thinnings are rare and fellings serve the interest of the purchasers; natural regeneration is thus from unselected seed. This state of affairs is due to lack of finance, indifference and insufficient forestry knowledge on the part of the woodland owners.

Simultaneous action on four fronts is needed to remedy the situation:

1) Increase in the size of operations

2) Training of woodland owners and workers

3) Specific, easy and rapid financing

4) Extension and incentives to technical progress.

The worst forest damage is caused by forest fires, especially in the forests of maritime pine which are particularly susceptible. Pests and disease which pose less of a threat, are often due to lack of silviculture or the use of species not adapted to the sites on which they are planted. Some measures have, however, to be taken in order to prevent spreading through outbreaks: that is the aim of recent legislation on the control of Phoracantha spp. which attacks Eucalyptus species. Pollution merits no special mention.

In spite of the various difficulties that have been mentioned, some progress has been made with fire prevention.

The Secretariat of State for the Environment is empowered to propose, after consultation with the various governmental departments concerned, the establishment and constitution of "recreation reserves" and "protected landscapes" in "national parks". Responsibility rests with the National Park Service. These developments constitute part of regional development policy and conform to the requirements of the fourth EC action programme for the environment, which came into force in 1987.

With regard to the management of game and of freshwater fishing, the main objective of the Directorate General of Forestry is to utilize the resource in a way that is compatible with its preservation and with multiple use forestry. Fish farming could be increased by using exotic species.

Recent hunting legislation aims at reducing the areas where hunting is unrestricted in favour of areas where hunting is managed and controlled. It also encourages the participation of hunting associations, farmers and other citizens in the management. The issue of hunting permits is now subject to the passing of an examination. It is envisaged that hunting will play an important role in the support of agriculture and of regional development. To some extent that also applies to bee-keeping. Recent different legislation on bees and honey is in force.

The afforestation of abandoned agricultural land is envisaged in Article 22 of the EEC programme for the development of agriculture in Portugal, but certain specific questions of timing and scope may limit its implementation.

4. UTILIZATION

There are no general laws concerning the harvesting and transport of forest produce, except for cork originating from estates which were nationalized or expropriated under the agrarian reform.

The Directorate General of Forests is responsible for enforcing this legislation and for maintaining a staff unit to give technical assistance and to control all operations connected with the harvesting and trading of cork from producer to primary user.

Forest produce from State forests is sold standing by tender after the trees have been marked and measured by the State Forest Service. The Service does all it can to promote the mechanization of harvesting.

In December 1983, the EC Council of Ministers approved a technological development plan for Portuguese industry; the provisions in this plan for the technological centres for wood processing and for the cork industries have not yet been realized. Forest industries may, however, benefit from a decision of the Ministry for Industry to promote the development of natural resources; they may also benefit from the European Fund for Regional Development.

As far as standardization is concerned, there are numerous Portuguese norms concerning terminology, classification and characteristics of various forest products, including cork.

The relations between the many small growers and the few large pulp industries are characterized by the weak bargaining position of the growers, minimized by lack of supply which causes the policy of the industries to be buying or renting considerable areas of land to grow timber.

The sawmilling industry is composed of some few well-dimensioned sawmills and many small units, some of them using rudimentary technology. It is geared to the sawing of small logs to produce utility lumber for export. The few forests that produce substantial quantities of large, high quality logs belong mostly to the State. That is why Portugal imports a lot of tropical hardwood logs.

Trees are always sold standing to merchants or intermediaries with the result that growers tend to get little for their wood. In the cork sector, the imbalance between growers and industries is less severe.

Forest industries are obliged by a law of 1966 to guarantee the health, well-being and safety of the public, but the law is vague and ineffective; its revision is now planned.

The National Plan for Energy of 1984 recognizes the possibility of encouraging, by means of government measures, the utilization of forest biomass for the generation of energy. The two sources of biomass to be studied are:

- residues from logging and industrial wood processing;

- forest energy plantations.

The implementation of the plan awaits further government decisions, but a study undertaken at the initiative of the Directorate General of Energy concludes that prospects for both the above approaches are favourable. Some points, however, such as the environmental and economic implications (in a global outlook), require clarification. Meanwhile, several industries generate energy from their own wood residues or from residues obtained from others.

5. EXTERNAL TRADE

Two general policy objectives are:

- to add as much value as possible to produce before export;

- to reduce imports of timber of large dimensions by promoting the growing of large trees at home.

6. EMPLOYMENT

The labour laws of November 1969 and December 1979 laid down detailed rules for individual contracts of employment and for general labour relations. The main provisions relate to rights and duties, discipline, security, health, safety, recruitment, working hours, paid holidays, wages, etc. The special conditions governing the employment of women and minors are also covered.

The provisions for general labour relations are concerned with the collective arrangements between employers and employees, including rules for solving disputes.

In general terms, the sequence of priority for employment measures is as follows: the young, the long-term unemployed, women, the handicapped. Account is also taken of regional problems and the prospects of particular industries.

In forestry, the main objectives have been:

- creation of supplementary part-time employment, e.g. for afforestation;

- stable employment in existing forests;

- additional employment in forest industries associated with rising production from the forest.

Forest and forestry enterprises try to recruit personnel locally, while the industries advertise their vacancies in the media, especially the press.

The planning and coordination of work safety measures at national level is mainly undertaken by the General Directorate of Hygiene and Safety on Labour in the Ministry of Labour. Forestry is covered by these general provisions.

7.   EDUCATION AND TRAINING

Education in Portugal is at three levels:

- elementary: 6 years

- secondary: 6 years

- higher: 3 years for the baccalaureat and 5 years for the diploma.

Technical education in forestry takes place at the upper level of secondary education (10th - 12th year) for forestry technicians. The higher level of education for professionals, leading to qualification as a forest engineer, is available at:

- Instituto Superior de Agronomia, which is incorporated at the Technical University of Lisbon which qualifies graduates as forest engineers;

- Instituto Universitário de Trás-os-Montes e Alto Douro.

A course leading to the baccalaureat in forest production is provided at the Instituto Politécnico de Castelo Bronco.

A start has been made at a few schools with "techno-professional" courses in the 10th year of secondary education.

Forestry training outside schools is the responsibility of the Directorate General of Forests, but certain private and public enterprises are also active in this field. For example, there is a centre for professional training for the timber industries in which the National Association of Wood Industries and the Federation of Trade Unions for Sawmilling and Joinery participate. Another example are some of the pulp industries which have systematic programmes of training and refresher courses for their employees at all levels.

At present there are about 170 forest engineers and 100 technicians. An estimate prepared in 1984 concluded that these numbers would have to be increased gradually to 340 and 720, respectively.

Future education and training for forestry personnel must take into account three important considerations:

1) the increasing need for an interdisciplinary and intersectoral approach to problems;

2) advances in technology, which in particular necessitate a higher standard of qualifications at technical level;

3) the need for more specific training for graduates who are appointed to undertake research.

8. RESEARCH

The only general programme of research in forestry is undertaken by the National Forestry Research Station of the National Institute for Agricultural Research. Priority species for research are: cork oak (improvement of cork quality and methods of regeneration); maritime pine; eucalypts (e.g. provenance tests of E. globulus); Quercus rotundifolia, Pinus nigra, Pseudotsuga menziesii, Castanea sativa. Other research topics include, for example: improvement of grazing under cork oak, multiple use forestry, agriculture, aromatic plants, utilization of forest residues for energy, biological and ecological studies.

Some forestry research is also undertaken by universities, the pulp and cork industries and various agricultural and technical institutes.

The results of research are published and, if requested, the results and also provisional results are passed direct to forest managers and other interested parties.

There are important research links with other countries. For example, there is a collaborative research project between Portugal, Spain, France and Italy on the micropropagation of eucalypts.

- 209 -

SPAIN

1. INTRODUCTION

Areas classed as forest occupy 25.6 M ha. or 50.8% of Spain's total surface area of 50.5 M ha. The areas classed as forest include some 13 M ha. of pastures and "matorral"; and of the 11.8 M ha. where tree crowns cover over 10% of the surface area, only 8.3 M ha. are closed forest and of these only 6.5 M ha. are exploitable.

Ownership of the 11.8 M ha. of tree-covered areas is as follows:

	M ha.	%	average area per property(ha.)
State	0.5	4	500
Other public ownership	3.5	30	600
Private	7.8	66	3
TOTAL	11.8		

Broadleaved species dominate in 6.1 M ha. and conifers in 5.4 M ha., while 0.3 M ha. are mixed.

Forestry policy in Spain is based on the following objectives:

a) The protection and rehabilitation of the resource with emphasis on:

   - protection against soil erosion, torrent control and watershed management;

   - protection of forests against fire.

b) The promotion and optimization of forest production, with emphasis on:

   - the needs of rural populations in disfavoured areas;

   - the principle of sustained yield and maintaining the productive potential of the ecosystem.

c) The contribution of forests to the environment and its enjoyment by the public through protection of flora and fauna, provision of opportunities for recreation and promotion of a better understanding of nature especially among children.

The main general statements of policy concerning the protection of the environment and natural resources including forests are:

   - Article No. 45 of the Spanish Constitution of 1978;

   - The message by His Majesty the King in June 1980 on the occasion of the World Day of the Environment;

- The agreement of the Council of Ministers on 6 June 1980 to approve the proposal of the Interministerial Commission for the Environment concerning the Spanish Strategy for the conservation of natural resources.

More specific statements concerning forestry policy are contained in twelve laws issued between 1941 and 1982.

2. ADMINISTRATION

Forest administration in Spain is rendered difficult by the fragmentation of ownership - there are 2,600,000 private owners with an average of only 3 ha. each. The 5,700 publicly owned forests with an average area of about 600 ha. present less of a problem.

Private owners can enter into an agreement with the Administration to have their woodlands reforested. About 9,000 properties, with a total of 2.9 million ha., are in this situation.

The administration of the State forests and other publicly owned forests passed from the Central Government to the Forest Services of the Autonomous Communities between 1980 and 1985. Since this decentralization, the Central Administration, which is still responsible for the National Parks, has been acquiring some private properties within or adjoining these parks.

The responsibility for most aspects of Central Forest Administration rests with the following organs of the Ministry of Agriculture, Fisheries and Food:

- Instituto Nacional para la Conservación de la Naturaleza (ICONA). This is an autonomous body charged with implementing conservation programmes: prevention of erosion and forest fires, management of protected areas and cattle routes, genetic improvement, reforestations of public interest, etc.

- Directorate General of Agrarian Research and Training. This is another autonomous body responsible for forestry research and the foresters' training schools, besides other agricultural and cattle research.

- Directorate General of Agrarian Production. This is responsible for forestry production and for administering grants to private forest owners, besides other agricultural activities.

- Directorate General for Agro-Industries. This is responsible for the primary wood processing industries, among other agro-industries.

Forestry education at higher and intermediate levels is the responsibility of the Ministry of Science and Education; secondary wood processing industries come under the Ministry of Industry and Energy; and trade in forest products comes under the Ministry of Economy and Trade. The organization of the forest services of the Autonomous Communities varies. For example, in some but not all, the responsibilities in respect of publicly owned forests and of private forests rest with different departments.

The Autonomous Communities are generally responsible for all aspects of forest management, harvesting, afforestation, hunting, fresh water fishing, cattle routes, etc. The Communities also have certain legislative powers within the framework of basic national legislation.

The Central Administration has retained the responsibility for matters such as: basic legislation, coordination of general planning, public works affecting more than one Autonomous Community, international relations, national statistics, national forest inventory, management of National Parks.

The Central Administration and the Autonomous Communities jointly deal with matters such as: watershed management projects involving more than one Community, some measures to prevent and combat forest fires, some aspects of planning in National Parks.

A body in which the Ministry of Agriculture, Fisheries and Food as well as all Autonomous Communities are represented is planned. Its functions will include, among others: establishing lists of protected species, issue of hunting and fishing licences, laying down rules of conduct for forest personnel, development of general training programmes for nature studies, distribution of tree seeds and plants.

The following main organs of government influence forest policy:

Executive Organs

- The Council of Ministers

- The Councils of the Autonomous Communities

- The Ministry of Agriculture, Fisheries and Food

- Various Commissions of the Government, especially the ones for Autonomous Matters and for Economic Matters

- The Committee for Public Investments

Legislative Organs

- The two Chambers of the Nation, which approve laws and important decisions

- The Commissions of these Chambers, which deal with State Budgets, Agriculture, Environment and International Affairs

- Various Commissions of the Senate on specific topics, e.g. forest fires, freshwater fishing, floods.

- The Parliaments of the Autonomous Communities.

There are three major constraints on the implementation of forest policy:

- the already-mentioned fragmentation of ownership

- the constraints, common to all countries, which arise from the multiple links of forestry with other sectors of the economy

- problems associated with the recent decentralization of forest administration.

In national development programmes, forestry plays a part mainly in those concerned with:

- the protection and improvement of the environment and natural resources, for which ICONA is responsible;

- the promotion of production in agriculture and fisheries where forestry accounts for some 35% of the subsidies and credits.

In 1986, forestry accounted for about 0.3% of the general budgets of the Central Government and Automonous Communities for current expenditure and investment.

3.   MONETARY AND FISCAL POLICY

The monetary and fiscal incentives to private forestry are mostly contained in the Law on Forestry Development of 1977.

Grants for forestry operations are available to private forest owners as well as to others to whom the owners have ceded the use of their lands. The grants vary between 25% and 50% of the cost. The operations which qualify include: planting, thinning, pruning, construction and maintenance of roads and firebreaks, etc. Credits up to 90% of the total cost of an operation are available in addition to the grants.

As an alternative to the above aid, an owner may enter into an agreement with the Administration to undertake the work for him. In this case, half of the cost is written off as a grant while the other half must be repaid by the owner at the time of harvest. The interest charged on this loan is very low.

Fiscal incentives include complete exemption from the rural land tax for reforested areas and reduction of up to 95% on certain other taxes, including capital transfer tax inter vivos, provided that certain administrative and technical conditions are met.

The establishment of forest cooperatives and associations of forest owners is encouraged by means of credits and grants.

Taxes

For woodlands not exempt from the rural land tax, the rate at which it is levied varies greatly according to the site potential and tree species. A contribution to social security is levied in the form of a tax on "theoretical" labour input, even when no actual work has been done during a year. In addition, there are some para-fiscal measures, such as payments for licences and technical services supplied by the Administration. Finally, there is a tax on the value of produce extracted from private forests. This value is added to income from other sources for tax purposes. Where there is an income only every few years, the tax is levied only on the proportion applicable to the particular tax year.

One cannot say that forestry policy and fiscal policy are incompatible, but it is true that forestry problems could be treated with greater sensitivity, bearing in mind the non-economic benefits of forests. There is a case for reducing some taxes and abolishing others.

4. FOREST MANAGEMENT AND PROTECTION

Spain has one of the worst and most extensive erosion problems in Europe. The starting point for tackling these problems is an inventory of the erosion zones. An outline plan will then be prepared jointly by ICONA and the Autonomous Communities:

a)   quantifying what needs to be done
b)   defining priorities
c)   defining specific projects which will then be planned in
     detail.

Independent of these efforts is the continuing programme for combating desertification in the Mediterranean Region, "LUCDEME", for which south-western Spain is a pilot area.

The first principle of forest management is to assure the permanence of the resource. The second principle is to achieve a harmonious balance between the supply of products and of environmental and social services.

Forest destruction through grazing, fire and conversion to other use, which has been going on for centuries, continues to this day. Fires constitute the worst problem. Ninety-four percent are caused by man, many intentionally (e.g. to provide grazing). Forest administrations are hampered in their efforts to prevent fire damage by an insufficient network of roads and fire breaks and by a not entirely adequate legislation.

Pests and disease, while not neglible, are far less serious. Damage from aerial pollution is not widely spread at present.

The establishment of a school for forestry engineers, the creation of the "Guardería Forestal" and the preparation of a catalogue of forest land of public interest are the main achievements of the 19th Century. During the early part of the present century, various laws were passed and conservation measures were taken. In 1941, the State Forest Resources Law led to the reorganization of a part of the forestry administration and the implementation of the National Plan for Reforestation which had already previously been envisaged. The Plan provided for the planting of 6 M ha. in 100 years, the emphasis being on ecological considerations. The Administrations have since then planted 2.4 M ha., but the private sector, in spite of the various incentives, has only achieved 250,000 ha.

ICONA was created in 1971. The object was to place under a single management all plant and animal natural resources and to establish a coherent concept for their conservation and protection.

The new decentralized administrative structure, as well as other considerations, have necessitated a redefinition of objectives, including:

- a greater participation by private woodland owners and the general public

- improved living conditions for rural populations in disfavoured areas

- promotion of a better understanding of nature.

The Law 15/75 on Protected Areas establishes four kinds of areas:

- National Parks (122,700 ha.) which alone continue to be managed by ICONA;

- Integral Reserves which are smaller areas of exceptional scientific interest; there are 27 at present (11,600 ha.).

- Natural Places (Parajes Naturales) for the conservation of specific flora or other components of nature of great national interest; there are 74 of these (21,500 ha.).

- Nature Parks, which are intended to promote contacts between man and nature; there are 63 of these (159,100 ha.).

A new law, inspired by Article 45 of the Constitution, is being drafted in order to adapt exising legislation to the new administrative situation. Forest Recreation Areas consist of:

a) Forest Parks: usually large areas near towns where other aspects of forest management are subordinated to the provision of opportunities for recreation;

b) Specific recreation areas which consist of a "nucleus" and a "surrounding zone" which is influenced by the "nucleus" and the facilities provided there. The facilities depend on location and demand, e.g.:

* recreation parks for a high density of day visitors; these are well equipped with swimming pools, dressing rooms, restaurant or bar, toilets, children's play equipment, etc. Such parks can be self-financing;

* picnic sites;

* large and small campsites catering for stays of several days by various
  kinds of visitors (groups of young people, families, etc.).

Game management: here the policy is to do justice to the various aspects of
the subject: environmental, scientific, educational, hunting, protection of
endangered species. The responsibility for policy implementation rests with
the Autonomous Communities, but ICONA has retained a general coordinating and
supervisory role.

There are a number of national laws concerning hunting and the protection
of wild animals and there are also the international conventions to which
Spain is a signatory (Ramsar, Bonn, Washington, Bern).

Up to now, cooperatives and other rural organizations have played little
part in planning forest management, but this is to change under legislation
now being prepared.

There are considerable areas of land abandoned by agriculture after they
had become degraded. Afforestation of such areas is urgent.

The aim for the development of the economy in mountainous regions is to
achieve the right balance between agricultural and other activities. Forestry
plays an important part in this development.

5.   UTILIZATION

The level of harvest is based on the principle of sustained yield and is
determined by working plans or, in their absence, by annual plans. Most timber
is sold standing and is extracted mechanically by the purchaser. Animals are
not used for extraction. Transport is mainly by road. There are only a few
forest areas which are still inaccessible, but the road network in and around
forests is being improved and extended by the Forest Administrations in
collaboration with the forest owners.

The links between forestry and the sawmilling, panelboard and pulp
industries are close. Most enterprises buy direct from the growers and some
enterprises own woodlands themselves. Annual or longer term contracts for the
supply of wood are not uncommon; sometimes these contain an undertaking by the
purchaser to replant and manage woodlands.

Logging and sawmilling residues are utilized as much as possible for
pulping, manufacture of panel boards or fuel. Logging residues for which there
is no market are sometimes burned in situ.

There are various regional financial incentives for the installation, expansion or modernization of wood processing industries, but these will be superseded by Law No. 50/1985 concerning regional incentives to correct economic imbalances between regions. Low-interest loans are available under the Decision of the Council of Ministers of April 1983. Finally, the forestry sector can benefit from the Royal Decree 1492/1986 concerning the processing of agricultural and fishery products. All the above incentives will have to be made to conform with the relevant rules of the European Community now that Spain has become a member.

Wood processing industries are subject to the same taxation and legislation as all other industries.

The panelboard industry is working at about 90% capacity. Many mills have closed down in recent years and new ones are unlikely to be established in the near future. The pulp industry is working at almost 100% capacity but major new developments are unlikely, partly because of objections by surrounding populations and partly because of the very high capital costs involved.

With the exception of a few small local sawmills and furniture factories, there is no participation of rural organizations in the wood processing industries.

The main pollution problems are caused by the pulp industries. This explains the objections to new plants and to the maintenance of existing plants in areas frequented by tourists.

The interest in wood energy which began in the late 1970s has now declined with the reduction in the price of oil. Two approaches have been adopted to promote the use of logging and industrial wood residues for fuel: the first has been to subsidize the installations to burn chips; this approach has proved very successful in the major wood processing industries; the other approach has been directed towards the development of improved methods and machines to bring chips to the market. ICONA and various other organizations are involved in the implementation of these policies.

6. TIMBER TRADE AND MARKETS

Timber prices have always been free in Spain with the exception of some years after the war. They tend to be low because the numerous small woodland owners are less well organized and therefore in a weaker bargaining position than the buyers.

In 1984, apparent consumption of wood products was 14.5 M m3 (roundwood equivalent under bark) and production 11.6 M m3.

International trade is generally promoted by associations of importers and exporters for specific products and is based on the principle of a free market. There are no specific market regulations for wood except for the classification of forest products, which is in accordance with European norms. It is worth mentioning that new technologies have made it possible to replace tropical and other high quality timbers with less expensive timber.

Equally encouraging is the fact that, in recent years, Spain has been able to halve its trade deficit in the forest products sector.

7. EMPLOYMENT

Labour legislation and social security in forestry is the same as for agriculture. Both employers and employees contribute to the cost of social security. With certain exceptions, these contributions are less than in other sectors of the economy, but these differences are likely to decrease.

There is no general employment policy for the forestry sector. There have, however, been some specific measures. These have not generated more employment but have helped to maintain employment in existing projects. The main need for more jobs in forestry is to increase the number of posts in the "Guardería Forestal" from the present 4,600 to 6,600 in order to achieve more effective fire prevention and reduce working hours which far exceed legal limits.

Up to now, most workers employed in the forestry sector have been small woodland owners who have contracted to do this work in addition to their own. Because of unemployment in the building industry, the Administration would like to absorb these unemployed into forestry to the detriment of the small woodland owners, who have responded to this threat by getting themselves registered as umemployed so as to qualify for employment in forestry.

Most forestry labour is casual and not organized, but the general trade unions for industry and services have some members in the forestry sector.

Until 1980, earnings at all levels in the forestry sector were lower and working hours longer than in most other sectors of the economy, but this no longer applies. The costs of forest operations have risen accordingly.

8. EDUCATION

Forestry education is at three levels:

- Superior level: this education is given at the "Escuela Técnica Superior de Ingenieros de Montes" in Madrid. The new emphasis here is to place forestry into the broader context of society.

- Technical level: for training at this level, there are three "Escuelas Universitarias de Ingeniería Forestal" situated respectively at Madrid, Albacete and Huelva.

- Vocational level: Here there has been the greatest progress. Up to 10-15 years ago, candidates for entry into the 'Guardería Forestal' merely had to pass an elementary test in basic education. Now they have to undergo a two-year training course at special schools organized by the Autonomous Communities.

Forestry plays no part in general education except that attention is drawn in schools to certain matters such as forest fires.

9.   RESEARCH, EXTENSION, INFORMATION

Forestry research falls within the National Plan for Agricultural Research. Responsibility within the Central Administration rests with the "Instituto Nacional de Investigaciones Agrarias" (INIA), which is an autonomous body of the Ministry of Agriculture, Fisheries and Food. In the Autonomous Administrations, responsibility rests with the organs to which responsibility has been transferred.

The main objectives for forestry research in the above Plan are:

1.   Improvement of trade balance in the sector

     (e.g. by introduction of new species, forest genetics)

2.   Development and rationalization of production systems

     (e.g. ecology and economics of fast-growing species)

3.   Improvement of inputs

     (e.g. fertilization, better and less costly methods of propagation)

4.   Rationalization of processing and marketing

     (e.g. improved pulping technology, commercialization of aromatic and medicinal plants, improved sawmilling technology)

5.   Conservation and utilization of natural resources

     (e.g. studies of ecosystems, fire prevention including social aspects, prevention of desertification).

INIA undertakes both fundamental and applied research. The units of INIA which are primarily concerned with forestry are:

- silvipasture and forest management
- wood
- cork production and processing
- cellulose and extractive industries.

In some instances, there are agreements between INIA and other institutions for the conduct of forestry research projects. The research departments for wood and cellulose are in close contact with other Ministries on such matters as establishing technical norms for specified products.

INIA participates in the activities of IUFRO and other international research organizations relevant to forestry. Bilateral research agreements exist, among others, with the USA, France and the Federal Republic of Germany.

Most of the funding for forestry reseach comes from the general allocation to INIA from the general State Budget. These funds are supplemented in the case of some projects by finance and facilities from other sources, public or private.

The diffusion of research results is undertaken in various ways:

- INIA issues a series of scientific publications (communications, monographs, technical leaflets, etc.)

- the agricultural extension service publishes practical advice based on research results

- many of the results of forestry research are transmitted to practice by personal contact as well as through publications.

The responsibility for general publicity is divided between the Ministry of Agriculture, Fisheries and Food and the relevant authorities within the Autonomous Communities. Television programmes, practical summer vacation courses in the field, and lectures at schools of agriculture all play a part.

10. INTERNATIONAL COOPERATION

National policy for international cooperation in forestry is executed by ICONA through the External Service of the Ministry of Agriculture and the Directorate General for Technical Cooperation in the Ministry for Foreign Affairs. The main objectives are to:

- contribute towards the international prestige of Spain

- improve and update the technical knowledge within Spain

- contribute towards the development of other countries

- promote the export of Spanish technology, machinery and equipment

- participate in international decisions concerning the natural environment, its conservation and the use of its resources.

In principle, cooperation extends to all states, but relations are closest with countries in Latin America and with a few countries in Africa.

Through the Ministry of External Relations, ICONA also participates in the activities of the following international organizations; FAO and ECE and the various bodies connected with these organizations, Unesco, OECD, Council of Europe, IUFRO, CIC, CEA, European Federation of Agriculture, IUCN, WWF.

ICONA's budget provides for the costs of meetings and other obligations arising out of the membership of international organizations, while the Ministry of External Relations finances bilateral cooperation.

SWEDEN

1. INTRODUCTION

The total land area of Sweden is 411,500 km^2, of which 236,000 km^2 or about 57% are classed as forest.

Broadly speaking, Sweden has had three different historical developments:

In South Sweden, one hundred years ago, most of the land was still used for extensive agriculture. In Central Sweden, there was an early industrial development based on iron mining and manufacture. In most cases the iron ore companies also became big forest owners since they needed wood for charcoal burning. With increasing demand for forest products, there was a continuous transition from iron manufacturing towards forest industries. The new forest companies introduced "scientific forestry" in Sweden. In North Sweden, with its sparse population and infrastructure, the forests were largely inaccessible until the beginning of this century.

The ownership pattern which emerged from the historical development had stabilized already by 1900 and has remained largely unchanged since.

Forest area and ownership. Million hectares. (NFI 1980-84)

Region	State	Other public	Companies	Private	All
North Sweden	3.5	0.8	3.8	5.1	13.2
Central Sweden	0.6	0.6	1.5	2.7	5.4
South Sweden	0.4	0.4	0.3	3.9	5.0
All Sweden	4.5	1.8	5.6	11.7	23.6

The national forestry policy in Sweden has emerged as a result of a general democratic, evolutional process aimed at consensus solutions of all matters which are of basic national importance. Non-governmental organizations inside and outside the forest and forestry industry sector thus have had, and still have, a big influence on the development of forest policy.

The basic ideas behind the forest legislation can be summarized by the following two principles:

*   Land which is suitable for forestry and not used for agriculture or other more important uses (nature conservation included) should be used for forestry.

*   Forests and forest land should be managed in order to give a high, valuable and sustained yield of industrial timber. Environmental and other common interests should also be satisfied.

It is a basic principle in the Forestry Act that reasonable environmental consideration should be given by the forest owner, subject to the condition that such measures would not seriously hamper the existing land use: that is, production of industrial wood. If more far-reaching environmental restrictions are necessary, the owner could get full compensation for his economic losses or the land could be set aside as a nature reserve according to special regulations in the Nature Conservation Act. In this case, the land is bought by the National Environmental Protection Board. This is an expensive measure for the State, and the available funds are limited.

Non-governmental organizations for nature conservation and environmental protection consider that the present Forestry Act places insufficient emphasis on the objectives related to the environmental, scientific and aesthetic values of the forests.

2. ORGANIZATION AND ADMINISTRATION

2.1 Organization

The National Board of Forestry is the central authority for implementation of the national forestry policy. Its work is carried out with the help of 24 County Forestry Boards.

There is no central forest industry association. Each branch of the forestry industry thus has its own organization.

Since Swedish forest industry companies also own around 25% of the forest area in Sweden, it is natural that their associations play an important role in the development of national forestry policies.

The State itself is a big forest owner. Around 19% of the total forest area, predominantly in northern Sweden, is owned by the State. The National Forest Enterprises of Sweden (Domanverket) is in charge of the State forests under the Ministry of Industry. It works on a commercial basis similar to a private company and is an important supplier of wood, part of which goes to ASSI, a State forest industry company which owns some big forest industries, mostly in northern Sweden. The NFE (Domanverket) plays an important role in forestry policy development. It is of special relevance that the NFE is in charge of almost all high mountain forests including some national parks and other forests reserved for conservational reasons.

Traditionally, most private forest estates have been combined with agriculture. The pattern has changed, however, and today the majority of private forests are owned by others than farmers. The share of absentee owners, elderly owners and of multiple ownership is increasing rapidly. This development poses one of the most serious problems to forest policy.

The private forest owners are organized in 12 regional Forest Owners' Associations which aim at promoting the economic interests of the individual forest owner. These associations are united in the National Federation of Swedish Forest Owners. The Federation is a branch organization of the Swedish Agricultural Organization, and represents the private forest owners in forestry policy matters.

The labour unions related to forestry and forest industries are also important actors in forestry policy making. The Swedish Forest Workers' Union, the Swedish Wood Workers' Union and the Swedish Paper Workers' Union also cooperate with each other by developing a common forest policy for the three unions. They also engage in international cooperation within this field.

In addition, there is a large number of other organizations which play an important role in Swedish forestry.

2.2 Administration

All Swedish forests are subject to regulations of the Forestry Act under the supervision of the National Board of Forestry, which is situated in Jonkoping and is a central administrative authority under the jurisdiction of the Ministry of Agriculture. It is responsible for the practical implementation of the forest policy established by the Government and Parliament.

There are 24 County Forestry Boards, one in each of the 24 provinces. Normally, the provincial governor is chairman of the board. The board members are selected from amongst local politicians and forestry professionals with a renowned competence in forestry matters.

The County Forestry Boards carry out activities which are financed by public funds, but undertake also contractual services on a commercial basis.

The County Forestry Boards have a central organization corresponding to the departments of the National Board and a district organization. Almost all contacts with the individual forest owners are directed from the forestry districts.

The district organization is the core of the National Forestry Organization.

One important feature of the Swedish forestry administration is the National Forest Inventory. The first and second NFI were carried out in 1923-1929 and 1938-1952, respectively. The present NFI is an inventory covering the whole land area of Sweden every year. It is performed as a sample survey with low sampling fraction.

The Department of Forestry Survey is one of the departments within the Forestry Faculty of the Swedish University of Agricultural Sciences. The faculty is situated in Umea.

2.3 Importance of the Forestry Sector

A new production and consumption study which is now being published will be a basis for an aggregate description of the size of the sector.

An important part of that study consists of "cutting calculations" which aim at describing possible developments of the Swedish forests over the next 100 years (100 years is an average rotation period in Sweden). As part of the study, there are also aggregate cost and revenue calculations.

The extent and nature of public grants to forestry is a greatly disputed matter in Sweden.

3. MONETARY AND FISCAL POLICIES

3.1 General Background

There is a continuous discussion going on, aimed at finding means for better adaptation of monetary and fiscal policies to general forestry policies.

A basic problem is that private forestry in Sweden to a large extent is combined with agriculture, at least in legal and fiscal matters.

Much of the regulation system within agriculture therefore also influences the forestry sector. The purchase of agricultural and forest land, for instance, is regulated by law and is subject to restrictions which tend to conserve the present fragmented ownership structure.

3.2 The Taxation System and its Implications in Forestry

There are five types of public taxes which are of importance to a private forest enterprise:

Income taxes: there is a progressive State income tax and a proportional community income tax. Depending on the net taxable income, the income tax may range between 30 and 80% of the net taxable income.

In the case of a forest estate, the main principle is that the annual growth is considered as an income subject to taxation. The growth is, however, not taxable until there has been a corresponding sale of wood.

Capital gains taxes: Generally speaking, the tax system on capital gains is fairly generous. The capital gains taxes favour a management strategy based upon a high initial cutting level followed by an accumulation of growth to a large growing stock which is transferred to the next generation by inheritance or gift.

Property taxes: Real estate and other property form a basis for a
progressive property tax. In order to get a legal basis for valuation of
real estate, there is a periodical official valuation based on the
estimated market values. The expectation value of the net annual yield may
serve as a basis for these estimates.

The forest owner does not have to pay property tax for more than 20%
of the market value of his estate. The property tax system in combination
with the legal restrictions for purchase of agricultural and forest estates
tend to conserve the present fragmented ownership structure.

It seems that the low property taxes, rather than the high marginal
income taxes, are the basic reasons for the pronounced tendency of too low
cutting intensity within the private forest sector.

Silviculture tax: There is a specific deductable silviculture tax amounting
to 0.8% of the taxation value of forest property. The proceeds from this
tax are used to subsidise silvicultural measures and forest road building
in northern Sweden.

4.   FOREST MANAGEMENT AND PROTECTION

4.1   Forest Management

The main principles of forest management are laid down in the Forestry
Act. Basically, all prescriptions in the Forestry Act are formulated as
minimum requirements.

The strategy of the National Forest Organization is to implement the
national forestry policy as efficiently and cheaply as possible by an
optimal mix of legislation control and extension services, to some extent
complemented by State subsidies. The regional standwise general forest
inventory mentioned earlier is an extremely useful aid for an efficient
allocation of the efforts made with the different tools of forest policy.

4.2   The Recreational Environment

The common right of access to all forest land is an old tradition,
according to which nature is an asset for everyone. There are all kinds of
organized activities in the forests, ranging from walks through the parks
to wilderness hikes. Approximately 100 million litres of berries and 20
million litres of mushrooms are collected every year.

There are about 300,000 moose (Alces alces) in the winter population,
around 200,000 roe deer and 500 bears. There are also around 300,000
hunters in Sweden. Sport fishing may have a bigger recreational value than
hunting, but it is a lesser problem from the point of view of public
access.

4.3   Nature Conservation

There is a Nature Conservancy Act which contains detailed rules
pertaining to the protection and care of the natural environment. Around 5%
of the Swedish land area is subject to some type of formalized nature
protection.

The protected areas are under the supervision of the National Environmental Protection Board. The NFE (Domanverket) mostly administers the national parks and protected areas on State land. The County Forestry Boards mostly administer protected areas on private land.

4.4. Forest Protection

According to the Forestry Act, the forest owner has to undertake far-reaching measures for forest protection.

Forest fire damage is normally of minor importance. The biggest damage hazard in the Swedish forests is windbreak followed by insect invasion.

Preliminary findings from the NFI show that the damage from atmospheric pollution is not too serious at present, as far as visible effects on trees including their growth are concerned.

The creation of a special Ministry of the Environment stresses the Swedish determination to cope with the increasing threats to the natural environment.

5. FOREST UTILIZATION

5.1 Primary Production and Potential Cut

There are two ownership categories in the table below. State forests and company forests are shown together under the heading "Large" (large scale forestry). Private forests and public forests other than State are shown together under the heading "Small" (small scale forestry).

Potential cut according to "AVB 85" option
"Present forest policy and estimated fellings 1980-1984
according to the National Board of Forestry estimates
Million cu.m. inventories volume

	Large	Small	All
Potential cut	25.7	50.3	76.0
Fellings 1980-1984	23.1	39.3	62.4
Difference	+2.6	+11.0	+13.6

Around 75% of the actual felling volumes come from clear-cutting and only around 25% from thinning. As a long-term average, 30-35% of the total cut may come from thinnings.

5.2 Logging and Transport

The mechanization process started with clear-felling. A successful mechanization of thinning, satisfactory from both ecological and damage points of view, had a breakthrough in Sweden as recently as during the last 2-3 years.

Around one-third of the annual harvest on private land is carried out by the forest owners themselves or by their family, mostly by means of motor-manual methods.

Long distance transport of wood is an important aspect of forestry in Sweden. River floating had been a prerequisite for the development of forest industries in northern Sweden, but has been substituted by truck transport over the last 2-3 decades.

5.3 The Forest Industries

It is the Swedish forest industry which has given birth to forestry, rather than the opposite.

During the major part of this century, wood supplies have kept pace with industrial development without any episodes of shortage. At the beginning of the 'seventies, however, the wood balance situation became critical. At the end of the 'sixties, there was a drop in current increment and at the same time industrial demand rose very rapidly. This somewhat alarming situation led to legislation to control the further increase of wood consumption.

Forest industry consumes around 70 million cu.m. of inventoried volume per year, whilst the domestic supply is about 5 million cu.m. less. For this reason, there is an urgent national objective to increase fellings by around 5 million cu.m. per year, mainly by promoting a higher felling intensity amongst less active private forest owners.

The industrial debarking of sawlogs which was introduced during the 'sixties has enabled almost 100% of sawmilling residues to be transferred to other industrial use.

Within the pulp and paper industry, there has been a development of utmost importance: it is the introduction of closed circuit processes which drastically reduce effluence and emission as well as energy losses.

Research and development within the forest industry sector is carried out by the Swedish Forest Products Research Laboratory which was founded in 1942 and by the Swedish Wood Technology Centre, which was founded in 1984. Both institutes are so-called branch research institutes which are financed jointly by the industries concerned and the state on a fifty/fifty basis approximately.

The three big categories of forest owners, namely the forest companies, the State and the private forest owners, are also the owners of the forest industries.

5.4 Wood for Fuel

The consumption of wood for fuel reached a minimum level around 1975.
The oil crisis and efforts by the Government to decrease dependence on oil
then led to a rapid increase.

Out of the total current wood fuel consumption of 7.5 million cu.m.
per year, it is estimated that 3.1 million cu.m. is roundwood and the
remaining volume is forest residues.

The present low oil price has made wood less competitive as a fuel.
Environmental considerations which favour the burning of wood rather than
oil and coal, and the long-term decision by Parliament to phase out the use
of nuclear energy, makes it likely that the use of fuel for energy will
continue at an increased level. There are trials with short rotation
plantations of energy wood. If these develop successfully, such plantations
may, under optimal conditions, reach a level of around 100,000 ha. by the
year 2000.

6. TIMBER TRADE AND MARKETING

6.1 Organization of wood scaling

There are detailed regulations for scaling of softwood sawlogs and
pulpwood. More than 80% of all wood scaling is carried out by Timber
Measurement Associations formed by interested parties from the sellers' and
buyers' side. There is also a Swedish Board of Timber Measurement,
consisting of representatives of the buyers and sellers.

6.2 The Roundwood Market

The domestic supply of roundwood has been insufficient during recent
years. This situation motivated the inclusion of certain minimum cutting
rules in the Forestry Act with effect from 1983. It also led to increased
wood prices and to a shift from sales of roundwood delivered at the
roadside to sales of standing timber.

The new market situation has led to the creation of strong purchasing
companies owned by the pulp and paper industry. These companies now compete
successfully with the Forest Owners' Associations and with private sawmills
on the market.

7. EMPLOYMENT

The total number of employees in forestry and forest industries
amounts to around 190,000, of which 50,000 are in forestry, 80,000 in wood
working industries, and 60,000 in pulp, paper and paper products
industries.

From 1960 to 1985, the labour input decreased from 0.6 to 0.1 man-days
per cubic metre of harvested volume as an average for all logging and
silviculture work. A corresponding modernization and structural
concentration took place within the forest industries.

The policy of the Forest Workers' Union mostly has been to support mechanization and rationalization in return for better wages and more acceptable working conditions, but at the cost of a successive loss of members.

Silvicultural operations have offered suitable objects for relief work. In addition to relief work for occasionally unemployed people, forest relief work has been arranged for unemployed elderly forest workers with a decreased working capacity and to a certain extent also for individuals with drinking and drug problems.

Occupational safety is another important aspect of the employment policy. Around-the-year employment, good occupational education and efficient safety regulations and control have been the main approaches towards decreased occupational injuries.

9. FOREST RESEARCH, EDUCATION AND TRAINING

9.1 Administration

On 1 July 1977, the College of Agriculture, the College of Forestry, the Veterinary College, the School for Forest Engineers and some institutes merged to become the Swedish University of Agricultural Sciences. Today, the Forest Institutes at Bispgarden and Varnamo also belong to this university. This means that the University is responsible for professional forestry education at all levels and also for further education at the respective levels. Courses for further education are also arranged by the National Board of Forestry and others. Around 85% of the budget of the Faculty of Forestry is spent on research and around 15% on education.

There are also so-called branch research institutes within the forest and forest industry sector, namely the Institute for Forest Improvement, the Forest Operations Institute, the Swedish Forest Products Research Laboratory and the Wood Technology Centre. At the Stockholm Institute of Technology for the education of professional engineers, there is also a Department of Wood Technology.

9.2 Forestry Education

The forestry education system may be summarized as follows:

Forest workers: After 9 years of compulsory comprehensive schooling, it is possible for a student to take a special course in forestry of 40 weeks' duration which gives basic training in forest work with special emphasis on work safety.

Forest technicians: A degree in forest technology may be obtained at one of three Forestry Institutes located in Varnamo, Skinskatteberg and Bispgarden. A future technician has a basic and occupational education which amounts to 13 years in total. In addition, one year of vocational training is compulsory as an entrance qualification to the Forest Institutes.

Forest engineers: As indicated by the name, the Institute of Forest Engineers lays emphasis on forest technology and forest operations and less emphasis on forest biology.

Forest officers: The Faculty of Forestry provides a basic degree in forestry after 4 1/2 years of university studies. It is a general rule in Sweden that universities should be open to everyone with certain general qualifications for university studies, regardless of previous formal education.

The Faculty of Forestry not only prepares students for a career in forestry but also for other tasks where the combination of biological, technical and economic competence is essential (for example nature conservation, community planning, assistance to developing countries and research).

9.3 Forestry Research, Extension and Information

The Swedish University of Agricultural Science has the main responsibility for forestry research. Direct allocations from the State only cover just over half of the total budget. The remaining part comes from research funds or from other sources which are funding certain research projects on the basis of contractual agreements.

The research within the University is divided into five big research programme sectors which are governed by research committees. These committees are mostly chaired by the head of the research department which dominates the programme sector. Research workers from related research departments and representatives of the forestry sector outside the university are members of the committees.

This arrangement aims at involving the consumers of forestry research in the research planning and promoting interdisciplinary research programmes.

It would not be fair to say that all expectations related to the creation of research committees have been fulfilled. The departmental boundaries are often of barrier-type and the State policy for fund allocation has not favoured the system either.

The State's funding of forestry research has a tendency to become more and more directed towards transferring money by means of research foundations. This system has some advantages in that the research foundations can buy "urgent" research projects from the institutions. A disadvantage is that what is "urgent" research tends to vary rapidly in time.

The dissemination of research results is an important aspect of forestry research in Sweden. In accordance with its arrangements for programme-bound forestry research, the university arranges a public two-day research seminar every autumn.

The big forest enterprises, the forest associations and the National Forestry Organization have research specialists who are the direct consumers of research results. They digest these results and are responsible for further dissemination and extension.

10. INTERNATIONAL COOPERATION

   Participation in development work within international organizations
related to forestry as well as bilateral efforts within the forestry sector
are aimed at supporting agreed objectives within the international and
national communities. "Sustainable development" according to the
definition by the Brundtland Commission may serve as a concentrated
description of these objectives.

   Swedish participation in UN-related agencies is coordinated by the
Ministry of Foreign Affairs. FAO-related activities are supervised by the
Ministry of Agriculture; ECE-related activites are under the Ministry of
Industry; and UNCTAD-related activities such as participation in the
International Tropical Timber Organization are under the Department of
Commerce of the Ministry of Foreign Affairs.

   The Swedish International Development Agency (SIDA), under the
Ministry of Foreign Affairs, is the executive agency for the major part of
Swedish bilateral and multilateral support to developing countries. Since
Sweden has a well-developed forestry sector it has been found feasible to
allocate a fairly large proportion of the total aid to that sector.
Besides bilateral programmes within countries such as India, Vietnam,
Tanzania, Ethiopia and Laos, substantial support has been given to FAO's
forestry programme for rural community development.

   Although there is a specialized agency for research cooperation with
developing countries, "SAREC", there have been so far very few research
projects related to forestry. This is mainly a sign of the fact that there
are very few and weak research organizations within the countries which
have been selected as main countries for Swedish development support. It
is expected that SAREC's support to the forestry sector will increase.

   The Swedish University of Agricultural Sciences takes part in
international forestry research via IUFRO. In addition, there has long
existed organized and formalized research cooperation within the Nordic
countries: Denmark, Finland, Iceland, Norway and Sweden. One way of
cooperation is a frequent exchange of research workers on the basis of a
common labour market.

   A basic pattern of international cooperation within the forestry
sector is the arrangement of ad hoc study tours to and from Sweden on a
bilateral basis. The National Board of Forestry, the Swedish University of
Agricultural Sciences, the National Forest Enterprises of Sweden, the
National Federation of Swedish Forest Owners and even the labour unions
related to forestry frequently arrange or take part in such study tours.

   Exchange visits are mainly with the Federal Republic of Germany, USA,
Canada, USSR, UK and France. The threat to the forests attributed to
airborne pollution has led to more intensified cooperation than hitherto
with some countries, notably the Federal Republic of Germany.

   Within the framework of international cooperation, the forest
industries of Western Europe must become more closely integrated and
dependent on each other. Swedish private forest companies should thus
enter into partnerships with forest industries in the EEC countries and
vice versa. Development of such partnerships would also lead to
cooperation within the forestry sector.

SWITZERLAND

1. <u>INTRODUCTION</u>

The total area of Switzerland is about 4.1 million ha.; forests occupy 1.2 million ha. (28.7%), of which 1.04 million ha. are classed as productive. Eighty percent of the forests are in the mountains.

Forest structure is as follows:

Managed high forest	58%
Selection forest	17%
Coppice (chestnut groves, etc.)	17%
Other (inaccessible, scrub)	8%

Seventy-three percent of the volume of the growing stock consists of conifers (spruce, larch, silver fir, pines) and 27% consists of broadleaved species (beech, sweet chestnut, oak, ash, sycamore).

The health of the forests in Switzerland has given rise to grave concern in recent years. Several causes have been known for a long time. They include forest grazing, fire, insect pests, abnormal weather, game damage and lack of silvicultural treatment. In recent years, air pollution has also resulted in a reduction of vigour in forests all over the country. The most recent inventory of damage conducted under the "Sanasilva" programme shows that, in 1986, 50% of the trees in Switzerland showed signs of damage. This compares with 34% in previous years. The proportion of damaged conifers (52%) is slightly greater than that of broadleaves (45%), but the difference is getting less. The proportion of damaged trees is particularly high in the Alps (60%) and south of the Alps (65%).

Seventy-four percent of all forests (871,000 ha.) are publicly owned, mainly by small communes of various kinds. Only some 6% of the total forest area is owned by the Federation and the cantons. There are 3,725 public owners.

The 26% (313,000 ha.) of private forests are divided among 252,000 owners, giving an average of only 1.2 ha. per owner. Over 90% of all private forest properties are under 10 ha. in extent.

The economic situation of forestry is becoming increasingly difficult and there are more and more forest owners who find that the income from the forest no longer covers expenditure. The consequences vary according to the circumstances of the owners. There is a risk that the level of management will suffer over very large areas, especially in the mountains.

2. THE INSTITUTIONAL FRAMEWORK OF FOREST POLICY

Forestry in Switzerland is extremely decentralized. The Constitution of the Federation (in Article 24) reserves to the Federal Government only very limited rights in forestry matters. The main legislative authority lies with the cantons, which are thus in a position to take account of regional differences and the particular circumstances of each canton.

The main forestry policy objectives at federal level may be summarized as follows:

- the conservation of the total area under forest and its general distribution;

- the development of the multiple functions of the forest;

- the promotion of measures for the protection of the countryside against natural disasters.

In recent years, Parliament as a whole, as well as the forestry group in Parliament, and many individual members have devoted much of their time to seeking solutions to the varied and complex problems associated with the protection of the environment, the fight against atmospheric pollution and forest decline. They have also drawn attention to the economic and structural difficulties of forestry enterprises and the wood economy. The emphasis in the statements by Members of Parliament has been on the interdependence of the problems facing the environment and forests. Several of the motions put forward have been adopted and have led to specific actions by the Government.

At federal level, the responsibility for forestry policy rests with the Ministry of the Interior. Since 1986, the forestry service in this ministry has also been given the responsibility of protecting the countryside. The forest service is now sub-divided into two main divisions: one is concerned with forest conservation and hunting, while the second deals mainly with the protection of the countryside and its use for recreational purposes. In addition, there are the administrative secretariat, the legal service, the press and information service and the institute for the study of snow and avalanches. The service employs a staff of 50 and the budget is of the order of 127 million SFR, of which 110 million are federal subsidies, 7 million investment credits and 4 million are for the institute for the study of snow and avalanches. The budget has been increased significantly since 1984, when it was 78 million SFR, and further increases are envisaged.

Also the political institutions of each canton have within their competence important decisions on forestry policy in such matters as the issue of regulations, the organization of personnel, budgetary affairs and the level of cantonal subsidies to forestry.

The forestry organization in the cantons generally operates at three
levels: the inspectorate of forests under the head of the department
responsible, regional offices to ensure territorial coverage, and the
forestry districts which constitute the operational units. The framework of
this organization is fixed by federal law.

The main local institutions concerned with forestry are the political
communes. Their role derives from their authority in land use planning and
from their ownership of forests. They are also often associated with the
management of other forests in common ownerships of various kinds (e.g. the
so-called bourgeoisies). The role of local institutions in matters of
forestry policy has hitherto been very limited but is likely to increase.

Other institutions and organizations which influence forestry policy
include:

-   the political parties at both federal and cantonal level, which in
    recent years have given their particular attention to
    environmental problems;

-   the organizations concerned with forestry and forest industries;

-   the associations for the protection of nature and the environment,
    which are playing an increasingly important role.

There are two main forestry associations, one representing the forest
owners and the other mainly the forestry personnel. In the forest industry
sector, there are a large number of professional organizations, most of
which represent particular sectors of the industry. Their activities are
coordinated by the Swiss Timber Committee.

At federal level, the Timber Forum acts as an advisory body to the
Department of the Interior. It comprises representatives of the different
sectors of forestry and forest industry as well as other relevant
interests. There are also several other advisory bodies associated with the
Federal Office for Forestry and Protection of the Countryside. Coordination
between cantons among themselves and between cantons and the Federation has
been placed on a formal footing by conferences of the authorities
concerned.

Government policy directives which are adopted by the Federal Council
and submitted to Parliament at the beginning of each legislature ensure
that forestry policy is integrated into the totality of government
measures.

The annual and longer term budgets of the Conferation also have a
decisive influence on the implementation of national forestry policy. In
1987, the various forestry programmes accounted for about 0.5% of the
federal budget of 22.4 bn SFR.

At cantonal level, forestry is integrated into general policy in a
similar way.

3. FORESTRY LEGISLATION

Federal legislation in forestry provides the framework for the more detailed forestry laws and decrees enacted by each canton. The cantons are also responsible for implementing most of the federal and all of the cantonal legislation. The competences and duties of the Federation in forestry matters are defined in the Forestry Act of 1902 and its subsequent amplifications and revisions. This legislation contains rules for maintaining the forest cover and protecting the forests; it also covers the organization of the cantonal forest services, but the various kinds of federal subsidies to forestry are only covered in a very general way in federal legislation.

Some cantons have gone much farther than others in amplifying federal forestry legislation.

During the past two decades, a number of studies and commissions have demonstrated the need for a revision of the federal forestry legislation. Several discussions in Parliament have also been devoted to the subject. In compliance with the mandate of the extraordinary session of Parliament in 1985, the Federal Council decided that the revision of the Forest Law should be treated separately from more general and complex proposals on the division of duties between the Confederation and the cantons.

This decision has speeded up the revision. The draft of a new Forest Law was drawn up by the department responsible and, in the second half of 1986, the Federal Council circulated it for comment to the cantonal governents and a large group of interested organizations.

The proposed new law is much more specific than the existing law and sets out its objectives in more detail as follows in a new section:

- the maintenance of the area under forest and its regional distribution;

- the protection of the forest as an aggregate of ecosystems and as a safeguard of the landscape against damage by natural causes and by man;

- the maintenance and development of all the functions of the forest especially its protective function against natural dangers, its recreational function for the population and its function to produce wood;

- the maintenance of sustained management of forests which are stable, diverse and protective;

- the promotion of a viable forest economy.

- 235 -

This section refers also specifically to the protection against
avalanches and other calamities and underlines the close relationship in
mountainous areas between maintaining the forest cover and other protective
measures.

During the preparation of the draft law, certain points of particular
importance to the evolution of forest policy became apparent, for example:

-   the fundamental importance of forests, especially in the
    mountains;

-   the difficulty of finding a legal definition of forest cover in
    view of the dynamic evolution of natural vegetation;

-   the need for a clear distinction between compensation paid to
    forest owners for services rendered in the public interest, and
    financial aid given to the owners to ease their financial
    difficulties.

4. FOREST PROTECTION AND MANAGEMENT

The main factors to be considered are:

-   the importance of forests, which has already been mentioned;

-   income from forests no longer suffices to cover the cost of
    management, so that forest owners depend more and more on
    financial support; in fact, forests will only be able to survive
    if society accepts the responsibility for their protection and
    management.

Conversion of forest to other use is only permitted in quite
exceptional circumstances if conversion is in the national interest and if
the purpose of the clearance cannot be achieved elsewhere. Financial
considerations do not influence the decisions. If a clearance of forest is
authorized, then an area of similar size must be afforested in the same
region. The maintenance of these restrictions is considered essential.

Some important measures to reduce aerial pollution have already been
taken. They include:

-   the prohibition of importing and selling petrol containing lead
    (1985 and 1986);

-   the application of car exhaust norms corresponding to those
    adopted in the USA;

-   the annual control of car exhausts;

-   the reduction in the level of customs duties on lead-free petrol;

-   a speed limit of 120 km/hour on motorways and of 80 km/hour on
    other roads.

Some other measures have also been taken to limit or reduce industrial and urban pollution.

In 1986, the Federal Council stated its objective to bring about a reduction of total pollution in Switzerland to the levels of 1960 by the year 1995. This can be achieved by the measures already taken, but supplementary measures are being considered to speed up the reduction.

The minimum norms of forest management laid down in federal legislation for public forests are more stringent than for private forests, for which the main restriction is the prohibition of clear fellings. The relationship between the production of timber and the essential service functions of the forest is being reconsidered; the aim is to arrive at a new balance between the responsibilities of the community at large and the forest owners. A larger contribution from public funds is considered essential.

The main federal measures in support of forestry are the following:

- Article 42 of the Forest Law provides in a general way for the support of reforestation, control of torrents and improvement of forest infrastructures;

- Article 42 bis deals more specifically with the protection of forests and other land threatened by avalanches, landslides and falling rocks;

- the urgent federal decision of 4 May 1984 concerning temporary silvicultural measures to prevent and combat extraordinary losses to forests caused by pests, disease and pollution, and to repair the damage;

- measures adopted in 1986 as a result of a motion of Parliament and in accordance with Article 42 bis of the Forest Law to take the necessary silvicultural measures to restructure the protection forests in the mountains.

In 1987, the budget of the Federal Forest Service for financial support measures for forestry was as follows:

Protection against avalanches	26 million SFR
Reforestation	13 million SFR
Combating losses from pests, diseases, etc.	19 million SFR
Construction of forest roads and land consolidation in private forests	35 million SFR
Total	94 million SFR

To these amounts must be added the funds made available in the budgets of other services; these include 7 million SFR for protective measures along roads and 24 million SFR for combating losses.

The approval of federal support for forestry is made dependent upon a contribution from the cantons, which is commensurate with their financial resources; the cantonal contributions are over and above the federal support. The total funds available for forest conservation and the improvement of infrastructures are thus considerable.

The policy on forest protection forms part of more general legislation, e.g.

- the federal law of 7 October 1983 on the protection of the environment;

- the federal law of 22 June 1979 on land use

- the ordinance of 22 March 1986 on land use

- the federal law of 1 July 1966 concerning the protection of nature and landscape and the executive ordinance relating to it;

- the federal law of 20 June 1986 on hunting and the protection of mammals and birds.

5.   PRODUCTION AND UTILIZATION

Production, which has fluctuated widely between 3.3 million and 4.6 million m3/year in recent years, was 4.2 million m3 in 1986. Two-thirds of the production comes from publicly owned forests and one-third from those which are privately owned. Conifers account for 70% and broadleaved species for 30% of the annual harvest. The pattern of utilization is as follows:

Saw logs	65%
Other industrial wood	20%
Firewood	15%

	100%

Consumption (in roundwood equivalent) sank from over 6 million m3/year during 1970-74 to only 4.5 million m3 in 1976, and has since then gradually risen to reach 7 million m3 in 1986.

Exports and imports have also fluctuated considerably. In 1986, exports amounted to 2.7 million m3 roundwood equivalent, of which 670,000 m3 were actually of roundwood, while imports were 5.8 million m3 roundwood equivalent. National production now covers 58% of consumption in volume terms.

The number of forest industrial establishments decreased from 12,500 in 1975 to 10,600 in 1985, while the number of people employed increased slightly from 81,500 to 83,000 during the same period. Over 90% of the enterprises have fewer than 20 employees, and only 2% have over 50.

The total value added by the industry at the average market prices ruling between 1980 and 1984 is estimated at 3.5 bn SFR per year. To this must be added around 600 million SFR in respect of the manufacture of paper and board, giving a total of a little over 4 bn SFR, which is about 2% of the gross domestic product.

In its report of 1985, the Timber Forum identified the following main difficulties which confront the industry:

-   the unsatisfactory condition of the forest;

-   insufficient knowledge of the markets;

-   problems of the roundwood market;

-   problems of the markets for primary and final products.

To counter and resolve these difficulties, the Timber Forum has proposed a series of ordinary and extraordinary measures involving all parties concerned: the Confederation, the cantons, the communes, the enterprises and the professional organizations.

The ordinary measures include the following:

-   the enterprises must invest in equipment, marketing and training;

-   timber growers must be able to ensure regular supplies which should gradually rise to the full sustainable yield potential of the forests.

The additional extraordinary measures which may be required depend on such factors as catastrophic damage to forests in Switzerland or abroad.

The Confederation has adopted a major programme to promote the use of wood, with a budget of 17 million SR for the period 1986-91. The programme covers the use of wood in construction, the manufacture of furniture, the packaging industry, the classification of produce at each stage from forest to final product, wood as a source of energy, business management, advertising and refresher courses for personnel.

6. EDUCATION AND TRAINING

For forest workers, a three-year training schedule has been introduced throughout the country. It consists of an apprenticeship interspersed with short specialized courses. In 1985, 340 candidates passed the final tests and received their certificates. The main objectives of the scheme are:

- gradually to replace temporary workers, whose numbers are decreasing, with permanent forest workers;

- adequate training for the increasingly complex and advanced methods used in forest operations;

- improvement of the social status of the workers.

These objectives have hitherto only partially been achieved, more than half of the workers trained having left to take up work elsewhere. Insufficient remuneration in relation to the qualifications and working conditions, and insufficient opportunities for further training to qualify for higher posts are quoted as the main reason for the exodus. These matters require further consideration.

Forest guards are trained at two technical forestry schools, one at Maienfeld founded in 1966, and the other at Lyss founded in 1969. To qualify for admission, candidates must have the forest worker's certificate plus two years' experience. The course lasts for one year. A total of about 60 candidates qualify as forest guards each year and that suffices to meet demand. However, there are great differences between cantons. These differences are due mainly to insufficient flexibility of forest owners and to a lack of mobility of some candidates.

The responsibility for training forest engineers rests with the Forest Service and with the Institute for Forest and Timber Research at the Eidgenossische Technische Hochschule (ETH) in Zurich, where most of the four-year course is common to all students, but provision for some specialization is made in the final year. Between the third and fourth year, the students have a practical period in the field, organized by the Federal Forest Service in close collaboration with the ETH. About 30 students graduate each year.

There is a need to maintain professional standards at all levels by means of refresher courses. At present, such courses are offered by a variety of organizations, especially the cantonal forest services, the technical schools and the Central Forest Service. What is missing is an overall framework to ensure that all needs are met efficiently and on a continuing basis. Proposals to meet this objective are at present being worked out by a working group set up by the Conference of Cantonal Inspectors and the Federal Forest Service.

Training in the various branches of wood processing is regulated by the Federal Law of 1980. The technical content of the various training programmes is determined by the relevant professional associations. At the level of specialized workers and foremen, the training is achieved by a combination of apprenticeships within the enterprise and theoretical and practical courses at the School of Wood Technology at Bienne.

Overall, forest industrial training at the practical level has been satisfactory in all branches of the industry, but there have been deficiencies at the technical and higher levels. These deficiencies are, however, being rapidly rectified by new courses at the School of Wood Technology at Bienne and at the ETH.

The school at Bienne started in 1986 with the training of engineers in the use of wood in construction and in business management. The ETH in Zurich introduced a postgraduate course in 1987 covering the technological and economic aspects of the structural uses of wood. A similar postgraduate course was introduced in 1987 at the Ecole Polytechnique Fédérale at Lausanne.

7.   RESEARCH

The Federal Forestry Research Institute is an organization attached to the Council of the Federal Polytechnical Institutes. It comprises research divisions on: forestry techniques and land use; national forest inventory; torrent control and hydrology. The Institute is the principal organ of applied forestry research in Switzerland and also plays an important role in designing and coordinating national programmes.

The Institute of Forestry and Wood Technology Research at the ETH in Zurich also carries out numerous research programmes, especially in forest botany, soil physics, silviculture, forest road construction and forest engineering, forest management, economics and policy.

The main institutions concerned with wood research are: the faculties of wood technology and timber construction at the federal polytechnical institutes at Zurich and Lausanne, which have already been mentionied, and the wood section of the federal laboratory for material testing and the Research Institute for Industry, Civil Engineering and Structures.

Several national research programmes under the aegis of the National Swiss Foundation for Scientific Research have included research directly or indirectly concerned wih forestry and wood technology, e.g. with the problems of regional development in Switzerland or with Switzerland's participation in Unesco's programme on Man and the Biosphere. The programme SANASILVA, managed by the Federal Forest Service and the Federal Forestry Research Institute, involves the participation of numerous institutions and the cantonal forestry services. Its main aim is to support the efforts of forestry practice at all levels to combat the consequences of forest decline and to coordinate the multiplicity of relevant activities.

8. INTERNATIONAL COOPERATION

The Ministry of Foreign Affairs, as well as other federal government departments and the professional representatives of the forestry sector, collaborate actively with numerous international organizations concerned with forestry, timber, the environment and the protection of nature. For forestry, the main international organizations with which Switzerland collaborates are: the ECE Timber Committee, FAO's European Forestry Commission, the forestry working group of the CEA (Comité Européenne d'Agriculture) and IUFRO. In matters of nature conservation, Switzerland is heavily involved with the IUCN (International Union for the Conservation of Nature) and with the specialist committees of the Council of Europe and of Unesco. Switzerland has also signed various international conventions on nature conservation and has recently participated very actively in a number of international conferences on environmental problems.

Development aid to the third world is the concern of various governmental and other organizations. Aid in the forestry sector has increased significantly in recent years and the Directorate of Development Cooperation and Humanitarian Aid in the Ministry of Foreign Affairs now finances some 30 forestry projects as well as several others with a forestry component.

Forestry aid is concentrated on three aspects of development: training and applied research, management of the natural forest, and community forestry.

The guiding principles underlying the programmes are: the socio-economic integration of forestry measures into rural development as a whole, the participation of the rural population and the planning of natural resource management on a long-term basis.

TURKEY

1. INTRODUCTION

Twenty-six percent of Turkey is covered by forests. This area corresponds to 20.2 million ha., of which 8.9 million ha. are covered with productive and 11.3 million ha. with unproductive forest.

Distribution of forest areas is shown in the table below.

Forest Areas According to Form of Exploitation (in 1,000,000 ha.)

Quality	High Forest				Coppice Quality	Forest Area	%
	Conifer	Broad-leaved	Mixed	Total			
Productive	4.6	1.0	0.6	6.2	(1) 2.7	8.9	44
Unproductive	3.9	0.5	0.3	4.7	(2) 6.6	11.3	56
Total	8.5	1.5	0.9	10.9	Total 9.3	20.2	100

(1) Cutting arrangement
(2) Area allocated for plantation

There are 17,000 villages inside and in the vicinity of forests, in which 9.4 million villagers live. The income level of these villagers is low and social pressures by them on forests is high.

For this reason, especially great importance has been given to policies concerning the protection, improvement and enlargement of such forests.

The main principle of Turkish forestry, however, is to meet the demand of the forest industries.

Technical and scientific forestry began in 1937, when Forest Law No. 3116 was enacted. In this law, the idea of State ownership and State exploitation was dominant and authority was given to the State to impose strict controls on the forests belonging to the private sector also.

With the enactment of Law No. 4785 in 1945, the bulk of the private forest was expropriated. People reacted against this expropriation, and many forests were destroyed by forest fires, grazing and illegal cuttings.

In order to placate those concerned, some of the forest areas expropriated were handed back to the private sector with the enactment of Law No. 5653. Under this law, some areas covered with maquis which had previously been classed as forest were excluded from that definition.

With the enactment of Forest Law No. 6831, the national park concept, which aims to increase social and cultural benefits of the forest, has been accepted.

Law No. 3302, put into effect on 19.6.1986, changed some articles of Forest Law No. 6831 and made some principal changes to the procedure of forest cadastral activities. The cadastral commission, which consists of two forest engineers, one agricultural engineer, one member of the municipality board, one person from the village and one person from the local association of farmers, was established.

2. ADMINISTRATION

In Turkey, almost all forests are managed by the State. This task has been entrusted to the General Directorate of Forestry, which works under the Ministry of Agriculture, Forestry and Rural Affairs by laws.

The duties and responsibilities of the General Directorate of Forestry are set out in Law No. 3234. They include the following provisions:

(1)   To protect the forests against illegal cuttings, natural disasters, fires and various other types of damage;

(2)   To manage and exploit the forests;

(3)   To improve the forests;

(4)   To create new forests;

(5)   To preserve, protect and manage the national parks, natural parks, natural monuments, recreational areas and other areas that should be protected, and to protect, develop and manage hunting and wildlife resources;

(6)   To manage matters arising from forest cadastral and ownership problems;

(7)   To organize initial and on-the-job training;

(8)   To prepare projects on research;

(9)   To prepare annual work plans for forest villages in cooperation with the General Directorate of Organization and Support;

(10) To prepare road networks and surveys for production, plantation, fire control, etc.

Influences which affect the preparation of national forestry policies may be summarized as follows:

1. The aims of forestry policy and measures which help the aims to be realized are largely determined by the constitution enacted in 1982, Forest Law No. 6831 and the Five-Year Development Plans.

2. There are 9.4 million villagers living in 17,000 villages located inside and in the vicinity of forests. These villagers believe that husbandry and livestock activities inside the forest do not damage forests. These views are taken into consideration in the preparation of legislation relating to forestry policy.

The Institutions which play a role in the formulation and implementation of forestry policies are:

1 - Legislative Body

According to the Constitution, the Turkish Grand National Assembly has the right to make forest law and policies related to forestry.

2 - Consultative Body

The highest ranking consultancy body in the State is the Council of State.

3 - Executive Body

According to Article 119 of Forest Law No. 6831, the implementation of the law has been entrusted to the Cabinet. With the enactment of Law No. 2384 which has been effective since 31.2.1981, the implementation of the law has been vested in the Ministry of Agriculture, Forestry and Rural Affairs on behalf of the Cabinet. In the Ministry, the duties relating to forest activities have been carried out by the General Directorate of Forestry.

In addition, the Ministry of Finance and Customs, Ministry of National Education, Youth and Sport, Ministry of Culture and Tourism, Ministry of Industry and Trade, Ministry of Transportation, Ministry of the Interior and Ministry of Defence have important roles.

4 - Technical Bodies

These include professional associations and associations concerned with nature conservation.

5 - <u>Scientific Institutions</u>

These are universities, especially faculties of forestry, agriculture and veterinary science.

<u>Budget</u>

The Budget of the Generate Directorate of Forestry is about 4% of the General Budget each year.

3.   FINANCIAL POLICIES

<u>Private Forests</u>

General financial policies are applied to private forests as well.

In addition, some new arrangements have been made to encourage the development and enlargement of private forests.

Credits at a similar rate of interest as for agriculture (30-34%) have been made available by the Agricultural Bank for private reforestation, but this rate of interest is too high to encourage private reforestation. In order to solve this problem, some arrangements have now been made to provide credit without interest through the Agricultural Bank and to establish a Foundation for Reforestation.

Technical assistance for the preparation of plans and projects, as well as seed and seedlings, are provided free of charge for private reforestation. Private forest roads necessary for transportation and protection measures are also provided by the State.

Despite all encouragements, however, the private sector has not generally given priority to investment in forestry.

<u>Tax System in Forestry</u>

Building and land taxes are not collected from private forests for 50 years after they are established, but income tax is collected on the profits from exploitation. The income tax for private forests is equal to the income tax for agricultural activities.

It has been accepted that some further amendments concerning financial regulations have to be made.

4.   PLANNING OF LAND USE

In Turkey, there are 19.3 million ha. of class I, II, and III lands (24.9% of total area) which are suitable for agriculture. 7.2 million ha. of class IV lands (9.3% of total area) are suitable for agriculture provided that appropriate protection measures are taken. 50 million ha. of class V, VI and VII lands (64.5% of total area) which are suitable for forestry and pasture and must be covered with vegetation, are not suitable for agricultural activities.

Nevertheless, 6.1 million ha. of class V, VI, and VII areas have been cultivated for agricultural purposes. Some class VI and VII areas in particular suffer from serious erosion when opened to agricultural activities.

The General Directorate of Forestry has been endeavouring to convert unproductive forest areas into productive forest by planting.

Protection of Forest Resources

Illegal fellings and forest fires are the most important harmful factor; according to statistics 1% of forest fires are caused by lightning, and 99% by human beings. 40% of forest fires which are caused by human beings are intentional. In order to decrease forest fires, the 5th Five-Year Plan provides for:

1 -   Educational and informational programmes about forest fires;

2 -   Measures to get accurate and speedy information about changing weather conditions in the sensitive areas for forest fires;

3 -   Improvements in the communication system;

4 -   Construction of fire breaks and fire safety roads;

5 -   Use of helicopters and aircraft to fight forest fires.

Protection of Forests and National Parks

The basis for the rules governing the selection, management and improvement of nature parks and national parks of international and national interest was provided by National Park Law No. 2873 of August 1983. Regulations relating to this law were put into effect by publication in Official Gazette No. 19309 on 12 December 1986.

The duties connected with the above have been carried out by the General Directorate of Forestry.

The duties of designating and managing the protected forest are also carried out by the G.D.F.

Protected Forests have also been established for scientific purposes, for the protection of nature, improving the landscape, for various sporting activities and for recreation for the public and tourists.

Protected areas are classified in 5 categories, which are as follows:

- National park

- Nature park

- Nature monument

- Nature protection areas, and

- Protected forests.

The rapid rise in population and social changes increased the migration from the rural areas to city centres; this resulted in illegal settlements and insufficient parks and recreation areas in cities. It also increased the need for rural green areas and forest near cities.

Because of this, suitable areas in our forest are designated and managed as forest recreation areas by the General Directorate of Forestry.

Forest recreation areas are classified in three categories:

Type A: areas that contain camping facilities and have a high visitor potential;

Type B: areas that contain only adequate facilities for day visits and have a high visitor potential;

Type C: areas established for day visits to serve local needs.

Hunting and wildlife resources, besides having very important functions in the balance of nature, also have great importance in meeting the needs for protein. In addition, wildlife management and hunting serve recreational, scientific and sporting objectives.

The activities regarding hunting and wildlife are considered in two categories:

A - Protection of species

B - Protection of areas.

According to the Law of Land Hunting, No. 3167, the Central Hunting Commission decides on the protection, reproduction and regulation of game and wild animals in meetings held every year. In the perspective of these decisions, the species protection activities of hunting and wildlife are carried out by the General Directorate of Forestry.

Activities relating to the protection of areas carried out by the General Directorate of Forestry are as follows:

1. The establishment of game protection and reproduction areas: The endangered populations of game and wild animals in established game protection and reproduction areas have been protected by their environments to date.

2. Twenty-eight game reproduction stations have been established for endangered species of game and wild animals to date.

Development of the Mountain Economy

According to the statistics of 1984, the animal population in Turkey was 68,522,000: 59% were sheep, 19% angora goats, 19% cattle, and 3% horses, donkeys, mules and pigs. Grazing thus has an important place in the development of the mountain economy.

In mountainous regions and forest areas, there are around 1,073,000 ha. which have been classified for range management activities. In the General Directorate of Forestry, 3,000 hectares of range-land rehabilitation areas are being developed every year. The objective is to increase this figure to 10,000 ha. over a short period.

Reforestation

At present, the annual reforestation programme of the General Directorate of Forestry is about 150,000 ha., but this is to be increased to 300,000 ha. in the near future.

Watershed Management

The potential areas for this activity are as follows:

Reforestation: 5,350,000 ha.

Erosion control: 886,000 ha.

Range management: 1,073,000 ha.

Socio-Economic Developments

The forest villagers are employed in all forestry production activities.

In addition, firewood and other requirements of the forest villagers are made available to them at reduced prices every year, according to Law No. 6831.

Besides this, sawlogs are made available for the construction of bridges, mosques, schools, etc., in forest villages also at reduced prices.

5.   UTILIZATION OF FOREST RESOURCES

Forest Production

The activities of production, transportation and marketing of forest products are carried out by State Forest Enterprises.

Felling, transportation and storage activities are carried out in accordance with the State Forest Enterprises Revolving Budget Rules. According to these rules, unit-price, contracting and daily payment systems are used in production activities.

National Wood Industry

From the production value viewpoint, the forest products industry ranks fifth in importance among the 34 production sectors. There are 7,960 sawmills of varying sizes in the private sector whose total capacity is 10.6 million m3/year; and there are 27 which belong to the State with a 1.1 million m3/year capacity. 54.9% of capacity is utilized in the private sector and 29.9% in State sawmills.

The packing box industry which is considered as part of the sawmill industry is located mainly in the region where fruit and vegetables are grown; these are small family establishments.

There are 33 veneer factories; 12 of them are units of larger establishments and 21 factories are independent.

There are 16 plywood factories in the private sector and 4 factories which belong to the State.

The particle board industry has expanded rapidly during the last 15 years and has now reached a capacity of 1,400,000 m3 per year; there are 24 factories, 3 of which belong to the State.

The parquet industry has shown rapid growth in recent years. There are plenty of factories which belong to the private sector and about 10 parquet factories working as part of the State's sawmill enterprises.

The wooden furniture industry employs some 300,000 people in 14 large and 40,000 small establishments.

Nearly 100% of the wood consumption of the forest products industry is supplied by State forests. Wood production is not sufficient to meet the demand of the forest products industry and the greater part of total capacity of this sector remains unused.

The special commission report in the fifth Five-Year Plan puts the allowable cut at 12.9 million m3 for high forests and 6.2 million stere for coppice.

The various taxes on the sales of forestry industry raw materials total about 27% in the case of auction sales and 21% in allocated sales.

6. TRADE POLICY OF THE FOREST INDUSTRY SECTOR

Principles and measures relating to National Trade Policies are clearly stated in the Five-Year Development Plans (by periods); priority in the plans will be given to products with export potential and to an improvement in the competitiveness of forest industry products. There is a modest but significant two-way trade in forest products with several EEC countries.

7.   EMPLOYMENT

The situation is shown below for 1986:

	Forestry Sector (General Directorate of Forestry)	Forestry Industry Sector (for State Sector)	TOTAL
Forest Engineer	2,700	110	2,810
Other Engineer	131	19	150
Forest Technician	655	-	655
Other Technician	429	43	472
Lawyer	140	2	142
Forest Guard	8,495	8,495	8,495
Other Staff	18,107	628	18,735
TOTAL	30,657	802	31,459
Worker (man/day)	53 million	1.4 million	54.4 million

In the Five-Year Development Plans and Government Programmes, the implementation and support of labour-intensive projects based on assumptions that the most important problems in Turkey are unemployment and inflation have been accepted as targets.

In accordance with the Forest Law on forest activities, employment priority has been given to villagers living either inside or in the vicinity of the forests.

Almost all workers who have been working for the Forest Industry Sector and some of the workers who have been working for the Forestry Sector are members of the unions concerned.

As many activities in the forestry sector are seasonal, generally seasonal workers are employed.

Wage and social security policies have been developed in the light of economic, social and living conditions. Measures in the field of protection of workers' health are covered by regulations.

In addition, workers' and pensioners' medical treatment and expenses in State or social insurance hospitals and necessary medicine are paid for by the State.

8.   FORESTRY EDUCATION AND TRAINING

For the training of professional and technical forestry staff, university level teaching is carried out at the following educational institutions:

1 -   Forestry Faculty, University of Istanbul

a)   Forest Engineering Section

b)   Forest Industry Engineering Section

c)   Landscape Architecture Section

2 -   Forest Faculty, University of Karadeniz

a)   Forest Engineering Section

b)   Forest Industry Engineering Section

c)   Landscape Architecture Section

3 -   Technical Training Faculty, Gazi University

Wood Working Industry Section

4 -   Engineering Faculty, Hacettepe University

Vocational Technology College for Wood Working Industry Engineering.

There are five Forest Protection and Forest Regeneration Training Centres for Forest Officers, in Trabzon, Eskisehir, Elazig, Kahramanmaras, Kastamonu-Arac; these belong to the General Directorate of Forestry.

The courses in education and training of these schools last one year and the students are selected from middle-school graduates.

Education and information programmes for the general public are prepared and implemented by the General Directorate of Forestry. In addition, World Forestry Day is celebrated during a nation-wide forestry week and plantation festivals are arranged.

9.   FORESTRY RESEARCH

There are two Research Institutes in the General Directorate of Forestry: one is the Forestry Research Institute with its central office in Ankara and Regional Directorates distributed throughout the various climatic regions. The other is the Poplar and Fast-Growing Exotic Forest Tree Species Research Institute in Izmit.

The research institutes cooperate with the Turkish Standards Institute, National Library, National Productivity Centre, and the Turkish Scientific and Technical Research Organization.

Research results are disseminated through publications, seminars, training symposia and technical meetings. Research programmes are practice-oriented.

The various interests concerned with the application of research results are consulted on the formulation of research programmes at annual meetings covered by the Research Institute Council.

UNITED KINGDOM

1. INTRODUCTION

The total land area of the United Kingdom – excluding inland water – amounts to 24,098,000 ha.; at 31 March 1986, there were 2,146,500 ha. of productive forest. Of this, 962,500 ha. were managed by the State forestry authorities, the Forestry Commission in Great Britain (England, Scotland and Wales) and the Forest Service in Northern Ireland, while 1,184,000 ha. were under private ownership.

Great Britain

The Forestry Commission was established by Act of Parliament in 1919. Under legislation now consolidated in the Forestry Act 1967, it is charged with the general duty of promoting the interests of forestry, the development of afforestation, and the production and supply of timber and other forest products in Great Britain. This general duty includes that of promoting the establishment and maintenance of adequate reserves of growing trees, and until 1958 the Commission's principal objective was to build up a strategic reserve of timber. Since then, the emphasis has moved towards economic, social and environmental objectives.

In December 1980, the Government set out its firm commitment to a continuing expansion of forestry, with a greater participation by the private sector in new planting to be encouraged by the introduction of a new and simplified system of grant-aid known as the "Forestry Grant Scheme".

A further change in objectives took effect on 26 August 1985 when the Forestry Act 1967 was amended to require the Forestry Commissioners to endeavour to achieve a reasonable balance between:

(a) the development of afforestation, the management of forests and the production and supply of timber; and

(b) the conservation and enhancement of natural beauty and the conservation of flora, fauna and geological or physiographical features of special interest.

Northern Ireland

The Forest Service in Northern Ireland, a division of the Department of Agriculture for Northern Ireland, took over the responsibility for forestry from the Forestry Commission following the Government of Ireland Act 1921. Its powers and responsibilities are contained in the Forestry Act (Northern Ireland) 1953.

A review of forestry policy was undertaken between 1968 and 1970. This culminated in the publication of a Government White Paper entitled "Government of Northern Ireland – Forestry in Northern Ireland Cmd 550". Among the provisions included in this were:

(a) the planned aim of eventual self-sufficiency to meet the province's needs of timber for constructional and agricultural purposes;

(b) a change in employment policy from one of emphasis on the provision of regular and permanent employment in rural areas to cost-effective working in the State sector. It was recognized that this could cause redundancies in the public sector work force;

(c) a recognition that recreation, conservation, amenity and public education were valid objectives and should be incorporated into State forestry objectives.

2.   ADMINISTRATION

In the post-war years the Forestry Commission and the Northern Ireland Forest Service expanded their woodland areas rapidly both by afforestation of former agricultural land and the purchase and reafforestation of private woodland when the owners felt themselves to be unable to undertake restocking of wartime-felled areas.

In Great Britain, the bulk of private forestry expansion has been carried out by forest management companies on behalf of their investor clients, many of whom were attracted by the tax arrangements for forestry. In Northern Ireland private planting has been undertaken mainly by private estate owners and farmers.

The Forestry Commission is directly responsible to the Minister of Agriculture, Fisheries and Food in England and to the Secretaries of State for Scotland and Wales. The Northern Ireland Forest Service, through its parent Department of Agriculture, is responsible to the Secretary of State for Northern Ireland.

The Forestry Commmission has the dual role of 'Forestry Authority' and 'Forestry Enterprise' and has to account for its activities to the Forestry Ministers and Parliament.

In its capacity as 'Forestry Authority' it is responsible for: advancing the knowledge and understanding of forestry and trees in the countryside; developing and ensuring the best use of the country's forest resources; promoting the development and efficiency of the wood-using industry; undertaking research relevant to the needs of forestry; combating forest tree pests and diseases including regulatory controls on imported wood and forest tree plants; advising and assisting with safety and training in forestry; encouraging good forestry practice in private woodlands through advice and schemes of financial assistance and by controls on felling; and preparing appropriate forestry legislation.

As the 'Forestry Enterprise' the Forestry Commission is responsible for: developing its forests for the production of wood for industry by extending and improving the forest estate; protecting and enhancing the environment; providing recreational facilities; stimulating and supporting the local economy in areas of depopulation by the development of forests, including the establishment of new plantations; and fostering a harmonious relationship between forestry and agriculture.

The Northern Ireland Forest Service has broadly the same responsibilities as the Forestry Commission except that there are no controls over felling in Northern Ireland other than through tree preservation orders administered by the Town and County Planning Service of the Department of the Environment, Northern Ireland.

The Forestry Commission is governed by a board of Commissioners, with ten members, four full-time and six part-time, under a part-time Chairman.

There is a three-tier administrative organization: Headquarters, seven Conservancies (Regions) - three in Scotland, three in England, one covering Wales - and 65 local Forest Districts (reductions by merger are contemplated).

In Northern Ireland the same responsibilities are covered by a similar, though smaller, hierarchy which forms part of the Department of Agriculture. Essentially, the Northern Ireland Forest Service approximates to a single Forestry Commission Conservancy.

The United Kingdom total public budget for 1986/87 amounted to £134.2 billion of which £58 million (0.04 per cent) was devoted to forestry.

3. MONETARY AND FISCAL POLICIES

It is Government policy that the bulk of new planting should be carried out by the private sector and this has been encouraged by the provision of grant aid and special tax arrangements. A new grant aid scheme, the Woodland Grant Scheme was introduced in 1988 with increased grants, while tax reliefs have been abolished. Grant aid has hitherto been provided under two schemes, the Forestry Grant Scheme and the Broadleaved Woodland Grant Scheme administered by the Forestry Commission, both of which were closed to new applicants on 15 March 1988.

(a) The Pre-1988 Forestry Grant Scheme was introduced in 1981 following the closure of two earlier schemes to new applicants. In order to receive grant aid, applicants are required to follow a five-year plan of operations, the primary objective of which should be the production of a utilizable crop of timber.

(b) In the Broadleaved Woodland Grant Scheme, which was introduced in 1985, the production of timber need no longer be the primary objective, although it is still expected to feature. The scheme is specifically directed towards rehabilitation of existing broadleaved woodlands (both by planting and natural regeneration), and establishment of new ones.

Woodland Grant Scheme. This new scheme introduced in 1988 replaces the FGS and BWGS referred to above, and combines the functions of both the earlier schemes with increased rates of grant, higher rates being paid for the planting of broadleaved trees. The enhancement of the environment is a feature of this scheme.

Farm Woodland Scheme. This new scheme to be introduced in 1988 is designed to encourage farmers in the UK to plant woodlands as part of their farm enterprise on land currently in agriculture. In the first experimental 3-year phase up to 36,000 ha. will be planted. Administratively, the scheme will be tied in with the Forestry Grant Scheme.

It is the Government's policy to leave the provision of loans for afforestation and woodland management to private financial institutions.

- 256 -

<u>United Kingdom forestry taxation</u> which hitherto has been based on similar
principles to those applied in other sectors of the economy, has been
developed and refined to take account of the long-term scale of forestry
investment and the absence of income in the years following establishment.

<u>Capital gains tax</u> applies to increases in the value of land carrying timber
crops, but not to the timber crops themselves.

<u>Inheritance tax</u> (formerly capital transfer tax/estate duty) is applied to
assets changing hands following a death and, in limited circumstances, to
lifetime gifts. Concessions include deferment of payment pending
harvesting of the crop.

4.   FOREST MANAGEMENT AND PROTECTION

Forestry policy within the United Kingdom has been dominated by the
need to create a forest resource especially after the exploitation of
already depleted reserves by the World Wars of 1914-18 and 1939-45.
Afforestation has continued so that by 1986 about 9 per cent of the United
Kingdom land area was being used for forestry compared with 5 per cent back
in 1919. The actual achievement in recent years has been as follows:

| Year | Area (K ha.) of new planting in Great Britain | | Total |
	State Sector	Private Sector	
1980	15.8	8.3	24.1
1982	11.0	12.6	23.6
1984	8.4	16.9	25.3
1986	4.3	19.0	23.3

The above figures reflect the switch of emphasis from State forestry
to private forestry.

In Northern Ireland, planting in recent years has averaged about
700 ha., mostly by the State.

Although by tradition reservoir catchments were often afforested in
the past, control of run off has not been a problem in the United Kingdom,
and greater concern is now expressed at the lower overall run off from
forested catchments both by water authorities and by the electricity boards
who are concerned by possible reductions in the hydraulic head in potential
hydro-electricity generation areas.

The most serious cause of damage to forests in the United Kingdom is
wind.

The phenomenon of 'acid rain' has apparently not affected forest crops
within the United Kingdom, but two air pollution surveys, including one on
the standard EEC 16 x 16 Km network are carried out to monitor the
situation.

The responsibility for fighting fires lies with the Local Authorities whose fire brigades deal with fires of all sorts. Close liaison is maintained locally so that access routes and emergency water supplies are reviewed and agreed. Advances in technique, such as the increasing use of helicopters, are examined and taken advantage of.

Damage from pests and disease occurs on a relatively small scale. For certain problems, statutory controls are in force in particular areas of the country, viz. against Dutch elm disease, watermark disease of willow and <u>Dendroctonus micans</u> (the Great Spruce Bark Beetle).

The Forestry Commission in Great Britain and the Forest Service in Northern Ireland have the protection and enhancement of the environment as one of their objectives, and the general aims of their conservation policies are:

a) to conserve, by appropriate management, scheduled special sites and additional sites of special nature conservation interest within the forest estate;

b) to enhance the nature conservation value of the forest estate as a whole;

c) in all forest or nature conservation activities to pay due regard to wider environmental values;

d) to promote the public use of areas of conservation interest where this is compatible with other conservation objectives. The general aims presented here apply equally to existing and newly created forests.

The Countryside Commissions in Great Britain and the Countryside and Wildlife Branch of the Department of Environment in Northern Ireland develop policies on recreation in the countryside generally. The Forestry Commission and the Northern Ireland Forest Service have continuing policies for developing their forests for recreation, providing facilities for informal leisure activities, and the enjoyment of quiet pursuits.

The Forestry Commission and Northern Ireland Forest Service welcome the public on foot to all their forests, provided that this access does not conflict with the management and protection of the forest, and provided there are no legal agreements which would be infringed by unrestricted public areas.

The main emphasis is on the provision of facilities for day visitors, such as car parks, picnic places, viewpoints and forest walks - particularly within easy access for visitors from towns and holiday centres. There are, however, also some camp sites and chalets for visitors who want to stay overnight in forest surroundings.

In Great Britain many private forests also welcome visitors and provide a similar range of facilities.

All government agencies dealing with countryside and conservation matters maintain contact with the relevant voluntary organizations.

5. <u>FOREST UTILIZATION</u>

<u>Harvesting operations</u> in the United Kingdom are dominated by even-aged coniferous crops. Approximately three quarters of the total cut is harvested by self-employed contractors working for private owners, timber merchants and the State Forest Services, while one-quarter is harvested by State forest service employees.

Since the end of the 1970s there has been a significant move towards shortwood harvesting by means of forwarder extraction. Fully mechanized methods employing harvesters and processors are used to a limited extent at the present time (less than 5 per cent of total cut).

Environmental restrictions, affecting mainly the size, shape and location of felling coupes, can usually be accommodated without serious effects on the cost of harvesting operations.

In general the <u>transport</u> of timber in the United Kingdoms is by road haulage with a maximum gross vehicle weight of 38 tons, allowing a maximum load of timber of just over 20 tons. The companies who carry out timber haulage are mainly small, often family concerns, and they tend to specialize in timber carriage. The use of rail transport is increasing.

While a number of public agencies in Great Britain have the aim of assisting <u>industrial development</u>, the main responsibility for promoting forestry and the forest industry sector falls to the Forestry Commission, as the national Forestry Authority.

In pursuance of this duty the Commission consults and takes advice from the Home Grown Timber Advisory Committee, a statutory body which comprises representatives of woodland owners, the timber trade and a range of land use interests. In Northern Ireland this function is carried out by the Industrial Development Board.

The Forestry Commission in Great Britain and the Industrial Development Board in Northern Ireland have taken a lead, together with the development agencies, in commissioning a series of national and regional studies to develop a strategy for the wood using industry. Recent initiatives to attract domestic and international investment for utilizing the rising wood supplies have proved extremely successful in Great Britain.

Wood has not been developed as a major energy source. There is, however, possible scope for utilizing forest residues as a fuel source, and this is being investigated by the Energy Technology Support Unit of the Department of Energy with assistance from Universities, the Forestry Commission and other government agencies.

6.   TIMBER TRADE AND MARKETING

The United Kingdom's market for wood and wood products relies on imports for about 90 per cent of its requirements at a cost, in 1985, of approximately £3,500 million. Total imports in 1985 were 37.6 million cubic metres expressed in terms of Wood Raw Material Equivalent (WRME).

The trade is largely without import restrictions except those required for plant health reasons.

Production of softwoods is currently about 4.2 million m3 per annum and will double within 15 years, while production of hardwoods is about 1 million m3 per annum and is expected to remain fairly level.

The international market exerts a crucial influence on specification and price. The policies in Great Britain and Northern Ireland are to encourage the development of markets for British timber which, in the long run, will provide the most profitable outlets for future production. The Forestry Commission markets its timber on a sustained and regular basis through a programme of regional tenders and auctions but some long-term negotiated supply arrangements are entered into with the specific objective of encouraging industrial development. These arrangements have proved to be a crucial factor underpinning a number of major expansions in Britain over the last few years in cartonboard, newsprint, medium-density fibreboard, particleboard and structural composition board. The marketing of timber in the private sector is inevitably more fragmented; in some parts of Great Britain, a system of joint tenders with the Forestry Commission has been established.

Research in wood technology and product development is undertaken by research establishments and Universities and is funded by the Government and all sectors of the industry. The two main institutions involved are the Timber Research and Development Association, largely funded by the timber trade, and the Building Research Establishment, funded by the Government.

In Britain, multi-national companies have invested some £650 million in wood processing capacity in the pulp, paper and wood based panels sectors since the trade recession in 1980. The market for British timber is currently reasonably balanced in supply and demand, and it is desirable that any further investment should take account of the available wood supply in relation to installed capacity in the wood processing industry.

7.   EMPLOYMENT

There is no industrial legislation specific to forestry employment in the United Kingdom; the Health and Safety at Work Act 1974 and the Employment Protection Act 1978 apply to all employees.

The State forest services employ forest officers who undertake professional forest management and advisory duties and forest workers who perform manual duties such as tree planting and timber harvesting. In addition there are a number of professional and industrial support groups, the main ones being: land agents, civil engineers and mechanical engineers with their industrial workers.

Forest workers are recruited locally at Forest District level. Administrative, professional and technical staff are recruited at national or Conservancy level consistent with recruitment standards laid down centrally by the Civil Service Commission for the recruitment of all government employees.

At each level in the organization there are consultative committees. All groups of employees are represented by trade unions who are consulted directly by management and who serve on the Consultative Committees.

The pay of professional and administrative grades is identical to the pay of equivalent Civil Service grades and is settled nationally by H.M. Treasury. The pay of industrial workers is negotiated directly within the highest level industrial consultation committee, i.e. The Forestry Commission Industrial and Trade Council.

There are no Social Security policies particular to forestry; only national policies for the whole population.

The Forestry Commission formed a Forestry Safety Council which includes representatives of trade unions and the private sector. The Council lays down safety standards which are set out in a series of Forest Industry Safety Guides issued throughout the industry. The Safety Guides are regarded by the Forestry Commission as the minimum safety requirements, and the observance of the guidelines is mandatory within the Forestry Commission.

There are no schemes for the reduction of unemployment specific to forestry but the Forestry Commission and private forestry employers provide work experience for young people under the national Youth Training Scheme.

8.   FORESTRY EDUCATION AND TRAINING

Three universities provide higher education and training in forestry and related subjects for undergraduates. The University of Aberdeen offers a Forestry Ordinary Degree (3 years) and an Honours Degree (4 years). The University College of North Wales combines forestry with wood sciences to Honours level (3 years) and the University of Edinburgh offers a 3-year course in Ecological Sciences followed by an elective 4th year at Honours level, one of the elective subjects being forestry.

The provision of undergraduate courses at Oxford University has ceased but postgraduate courses of one year continue to be available leading to the award of a Master's Degree.

The orientation of university level training has undergone evolutionary changes in recent years in order to reflect the increasing environmental pressures and the multiple land use aspects of modern day forestry.

Courses leading to the award of a forestry diploma are available at the Scottish School of Forestry (Inverness) and the Cumbria College of Agriculture and Forestry (Newton Rigg). The majority of students undergo a 5-year full-time training period comprising two years pre-college practical experience followed by a 3-year college-based course in which the middle year is an industrial "sandwich" aimed at developing supervisory and administrative skills.

In addition, there is provision for part-time study for those forest workers who demonstrate ability and aptitude for work at technician/supervisory level.

Once qualified and following a period of not less than 2 years' experience as a manager or supervisor, graduates and diplomates may apply for corporate membership of the Institute of Chartered Foresters. The examinations set by the Institute are designed to assess professional competence rather than academic ability.

Most forest workers are trained at the worksite in a range of skills which reflect the nature of the work within the undertaking. However, a significant number of young workers undergo more formalized training at one of the several colleges which provide forestry courses at craftsman level.

A recent government initiative is the creation of a national Youth Training Scheme (YTS) under which all school leavers who have not been able to obtain employment are entitled to participate. Forestry is one of the many recognized subjects and a significant proportion of YTS trainees are expected to be able to obtain vocational qualifications by the end of the 2-year training period.

In secondary education, forestry continues to be dealt with in general subjects such as geography, botany, biology and environmental studies but it does not constitute a separate subject.

The Forestry Commission and the N. Ireland Forest Service have developed their own "in-house" training service which provides job-related training for most levels of staff and in a wide range of operational activities. This service is available to the private sector on demand although capacity is limited.

The responsibility of the private sector is discharged under various statutory and non-statutory obligations, many of which are satisfied by the activities of the Forestry Training Council and Forestry Safety Council.

These Councils, which were created by the G.B. Forestry Authority, set the standards for the industry and their constitution enables a wide spectrum of representation including growers, timber merchants, trade unions and the education and safety authorities.

The problem of identifying and satisfying the training needs of harvesting contractors has still to be solved.

9.   FORESTRY RESEARCH, EXTENSION AND INFORMATION

The principal organizations financing and/or carrying out research
into the growing and harvesting of forests are:

The Forestry Commission, the Forestry Division and Research Division
of the Department of Agriculture Northern Ireland, the Natural
Environment Research Council, the Department of the Environment, the
Ministry of Agriculture, Fisheries and Food, the Nature Conservancy
Council, the Agriculture and Food Research Council, the University
Grants Committee and the Science and Engineering Research Council.
Research funded by private agencies is less than 1 per cent of total
research expenditure in forestry.

Forestry research is reviewed and coordinated by a Forestry Commission
Committee entitled the Forestry Research Coordination Committee (FRCC).

There are important connections between forestry research
organizations and researchers in public agencies responsible for nature
conservation, countryside amenity, environmental pollution, agroforestry
and building research, as well as with researchers in institutions financed
by these agencies. Some growth can be foreseen in research into economic
and social aspects of forestry.

Total annual expenditure on forestry research is about £12 million per
year (1987) of which the Forestry Commission accounts for about one half;
expenditure in N. Ireland is approximately £250,000.

A major concern of the Forestry Commission is to communicate research
results and to improve the speed and scale of application. Some 15 per
cent of the gross expenditure of the Forestry Commission Research Division
is concerned with communication with both users and other scientists, with
the bulk of this effort being devoted to the transfer of technology to
forest managers, arboriculturists and other users.

A major effort in recent years has been the initiation, writing,
procurement and siting of a Forestry Commission display at the major
agricultural shows throughout the country.

In Northern Ireland, a Forest Education and Public Relations Officer,
supported by a Forest Graphics Unit, has responsibility for public
relations and is responsible for mounting forestry exhibits and providing
interpretative materials.

10.   INTERNATIONAL COOPERATION

In international cooperation with developing countries it is the
national policy of the aid recipient country which determines the nature of
the cooperative action.

Emphasis is given to:

- fast-growing plantations capable of reclaiming previously
  deforested and degraded land;

- improved management of remaining areas of natural forest in the
  tropics;

- regeneration of the forests after logging;

- meeting the basic needs of the local people for fuelwood, fodder
  for livestock, poles and other forest produce.

- the exploration, collection, evaluation and conservation of
  potentially valuable species and provenances.

The British Overseas Aid Programme is administered by the Foreign &
Commonwealth Office, through the Overseas Development Administration (ODA).
The Forestry Commission is also an important source of expertise in this
field. Four British universities (Aberdeen, Edinburgh, North Wales and
Oxford) contribute to teaching, research and advice overseas and the Oxford
Forestry Institute is a major international centre for tropical forestry.
The Commonwealth Development Corporation supports major forestry
development schemes.

The proportion of the bilateral aid programme devoted to forestry has
been increasing in recent years andd has reached approximately 2 per cent
of the total bilateral aid. In addition, substantial assistance is given
to forestry through multilateral aid which now constitutes nearly 40 per
cent of the total United Kingdom's aid programme.

Priority is given to assisting the poorest countries but, following
bilateral ties, approximately 65 per cent of United Kingdom's bilateral aid
goes to Commonwealth countries, particularly in Africa and Asia.

UNION OF SOVIET SOCIALIST REPUBLICS

1. INTRODUCTION

The branches of the forest complex of the USSR include forestry, and the timber, woodworking and wood chemistry industries, and figure prominently among the branches of the national economy, both in terms of output and numbers employed.

Forestry in the USSR is conducted according to the 'Fundamentals of Forestry Legislation of the USSR and Union Republics' established in 1977 by the supreme organ of the country, the Supreme Soviet.

According to the relevant legislative provisions, based on national economic values, location and functions, all forests in the USSR are divided into three groups.

The first group includes protection forests for soil and water conservation, forest parks, national and nature parks, forests of scientific or historical value, nature monuments, tundra and sub-alpine forests. The role of forests in this group is constantly being enhanced.

The second group includes forests in densely populated regions with a developed network of transport routes, which have a protective and limited exploitation value, as well as forests with inadequate raw material resources which require a stricter exploitation system to ensure their protective functions.

The third group includes forests in well wooded regions which have an essentially exploitative value and are intended to meet national timber requirements without detriment to their protective functions.

The USSR has 21.9% of the world's forests and 25.6% of all standing timber. The following table gives data on the forests of the USSR.

Distribution of area and reserves of
the common State forest stock for public use *

Category of Forest by Use	General Area of Forest Stock (million ha.)	Forested Area	Reserve of Wood (1,000 M m3)
State Forests including:	1,239.7	792.1	83.94
a) forestry managed by State bodies	1,182.8	745.5	78.65
b) urban forests and forest reserves assigned to ministries and departments	56.9	46.6	5.29
Collective Farm Forests	19.7	18.8	1.96
TOTAL	1,259.4	810.9	85.90

* Forestry of USSR, Gosleskhoz USSR, PPSTI, 1984, p.5.

Economically, the greatest value is attached to forests that are essentially made up of coniferous trees, which represent 72.3% of the forested area under the jurisdiction of State forestry bodies.

Under the Soviet regime since 1917, substantial measures have been implemented to develop and improve the geographical location of the logging and wood processing branches of the industry in order to bring the volumes felled in thinly-forested areas of the country in line with available resources.

The USSR has decided to promote the use of all harvested timber, including residues.

In the USSR, the volume of harvested timber in recent years has stabilized at around 360 million m3 per year.

Production of main types of wood and paper products in the USSR

	1960	1970	1980	1985
Production of sawnwood, million m3	105.5	116.4	98.2	98.2
Particle board, thousand m3	161	1,191	5,118	6,327
Fibreboard, million m2	67.6	208	469	561
Plywood, thousand m3	1,354	2,045	2,022	2,187
Cellulose, thousand tonnes	2,282	5,110	7,123	8,374
Paper, thousand tonnes	2,334	4,185	5,288	5,986
Paperboard, thousand tonnes	893	2,516	3,445	4,034

The great rise in production is largely explained by the increased utilization of logging and wood processing residues.

Change of export of main types of wood and paper production*

Indices	Unit of Measurement	1960	1970	1980	1985
Roundwood	million m3	4.4	15.3	13.9	15.4
Sawnwood	" "	5.0	8.0	7.1	7.8
Plywood	thousand m3	131	281	314	410
Particle board	" "	–	145	332	298
Fibreboard	million m2	–	41.6	90.8	71.7
Cellulose	thousand tonnes	243.7	447.8	821.3	965.0
Paper	" "	122.5	474.6	646.5	708.1
Paperboard	" "	–	247	371.9	392.1

* Foreign Trade of USSR. Statistical reference books for 1960, 1970, 1980 and 1985. M.: Finances and Statistics.

2. MANAGEMENT OF FOREST RESOURCES

The supreme State organization is the State Committee for Forestry (GOSLESHOZ). In republics and autonomous regions, there are Ministries or State Committees for Forestry, e.g. in the Russian Federation there is the Ministry of Forestry and in republics with small forest resources such as in Kirgiz SSR, there is a State Committee for Forestry. In regional and provincial administrations there are units for forestry management. The basic management unit is the woodlot (Leshoz). The Ministry of Forestry is in charge of forestry development as an integral part of the national economy, establishment of basic development programmes and annual planting. These tasks include: improvement of quality of forests, increasing forest productivity, establishment of protective and anti-erosion plantations, organization of continuing supply of forest products to industry and to the population, organization and implementation of measures aimed at improving the non-timber-producing function of the forest (i.e. function other than economic one), protection of the environment, control of and protection from forest fires and theft, and phytosanitary protection.

At local level, the organization of forestry management varies according to the importance and the size of the forests. In regions with small forest resources, one organizational unit is in charge of forest management, export and wood processing industry.

The main State organization in wood industry is the Ministry of Wood, Pulp and Paper Industry.

The establishment of units in charge of forest management, protection of forests, export and wood industry is considered to be the main task in the process of modernization and management of the forestry sector in the USSR.

Forestry and the timber and wood processing industries are developed on a planned basis. The main basis of management in the socialist economy is long-term forecasting and planning, the principal task of which is to achieve set growth rates of production in the branches so as to better meet national requirements with minimum production expenses and rational and comprehensive use of natural resources.

Forecasts are long-term - 20 years or more. Long-term plans are made for 10 years in the context of the Five-Year Plans. The Five-Year Plan is the main way in which industrial production is planned and organized; it is a State document, determining the main thrusts of industrial activity in forestry, its territorial industrial forestry associations and enterprises.

Economic and mathematical models are applied in the preparation of long-term forecasts and plans.

In defining a development strategy for the forest complex, the siting of industrial wood production in the country is optimized, and the raw materials policy and trends for the rational use of raw timber and the size and structure of timber exports are determined. Of the many variants, the one is selected that minimizes production and transport costs and best meets national wood production requirements and the optimum development of timber exports. Thus account is taken of the important principle of the location of production forces in the USSR - the rational distribution of labour between economic regions in order comprehensively and effectively to use the natural resources and ensure the complex development of each region's economy.

The essential projected growth of the branches of the forest complex is determined by the main economic and social development trends in the USSR up to the year 2000, adopted by the XXVII session of the CPSU in March 1986.

The fundamental task of the 12th Five-Year Plan (1986-1990) for the national economy of the USSR is to increase economic growth rates and efficiency by expediting scientific and technological progress, technologically re-equipping and reconstructing production, intensively using the created production potential, and improving the management systems and economic machinery, thereby enhancing the welfare of the Soviet people.

On the basis of this fundamental task, the national income spent on consumption and accumulation must increase by 19-22% through increased labour productivity.

In the USSR, forest management is intensified on the basis of socialist ownership and collective work in enterprises and associations, a fact which excludes exploitation. Under socialism, this means that the growing requirements of workers have to be met.

3. FOREST UTILIZATION

The USSR has elaborated, and has been using for a long time, progressive technology in logging operations on the basis of hauling timber in tree lengths; this technology will continue to predominate, although whole-tree logging will increase when tree biomass becomes more widely used.

Greater efficiency in the timber industry depends essentially on finding a timely and appropriate solution to the problem of timber transportation by land and water. In lumber camps in the USSR, the trend to increase removal by road will continue, and the construction of more log trucking roads that operate all year round (gravel and reinforced concrete) is planned to achieve smoother logging.

The introduction of new machines and equipment will do away with heavy manual labour in the most labour-intensive operations, the replacement of which is a most important social task in the USSR.

Increased mechanization significantly lowers the numbers of unskilled workers and sharply increases the numbers of machinists and operators of felling, bunching, chipping machinery, semi-automatic lines and automated conveyors.

To this end, the industry in the USSR has organized a broad and active system for training and retraining skilled workers to manage and service new machines and equipment (technical forestry schools, vocational and technical institutions, advanced schools and others).

The new sawmilling production technology is moving towards the output of specified products (glued components, planed sawnwood and other semi-processed products) that have a special (functional) purpose. This virtually means a gradual shift from the universal technology of general purpose production of sawnwood, to specialized technology and equipment.

The programme to concentrate and specialize sawing and wood-working enterprises aims to:

- intensify coniferous sawnwood production in large combines which produce lumber for export and domestic use according to consumer specifications;

- to sort deciduous timber at logging sites into wood for sawing, packaging, parquet and other forms of wooden wares;

- to promote technological specialization at sawmills through direct economic links with product users.

By 1990, these programmes will make it possible to increase sawnwood production per enterprise 1.4 fold, to create the conditions to automate and mechanize sawing output, effectively to apply new high-productivity technology and to raise the degree of raw timber use by increasing technological chip output from sawmill residues.

The growth of wood-based panel production will essentially be achieved by introducing new equipment which will also be used to treat low-quality hardwood timber, sawmilling and harvesting residues.

A much wider range and improved quality of particleboard and fibreboard (thin boards, reduced toxicity, improved surface, less material capacity, etc.) will constitute the main development feature of projected board production.

When designing and planning the home environment, efforts will be made to achieve functional and aesthetic harmony in the various domestic elements (furniture, consumer goods, lamps, decorative wares and ornaments) by taking into account the fact that a number of domestic appliances in furniture, intended not only for the kitchen but also for other rooms in the home, will be built-in.

Increased house-building is a component part of the social policies of the Party and Soviet Government, in order to improve housing and everyday living conditions for the Soviet people. Between 1986-1990, the overall number of houses built of wood will increase 1.3 fold, and after 1990, 2.5 fold.

4. ORGANIZATION OF FORESTRY RESEARCH

The leading institute within the system of the State Committee for forestry is VNIILN, the All-Union Research Institute for Forest Management and Mechanization. Its main tasks are: development of programmes for the rational utilization of forest resources, the introduction of new technologies in forest management and exploitation, the ecological role of forests, optimization of forest units, and particularly the anthropogenic influence of forests on the environment.

The Central Institute for Forestry Mechanization and Energy is the main organization in charge of development of mechanization of timber yards, the wood processing industry, and transport. Particular attention is given to the utilization of by-products (e.g. sawdust, branches, etc.), including energy production. A special institute deals with problems of forest economics and organization of forest industry.

Each of the institutes has pilot and experimental forests and processing units.

5. TRAINING

Forestry specialists are trained at universities and faculties which provide training in the field of forest management, transport and wood and timber, forestry economics and wood processing technology. The main schools are the Forestry Academy, Leningrad, and the Forestry Institute in Moscow. Forest technicians are trained in secondary schools and forest workers in special schools for tractor-drivers and workers in transport, wood processing and wood-cutting.

The larger forestry units organize on-the-job training for workers.

6. MAIN TRENDS AND DEVELOPMENTS

The main trends of economic and social development in the USSR between 1986 and 1990 and for the period until the year 2000 have resulted in forestry being given the task of improving the regeneration and use of forest resources, broadly implementing scientific achievement, zonal systems of the economy, chemicalizing and mechanizing production, intensifying the use of forest lands, increasing operations to cultivate protective trees and afforest pastures in desert and semi-desert regions, enhancing supervision of the use of raw timber resources and also protecting forests from fires, pests and disease.

Taking this fundamental task as a basis, forestry in the USSR will include a whole host of trends:

-   implementation of technical, technological, organizational and economic measures to enhance the productivity and quality of forests as a reliable raw material base for the logging industry, and the protective, water-retaining, sanitary and other useful properties of the forest, to expedite the economic development of the country;

-   securing of the timely restoration of valuable species, introduction of industrial growing methods, wide use of chemical means and fertilizers in arboreta and on forest planting areas, application of forest genetics and selection, setting up of complete drainage systems;

-   expansion of operations to protect forests from fires, harmful insects and disease;

-   development of operations to plant anti-erosion and field-protecting forest plantations in order to strengthen soil protection against wind and water erosion and enhance agricultural crop yield;

-   establishment of new, green areas around towns and settlements, equipped with services and utilities;

-   extension of forest use for recreational purposes;

-   fuller and more rational use of forests to obtain wood-chemical, technical and medicinal raw materials, food products, and greater overall timber production from every unit of forested area.

During 1986-1990 alone, reforestation operations will be carried out on about 10 million ha., over half of which are concerned with sowing and planting trees. The planned reforestation takes account of natural regeneration and will restore forests in all cleared areas.

To increase raw material resources, great significance will be attached to sanitary and maintenance felling. On the whole, intermediate fellings may grow 1.4 times over the country in the near future.

To improve quality and productivity, there will be more high-grade seed-growing with due attention to modern genetics.

The drainage of land and use of mineral fertilizers will remain an effective method by which to continue to increase productivity of forest areas. Drainage raises the growth of timber by 3-4 m3 per hectare per year. It is envisaged that forest drainage will be combined with road-building, fire-prevention installations in forest tracts and the assimilation of drained areas into the economy.

To raise the quality and effectiveness of forest regeneration operations, emphasis will be placed on accelerated scientific and technological progress in forestry planting operations.

Because of the variations in the forest growing stock and the ecological and economic characteristics of the diverse regions, monitoring is necessary in order to resolve a broad range of tasks: priorities, intensity of management and data-collection methods may differ from region to region.

In the initial stage, the most important tasks which secure the rational use and reproduction of the useful resources and properties of the forest have to be resolved: examples of these which are applicable to the taiga zone of the country, are the protection of forests against fire, harmful insects and other harmful influences, and the organization of the rational use of forest resources and opportune restoration of economically valuable timber species.

Remote sensing methods make it possible to carry out a range of tasks, which include:

-   compiling maps to show the current and intended future use of available forested areas;

-   their hydrological assessment in order to project water-retaining and water-improvement measures in forests;

-   studying the condition of field-protecting and mountain-protecting forests to combat erosion;

-   drawing up charts of hunting grounds, etc.

It should be emphasized that in these areas, in addition to timber harvesting, the forest is used in different ways: for resin harvesting, hunting, and minor forest products (haymaking; livestock grazing; apiculture; harvesting of fruit and sap from wild trees; nut, mushroom, berry, medicinal plant and technical raw material harvesting).

In order to use and reproduce forest resources more efficiently, new enterprise complexes, combining forestry, harvesting and woodworking operations, are functioning and being established in the USSR.

In the USSR, a series of State and public measures to exploit, renew and increase natural resources and prevent environmental pollution are being implemented.

In "The Main Trends of the Economic and Social Development of the USSR for 1986-1990 and for the Period up to the Year 2000", it is noted that the effectiveness of measures to protect nature and to implement low-waste and waste-free technological processes more widely has to be raised; combined production, which provides for the complete and complex use of natural resources, raw materials and materials, excluding or substantially reducing any harmful impact on the environment, has to be developed.

Forests in the Soviet Union, which are State property, are important for environmental protection. The Constitution of the USSR states that, in the interests of present and future generations, necessary measures are adopted to protect and use lands, forests and the plant world in a scientifically-based and rational manner and to secure the reproduction of natural wealth, including forest resources.

Measures to augment maintenance felling occupy a prominent place in the system of measures to protect the surrounding natural environment.

Considering the peculiarities of mountain forests, the entire exploitation activity here is carried out by methods which have been coordinated with nature protection requirements.

Taking into account the fact that in the USSR the forest has a favourable influence on raising the productivity of farming lands in steppe and forested steppe zones and on ploughed land, there are plans to extend the protective tree shelter belts. These belts reduce wind speed on enclosed fields, attenuate whirlwinds, increase air moisture and reduce evaporation of moisture in soil.

In the USSR, the State aviation and ground protection services operate to protect forests from fire. To protect the forest against harmful insects and disease, a system of forest protective measures has been devised.

In the USSR, the forest constitutes a base for the leisure time and rest of workers which is free of charge; forest parks, green area forests and also protection forests located in the vicinity of towns are used for recreation purposes.

Therefore there are plans to set up new green areas in towns and settlements, equipped with services and utilities, in the 1986-1990 period. More special facilities, leisure-motels, camping sites, etc., will be established to help reduce the negative influence of mass influxes of people to forests for pleasure. Research and scientific studies to organize and manage the economics of recreational forests will be expanded.

7. INTERNATIONAL COOPERATION

State forestry organizations cooperate with institutions and administrations of other countries, both bilaterally and multilaterally, on the basis of their long-term cooperation programmes. Fields of cooperation are: technology of forestry operations, management of recreational forests, development and utilization of micro-biological substances for forestry protection, control of forest fires, establishment of anti-erosion plantations, afforestation of deserts and sandy areas, and development of methods for early diagnosis of genetic characteristics of trees.

Cooperation with Finland is mainly on the exchange of genetic material and in the field of wood processing; with the German Democratic Republic, implementation of mathematical models in forest management; with Bulgaria, utilization of hardwoods.

Cooperation within the Council for Mutual Economic Assistance (CMEA) is concerned with the development of complex mechanization of forestry work and wood processing and development of inter-sectoral forecasting of future demand for forest products.

A new form of technical cooperation is the establishment of joint ventures with Japan and Finland.

Soviet experts participate in activities carried out by the Economic Commission for Europe (ECE) and also in forestry congresses and symposia organized by IUFRO. Soviet forestry and wood industry regularly participate in international forums and exhibitions.

YUGOSLAVIA

1. ## INTRODUCTION

The forests and woodlands of Yugoslavia are accorded special attention and care on the part of the social community. Such treatment of forests and woodland is guaranteed by the Constitution (Federal, republican, provincial). Forests cover 9.1 million ha., i.e. 35.7% of the area of the country. They are not evenly distributed throughout the territory of Yugoslavia, which is composed of six socialist republics: Slovenia, Serbia, Croatia, Bosnia-Herzegovina, Macedonia and Montenegro and two socialist autonomous provinces: Vojvodina and Kosovo.

Public forests account for 66.14% and private ones for 33.86% of the total forest area. The quality of public forests is better than that of private forests, the best of which are to be found in the S.R. of Slovenia.

High forests account for 54.1% of the total area under forests, and yield over 90% of the forestry output.

The most common species are beech, oak and spruce.

The annual gross increment is 29 million m3, of which public forests account for 21 million m3 and private ones for 8 million m3; the gross increment of deciduous species is 21.7 million m3 and of conifers 7.6 million m3. The annual cut in 1985 totalled 22.4 million m3 (16.1 million m3 broadleaves and 6.3 million m3 conifers).

On average, the growing stock per ha. amounts to 140.4 m3 in public forests and 92.8 m3 in private ones. The largest average growing stock of 205.1 m3 per ha. is in public selection forests.

The main objectives of the forestry policy are:

-   to improve the existing growing stock, with a view to attaining the highest possible increment and to expand the area under forest;

-   to make possible the regular, continuous supply of wood and wood-based products to industries and the population;

-   to upgrade the other benefits and services derived from forests;

-   to change the export pattern of forestry products and wood processing industries (step up exports of downstream products).

The set objectives will be attained through:

-   improvement of degraded forests and transformation of coppice into high forests;

-   the afforestation of bare forest land;

- increasing areas under plantations of fast-growing species;

- radical promotion of silvicultural and forest management methods;

- promotion of other beneficial functions of forests;

- introduction of higher value species, particularly conifers;

- the full use of the total biomass in forestry and of residues in wood processing industries;

- the better use of forest by-products (fruit, resin, fungi, medicinal herbs, etc.);

- making forests more accessible by construction of a new network of forest communications.

The area under forests can be expanded considerably, as about 800,000 ha. of bare forest land is publicly owned. There are about 250,000 ha. of abandoned agricultural land in private and public ownership which are suitable for plantations of fast-growing species.

2. ADMINISTRATION

2.1. Forest Ownership

Forest ownership changes slowly. In any case, areas under forests, both public and private, are increasing. In some mountainous regions, characterised by large outward migrations, organizations managing public forests buy forests from private owners. Besides that, public forests are expanding through the afforestation of bare areas, and forests in the private sector through the natural spread of woodland on abandoned agricultural land. There is no administrative influence on ownership changes.

2.2 Forestry Administration

The degree of decentralization in the forestry and wood processing industry is complete. Federal organs have retained only certain competences stipulated by the Constitution. Forests are managed not only by collectives in charge of public forests or by private forest owners, but also to a certain degree by society through its competent organs (in the Federation, republics, provinces, communes).

Wood processing and pulp and paper industries are in the competence of the Federal Committee for Energy and Industry at federal level (Federal Executive Council), and of committees or secretariats for industry in general in the republics and provinces.

The main guidelines for forest management are set out in the forestry laws of the republics and provinces.

2.3   Forestry Policy and Development

All the development plans of Yugoslavia, the republics, provinces and regions, give special emphasis to the development of natural resources, including forests, which account for about 10% of the total national wealth and for about 6% of employment in the economy.

Forestry financing is only partially of a budgetary nature. Organizations managing public forests and owners of private forests in principle reforest felled areas from their own funds. The afforestation of bare areas, improvement of degraded forest and the construction of forest roads is partially financed out of the budgets of the republics and provinces, bank credit and resources pooled by organizations outside forestry. The manner of financing differs in the various republics and provinces and is subject to change.

Young people also make a significant contribution to afforestation, e.g. through Young Nature Lovers' Associations.

3.   MONETARY AND FISCAL POLICY

3.1   Private Forests

The Forest Law and other regulations on forests apply equally to public and private forests. Private forest owners are obliged to ensure the simple reproduction of forests. Financial support to owners of private forests differs, depending on the republic and/or province. Private forest owners receive seedlings for afforestation free of charge or for a nominal sum.

Technical departments in communes carry out professional supervision and render professional services free of charge. These communal organs are also responsible for enforcing forest law regulations in private forests.

The Forest Law provides for the pooling of resources of private forest owners into agricultural cooperatives or other forms of association.

3.2   Taxation in Forestry

No taxes are levied on forests in public ownership, nor are there any special taxes applicable to private forests. Owners of private forests only pay taxes on land registry revenue, which is minimal.

4.   FOREST MANAGEMENT AND PROTECTION

4.1   Land Use and the Scope of Forest Management

The forest laws of the republics and provinces prescribe that the existing forests must be maintained. Regardless of their ownership, they may be cleared and transformed into other types of cultures only in the cases stipulated by law. These are: the construction of roads and transmission lines, canals, reservoirs, settlements, etc. Forests must be maintained not only with a view to the production of wood, but also because of the other benefits they yield, particularly the protection of soil against erosion and water regulation.

Rational management both in public and private forests is ensured
through working plans, general and specific. General plans are made for the
whole forest economic region and specific ones for each management unit.
These working plans, the contents of which are prescribed by law, are
prepared for 10-year periods and are subject to compulsory revision after
their validity expires.

The authorities responsible for approving forest working plans differ
between republics and are prescribed by the Forest Law. In most cases, the
working plan is approved by the competent organ of the republic and/or
province (Committee for Agriculture and Forestry or the Executive Council).

The costs of preparing working plans for private forests are defrayed
by the forest owners. In most cases these costs are minimal.

Inspection organs (communal, provincial, republican) see to it that
all forest users adhere to legal regulations and forest working plans,
especially those concerning the volume of felling, afforestation and forest
upkeep.

4.2   Afforestation and the Tending of Forests

In 1982, the Association of Forestry Engineers and Technicians and the
Timber Processing Industry of Yugoslavia and the General Association of
Forestry and the Wood Processing and Paper and Pulp Industry of Yugoslavia
prepared a forestry development programme up to the year 2000. This
envisages an increase in annual afforestation from the average of 34,000
ha. achieved in 1976-79 to a minimum of 60,000 ha./year between 1980 and
2000.

Increasing attention is being devoted to poplar and willow
plantations. Poplar accounts for about 0.85% of the forest area, and its
share of wood production is about 7.3%. The aim is to raise these figures
to at least 1.5% and 12.5%, respectively, by the year 2000.

4.3   Basic Guidelines for the Protection of Forests

In recent years there have been no major problems in forest
protection, as there have been no severe attacks from insects or fungi.
However, some pests have been appearing for years. Elm dieback for example
started 50 years ago and oak dieback also started a long time ago but has
not caused very serious damage. Neither have there been any disastrous
losses caused by abiotic factors, although there are some losses every
year, especially through forest fires in the coastal region.

In certain parts of Yugoslavia, particularly in the S.R. of Slovenia,
in the vicinity of ironworks, mines and power plants, forest dieback occurs
as a result of excessive air pollution. According to the latest data, in
Slovenia, 20% of the forest shows greater or lesser signs of damage. The
most endangered species are fir and spruce. Beech is the most resistant.

4.4   The Management of Protection Forests

Protection and special purpose forests account for 6.6% of the total forest area. Protection forests (235,000 ha.) protect economic and other facilities, settlements and watercourses.

National parks and reservations of natural rarities are forests of exceptional rarity and beauty or forests of special historic and national significance (132,000 ha.). They include not only forests, but a much larger area. Yugoslavia is one of the very few European countries where a number of virgin forests have been preserved.

Forests used for rest and recreation account for 14,000 ha. "Special purpose" forests (221,000 ha.) are forests for military needs, experimental plots of Faculties of Forestry, etc.

The trend is to increase national park areas.

Unless otherwise stipulated by law, the communes in which forests excluded from normal activities are located see to the application of the relevant legal requirements.

Organizations or legal persons engaged in forest management, or private forest owners, whose forests are excluded from normal economic activities, are entitled to compensation for loss of income.

4.5   Hunting Management

Hunting has always been an important economic activity in Yugoslavia. The basic unit which is managed and on which game is raised is a hunting district. These are units which have the necessary ecological conditions for game management.

Hunting districts are established and assigned to economic and social organizations (hunting societies) by the commune, province or republic of the territory in which they are located.

In some parts of Yugoslavia, hunting tourism is highly developed (bear, deer, boar, small game and game birds). Yugoslav hunters have won numerous awards for their trophies at international exhibitions. Types and size of game populations are restricted so as not to hamper the normal management of forests.

4.6   The Use of Abandoned Agricultural Land

The aim of forestry policies is to expand the area under forests on abandoned agricultural land. In mountainous regions in which agricultural land is abandoned due to the migration of the rural population, such areas revert to forest naturally as they mainly border on forests. In rare cases, this land is bought by organizations managing public forests or by the paper and pulp industry for the establishment of plantations of fast-growing species.

4.7 Management in Mountainous Regions

Forests generally cover the sparsely populated mountainous regions of Yugoslavia and make possible the development of mountainous agriculture, mainly livestock breeding.

Such forests are considerably burdened by grazing. In 1947, goat breeding was prohibited because of the great losses they caused by grazing particularly in coppice forests. After the passing of this law, forests in protected areas regenerated. In recent years the number of those in favour of allowing goat breeding is again rising.

A major problem in mountainous karst regions is soil protection and water regulation. Special work organizations deal with the protection of soil against erosion and torrent regulation. Most of them are in the SR of Serbia and the SR of Macedonia, where erosion is most widespread. One method of torrent regulation is the afforestation of soil exposed to erosion. Afforestation is facilitated by the fact that the rural population is gradually leaving such areas.

5. FOREST UTILIZATION

5.1 Harvesting

Slovenian and Bosnian coniferous sawn timber and Slavonian sawn oak timber already had an important place in the international timber market in the 19th century. Oak was initially used for the production of French and German staves, and by the mid-19th century, when steam sawmills were introduced, for the production of sawn timber. The processing of beech into sawn timber started only in the second half of the 19th century.

The allowed annual cut in public and private forests is specified in working plans. Tree marking for felling, both in private and public forests, is carried out by professional bodies, organizations or communes. Forest exploitation must comply with the conditions stipulated by the forest laws, i.e. the principle of the permanence of forest resources must be respected, and ecological conditions as well as the type of trees and stands must be taken into account so that optimum biological reproduction is ensured.

Since the mid-'50s, felling in public forests has been carried out by forest management organizations. In private forests, felling is done by forest owners, except in the S.R. of Slovenia where in most cases it is done by organizations managing public forests on behalf of private owners.

The Forest Law defines the season of felling (as a rule outside the growing season) and the maintenance of forest order. Forestry inspectors (communal, republican, federal) see to it that the provisions of the Forest Law and forestry economic working plans are observed.

A problem in Yugoslav forestry is the poor access to forests. On average there are only 5.6 km of roads per 1,000 ha. of forest.

Forestry policy aims at building another 15,000 km of forest roads by the year 2000, i.e. increasing the average road network to 10 km per 1,000 ha. of forest.

All felling and processing stages, both in public and private forests, are completely mechanized. About 60% of hauling from stump to truck road is mechanized as mechanical equipment cannot be used efficiently on all types of ground.

The aim of forestry policy is to increase felling from the present 22.4 million m^3 to about 26 million m^3 by the year 2000.

5.2 The Development of the Wood Processing Industry

The present pattern of total production in forestry and in the timber products industry (1985, according to value)

Production	%
Forestry products (logs, pulpwood, fuelwood, pit timber and other roundwood)	14.5
Sawnwood and panels	18.2
Final wood products	35.5
Cellulose and paper	29.0
Other products (musical instruments, brushes, etc.)	2.8
Total	100.0

In most of the country, forest residues are not used for industrial purposes because of the high cost of gathering and transport, but some are sold to the rural population for use as fuelwood.

Felling equipment is undergoing constant improvement. Particular use is made of the experience of countries with a similar structure of forests and similar topographic conditions. Of great help also are seminars organized by the Joint FAO/ECE/ILO Committee for Forest Work Techniques and forest workers training. The Yugoslav Agricultural Forestry Centre organizes annually an exhibition and demonstration of new equipment and machines at the Agricultural Fair in Novi Sad. The domestic industry manufacturing equipment suited to the specific Yugoslav conditions is also developing.

Some pulp and paper factories are establishing their own plantations of poplar and willow.

The Associated Labour Act is the legal basis for forming organizations dealing in the industrial processing of wood. These organizations are obliged, when a new factory is being built or an existing one expanded, to obtain an opinion on the socio-economic justifiability and evidence concerning the availability of the raw material supplies. This opinion is issued by chambers of the economy and self-management communities of interest for forestry.

Citizens or a group of citizens may privately own craft workshops (small-scale industry) for the mechanical and final processing of wood, the number of employees being limited by statute.

The construction of small factories in small towns or villages with abundant labour has been encouraged recently in mountainous regions with sufficient forests.

5.3 Wood-based Power Generation

Fuelwood is mainly used by households which have their own forests and by rural households in mountainous areas. Since the energy crisis, wood is increasingly being used for power generation to replace oil. It is, however, widely believed that wood is an industrial raw material and that it should not be used for heating. Nevertheless the demand for fuelwood has been growing recently.

6. TRADE IN WOOD

Forestry and the wood processing industry are export-oriented. Yugoslavia is currently the largest European exporter of sawn beechwood, third in the world for sawn oak, and sixth in Europe for furniture. The share of forestry products and the wood processing industry in total exports in the 1946-1955 period was 25.9% by value. In recent years, the value of exports has increased but their relative share has fallen to 10% because of the increased exports of other products.

About 52% of wood exports are effected by 5 large trade and production organizations. Some of them have been operating for over 60 years and are very well known in the international timber market. These organizations are part of large systems of forestry and wood processing industry work organizations.

Yugoslav standards and rules are in compliance with the requirements of importing countries. The products manufactured pursuant to Yugoslav standards may, by sorting, be adapted, on request, to the standards of importing countries.

The marketing concept is fully applied to trade in wood.

Due to the increased domestic needs and the low accessibility of forests, Yugoslavia, which had been a net exporter in earlier years, has become a net importer of coniferous and deciduous cellulose.

7. EMPLOYMENT

The Associated Labour Act and other laws and regulations regulate the manner of employment in general as well as employment in the sector of forestry and the wood processing industry.

Total employment (man years) was as follows in 1985:

Forestry	67,000
Manufacture of sawnwood and panels	61,000
Manufacture of final wood products	143,000
Pulp and paper manufacture	45,000
Total	316,000

(Source: Federal Bureau for Statistics, "Statistical Almanac")

In 1984, 1,726 forest engineers and 3,247 technicians were employed in forestry. Constant difficulties are encountered in recruiting workers, although the work is well paid and free transport to the worksite, hostel-type accommodation and meals are provided (food is very cheap as it is subsidised).

Jobs are obtained through public advertisements. Employed workers are organized (on a voluntary basis) in the Trade Union of Workers in Forestry and the Wood Processing Industry. Employed workers are entitled to retirement and health insurance. Health services, including hospital treatment and medicines, are free of charge. Full-time workers enjoy full social security. They cannot be dismissed, even when the volume of work declines. In cases of financial difficulties, the law guarantees minimum personal incomes.

The law prescribes the measures to protect the health of workers and prevent injuries at work. Inspection organs strictly control adherence to the measures prescribed by law.

8. EDUCATION IN FORESTRY AND THE WOOD PROCESSING INDUSTRY

    Forest workers (felling, afforestation) must have received elementary education (8 years) and have attended professional courses (from 6-12 months) organized by the appropriate secondary schools.

    Vocational (secondary) education lasts 4 years. During the first two years, students have a joint curriculum and during the next two years they are oriented towards forestry or wood processing studies, etc. Pupils who graduate from such schools hold the title of technician in the respective field. After this, they can enrol in faculties and attend post-graduate studies to get masters or doctorate degrees.

    University education is acquired at five faculties of forestry and one machine building faculty.

    Life-long education is a constant practice in forestry and the wood processing industry. It is carried out at faculties, education centres; professional associations and work organizations also play a part.

    Great attention is devoted to forestry in general education. It starts at primary school and is developed through various drives such as "landscaping of the school grounds", "days of forests", "weeks of forests", etc. Through organizations such as Young Nature Lovers, "Friends of Forests", Horticultural Societies, etc., young people organize drives for voluntary afforestation and other work in forests.

9. RESEARCH IN FORESTRY AND THE TIMBER INDUSTRY

    Forestry faculties are the leading force in the field of scientific research in forestry and the timber industry.

    Concurrently with the development of scientific research at faculties, a broad network of scientific research institutions has developed in Yugoslavia, specialized in various types of activities in the field of forestry and the timber products industry. In addition to scientific research as the main activity, these institutions deal with designing and executing projects and the transfer of know-how and technology. Some forestry institutes have set up departments for the timber industry.

    Research programmes in the field of forestry and the timber industry are examined and approved by the federal and/or provincial interest communities for scientific work.

10. INTERNATIONAL COOPERATION

    The aim of national policy is to expand the already intensive international cooperation in the field of forestry and the timber industry. Numerous institutions and work organizations take part in the cooperation. For instance, the Yugoslav Agricultural Forestry Centre has developed successful cooperation with Bulgaria, Czechoslovakia, Hungary, Austria, the GDR, Sweden, Finland, Norway, Italy and other countries.

    Yugoslavia, one of the founders of the Non-Aligned Movement, is particularly interested in cooperation with developing countries.

    Cooperation is supported by government institutions, business associations in forestry and the timber industry, business communities, etc.